LUCAS & BÉDART
BRUXELLES

The
Factory
of
Facts

Also by Luc Sante

Low Life: Lures and Snares
of Old New York

Evidence

The
Factory
of
Facts

Luc Sante

Pantheon Books   New York

Library of Congress Cataloging-in-Publication Data

Sante, Luc.
    The factory of facts / Luc Sante.
        p. cm.
    Includes bibliographical references.
    ISBN 0-679-42410-5
    1. Sante, Luc—Childhood and youth. 2. Belgian
Americans—Biography. 3. Belgian Americans—
Belgium—Verviers—Biography. 4. Sante
family. 5. Sante, Luc—Family. 6. Verviers
(Belgium)—Biography. I. Title.
E184.B2S36   1998
973'.043932'0092—dc21
[B]   97-25814
                    CIP

Random House Web Address
http://www.randomhouse.com

Book design by Fearn Cutler

Printed in the United States of America
First Edition

2   4   6   8   9   7   5   3   1

This is for Melissa

Some people tell me them overseas blues ain't bad.
Some people say them overseas blues ain't bad.
It must not have been the overseas blues I had.

Charlie Patton,
"Down the Dirt Road Blues"

Cours, camarade, le vieux monde est derrière toi.
(Run, comrade, the old world is behind you.)

Graffito, Rue Rotrou, Odéon, Paris, May 1968

Contents

I Résumé 3

II Cargo 13

III Fait-Divers 35

IV Flood 53

V House 69

VI Caesura 87

VII Escutcheon 105

VIII Via Crucis 129

IX White Flag 151

X Spleen and Ideal 173

XI Mirage 197

XII Atlantic 217

XIII Gloss 241

XIV Dummy 261

XV Non-Site 287

Sources 297

Thanks 305

The
Factory
of
Facts

ı Résumé

I was born on May 25, 1954, in Verviers, Belgium, the only child of Lucien Mathieu Amélie Sante and Denise Lambertine Alberte Marie Ghislaine Nandrin. Following the bankruptcy of my father's employer, an iron foundry that manufactured wool-carding machinery, and at the suggestion of friends who had emigrated earlier, my parents decided to move to the United States in search of work. We arrived at Idlewild Airport in February 1959, and moved in with my parents' friends in Summit, New Jersey. Prospects were not as bright as they had been depicted, and that November we sailed back to Belgium, but the situation there was no better, and early in 1960 we re-emigrated. Several more such trips occurred over the next few years, spurred by momentary hopes, by the Cuban Missile Crisis, by the illnesses and deaths of my maternal grandparents. At length my parents decided to remain in America, at least until the time came when they could retire to Belgium.

I was born in 1954 in Verviers, Belgium, the only child of Lucien and Denise Sante. Following the bankruptcy of my father's employer, an iron foundry that manufactured wool-carding machinery, and at the suggestion of my mother's brother, René Nandrin, my parents decided to move to the Belgian Congo, where my father would take up a position as local field director for a palm-oil concern. In February 1959, we arrived in Coquilhatville, on the banks of the Congo River, and moved into a company-owned villa in the European district. Suddenly we had servants and a chauffeured car. On the other hand, I came down with a succession of ailments aggravated by the climate and spent most of my time in bed. Barely a year later the Belgian government announced that the Congo would be granted its independence that June, and my parents' friends and colleagues began to show signs of alarm, sending prized possessions, for example, back to their families in Belgium. Emotions had risen to a point of panic by late May, when the first general elections were held. My parents and their friends dismissed their servants, fearing treachery. My father barricaded my mother and me and would himself not leave the house without a loaded revolver on his hip. Violent incidents began occurring, most of them in the south of the country, but some close enough that my father, over my mother's protests, sent us home. He followed a little over a month later, when fighting had become widespread; his employer turned over local control to native African managers. Connections made in the Congo led my father to a job with the Ministry of Commerce, and we moved to Berchem-Ste. Agathe, a suburb of Brussels, where I recovered and later found I had a surprising aptitude for competitive cycling.

I was born in 1954 in Verviers, Belgium, the only child of Lucien and Denise Sante. Following the bankruptcy of his employer, an iron foundry that manufactured wool-carding machinery, my father tried to find another job, but without success. After depleting their savings and selling our house in Pepinster, as well as most of the major household possessions, my parents moved into a succession of progressively smaller and dingier apartments, finally winding up in a single room in Seraing, an industrial suburb of Liège, where my father got a barely remunerative stint as nightwatchman in a warehouse. We endured two years of this as a family. My mother became chronically ill, probably due to stress as much as to bad food and lack of heat, and consequently I was taken in by my Remacle cousins in the country. They, too, were feeling the pinch of the economy, however, and palmed me off on other relatives, who in turn passed me along after a while. I spent three years being thus shunted around, until the Christian Brothers admitted me as a hardship case at their boarding school in Liège in the winter of 1964. By then my mother had been hospitalized full-time and my father had retreated into a vigilant and apparently unbreakable silence. At the school I was constantly victimized by the other pupils, most of them offspring of well-to-do families. Finally, at thirteen, I snapped. I set a fire that consumed the dormitory and took the lives of five boys.

I was born in 1954 in Verviers, Belgium, the only child of Lucien and Denise Sante. My father's employer, an iron foundry that manufactured wool-carding machinery, miraculously escaped the effects of the recession of 1958 and the collapse of Verviers's textile industry by a rapid and timely change to the manufacture of radiators. My father, who had worked his way up to junior management from the labor ranks, devised a streamlined method of cooling molds that earned him a succession of promotions, ultimately to the top seat. By 1968 we had sold our row house in Pepinster and moved into a villa in a parklike setting on the heights of the "boulevard" district of Verviers. I grew up fast, and was quickly bored by the provincial life around me. I barely maintained passing grades at St. François-Xavier, the local Jesuit *collège,* and would surely have failed and been expelled had it not been for my parents' social and political prominence. As it was, I was taking clandestine excursions—longer and longer ones—out into the world: to Amsterdam, to Paris, to London, to Majorca. I took every drug I could get my hands on, and I was possibly a father several times over; I was adept at vanishing when matters came to a head. My parents' threats to cut off my allowance became steadily more credible until, in the spring of 1971, I bribed the manager of the Place Verte branch of the Générale de Banque and withdrew my entire trust fund in cash—or nearly entire; I left a token five hundred francs. I flew to Marrakech, where I lived for eight months in a hotel frequented by members of British rock groups, until a run-in with one of the Berber chieftains who controlled the hashish traffic from the Rif caused me to fear for my life. I snared a series of van rides that took me to Goa, on the Indian Ocean, where I dwelt in a permanent cloud of dope in a waterfront flat. When my money ran out, I relocated to the beach. I contracted scabies and syphilis, but I didn't care.

I was born in 1954 in Verviers, Belgium, the only child of Lucien and Denise Sante. Following the bankruptcy of my father's employer, an iron foundry that manufactured wool-carding machinery, my parents decided to emigrate to the United States. We arrived at Idlewild Airport in February 1959, with eight suitcases and an address in Johnsonburg, Pennsylvania. The address belonged to a family whose son had died near Henri-Chapelle in the terrible winter of 1944, and whose grave my mother had maintained as part of a program in which young Belgian women "adopted" the remains of American servicemen. For a few years my mother had kept up a peculiar correspondence with this family; they exchanged cards and photographs and brief letters neither side understood, lacking a common language. Upon deciding to come to America she had dug out the address, writing this time in laborious, dictionary-assisted English, but had not received a reply. She maintained, however, that they must have gotten her address wrong, misreading her Belgian script; their return letter surely lay in some bin in Brussels. She was determined to call on them upon our arrival, but, after many halting inquiries, discovered that there was no public transport that went anywhere near Johnsonburg, Pennsylvania. My parents were directed by Travelers' Aid to an agency that helped them find an apartment in Ozone Park, Queens, and after a time my father found work as custodian at a doughnut franchise in Long Island City. My parents were miserable, impoverished and isolated and increasingly without hope, but lacked the means to return to Belgium; all their savings went into a fund that eventually enabled them to send me to boarding school with the Christian Brothers in Liège. I languished there, dreaming only of returning to America.

I was born in 1954 in Verviers, Belgium, the only child of Lucien and Denise Sante. Following the bankruptcy of his employer, an iron foundry that manufactured wool-carding machinery, my father miraculously got a nearly identical job with another iron foundry, which made structural supports for con-

crete constructions. I grew up in Pepinster, attending the
Catholic primary school and then St. François-Xavier, the Jesuit *collège* in Verviers, with money my grandmother had provided for this purpose in her will. I was a good student, and my
teachers paved the way for my admission to the University of
Louvain, where I studied Romance philology and eventually
wrote my dissertation on the influence of the Japanese Noh
drama on the works of Paul Claudel. In the course of my studies there it occurred to me one day that I had a calling, that I
had in fact long had this calling but had been inattentive to it.
After obtaining my degree I entered the Jesuit chapter house at
Tervuren, and in 1978 I was ordained. I celebrated my first
Mass at St. Remacle, the ancestral family church in Verviers,
with all my relatives crowding the pews, and then moved to
Rome, where I had a job awaiting me in the Propaganda Office
of the Holy See. Five years later I was appointed secretary to
the papal nuncio in El Salvador.

   I was born in 1954 in Verviers, Belgium, the only child of
Lucien and Denise Sante. Following the bankruptcy of my
father's employer, an iron foundry that manufactured wool-
carding machinery, my parents decided to emigrate to the
United States, on no more firm a basis than a visit to the U.S.
pavilion at the 1958 Brussels World's Fair. We arrived at
Idlewild Airport in February 1959, with eight suitcases, my father's prewar memories of high-school English, and the name
of someone's cousin who apparently lived in Long Island, New
York, which my parents thought was a town. A taxi driver who
knew some French took us to a hotel in Manhattan, which
turned out to be a clip joint. We lost three of our suitcases be-

fore fleeing to another hotel, respectable enough but commensurately expensive. My parents combed telephone books in search of the cousin, but to no avail. They applied for help from the Belgian consulate, and were turned away with frosty finality. They spent days on complex and indeterminate errands, looking for chimeric friends of relatives of friends, my father trying to look for jobs in his field without much idea of where to start. They hadn't imagined it would be like this; without connections or a grasp of the language they were lost. The money was rapidly dwindling, too; already there was not enough left for passage back to Europe, and soon they would no longer be able to foot the hotel bill. On the advice of the chambermaid, a kind woman from Puerto Rico—communication between her and my parents, conducted around a tongue none of them possessed, was comically histrionic—my parents relocated to a dank hostelry near Herald Square where the rooms were lit by fluorescent tubes. We lived on rolls and hot dogs. My mother made me sleep wrapped in a chiffon scarf to protect me from the cockroaches. My father took his watch, of a decent but undistinguished Swiss make, to a pawnshop, where he was given five dollars in return. Our suitcases, minus their contents, followed, and soon my parents' overcoats and their extra pairs of shoes went as well. They were beginning to consider applying to a church for assistance, but were hindered by their pride. One day, when it seemed no other option remained, a man who lived down the hall from us offered my father a job. He was to deliver a manila envelope to an address in Newark; he would be paid fifty dollars. He accepted with alacrity and set off. That night, after I had fallen asleep, while my mother wept with fear at having heard nothing from him, two men in dark suits came to our room and took us away. They were FBI agents. My father had been arraigned for interstate traffic in narcotics; the house to which he made his delivery had been under surveillance for several weeks. My mother was held as a material witness in the Essex County Women's Correctional Facility. I was kept in a wing of Juvenile Hall for four days, in the course of which I repeatedly wet my bed and was punished by being deprived of food. Then I was sent to a foster home, with a large and strict Irish-American family in Irvington. My inability to speak English enraged the father, who would take me into the vest-pocket backyard and beat me with a razor strop. I was moved to another foster home, and then another and another—I lost count. I had no news from my parents. After a while I couldn't remember their faces.

I was born in 1954 in Verviers, Belgium, the only child of Lucien and Denise Sante. Following the bankruptcy of my father's employer, an iron foundry that manufactured wool-carding machinery, and with the knowledge that there were no other jobs to be had, a combined result of the collapse of the centuries-old Verviers textile industry and of the recession of 1958, my parents decided to go for broke. They sold our row house in Pepinster and the bulk of its contents, and we set off by train for Biarritz, the beautiful city in France fronting on the Bay of Biscay and backed against the Pyrenees. The trip was glorious; we laughed and sang songs and pointed out the window at the spectacular scenery. When we got there my parents checked into a modest hotel, left me with sandwiches and a pile of comics, and went to the casino. My father's plan was to parlay the stake amassed from selling off their possessions into a small fortune at the baccarat table. It didn't work.

• • •

I was born in 1954 in Verviers, Belgium, the only child of Lucien and Denise Sante. Following the bankruptcy of my father's employer, an iron foundry that manufactured wool-carding machinery, my parents sat on the floor. Dust accumulated. Things fell and were not picked up. Mold grew on the potatoes in the cellar. The milk solidified. The electricity was cut off. Neighboring boys threw stones that broke the windows, and cold air blew in. First insects, then rodents, and eventually birds arrived to make their homes with us. Soon snow covered the dust, and then soot covered the snow. We grew increasingly warm as we slept.

II Cargo

On the night of August 13, 1995, I had an apparently in-
nocuous, even pedantic dream. An unseen narrator was showing me photographs. They were portraits and full-length
studies of what looked like ancient Romans or Byzantines.
The men wore gold breastplates and leg armor, leather-thong
skirts and high-laced sandals, and carried plumed helmets in
the crooks of their arms. The women were clad in long,
loosely draped robes, and displayed a dazzling assortment
of jewelry—tiaras, coin necklaces, heavy earrings, elaborate
bracelets. The pictures themselves were faded sepia. "How
could such photographs exist?" asked my host, anticipating my
question. "Even the Byzantine Empire fell nearly four hundred
years before the invention of photography. But in fact, you see,
these were taken in the 1930s." I was appropriately taken aback.

"None of these artifacts—that gold, those stones—have
survived," he went on. "The treasure of the X family [I heard
the name in the dream, but could not remember it upon awak-
ening] was completely and systematically destroyed by its subjects, along with most of the standing structures in the country
they inhabited." It seemed that this country, once a far-flung
outpost of the Byzantine Empire, had managed to remain outside history, being run as an unchanging feudal state for many
centuries. Its subjects were kept closed off from the world, ignorant, illiterate, superstitious, dirt-poor, by an upper class
who themselves maintained the life of fifth- or sixth-century

aristocrats. Oil lamps, wood fires, iron tools, ox carts, horse-driven plows were the extent of their technology. The poor were tenant farmers; the rich reveled in idle luxury. The former knew nothing of the rest of the world, while the latter refused to know—getting themselves photographed must have represented a singular aberration.

Everything changed in the 1960s, however. The catalyst was the unauthorized incursion of a Hollywood film crew, which was shooting a James Bond knockoff starring Robert Wagner and Stephanie Powers. The peasantry, suddenly confronted with evidence of what lay beyond their borders, overwhelmed by the force of this knowledge, rose up in revolt. In the process they obliterated every trace of their former rulers. They did not seek to keep any of their riches, not a single one of their possessions, but destroyed them utterly, burning what would burn and burying the rest. "This," said the narrator, "is a story that has been completely suppressed. You will not find it, nor so much as the name of the country, in any printed source."

I awoke from the dream trembling, somehow badly frightened, and could not get back to sleep for several hours. I got up the next day and wrote it all down. By then I was bemused, but at the same time I still felt an inexplicable tremor. Parsing the dream, I could find many strands of conscious residue, all of them cultural. The most obvious source was Ryszard Kapuściński's account of Ethiopia under Haile Selassie—an actual example of an empire maintained in an archaic vacuum until very recently. The blind destructive rage of the populace, meanwhile, surely derived from what I had read of the overthrow of the Ceauşescu regime in Romania. The story's suppression, the notion of an entire country purposely removed from printed records, was undoubtedly inspired by Jorge Luis

Borges's "Tlön, Uqbar, Orbis Tertius," which I had recently reread. The photographs—I can still see them clearly in my mind's eye—probably bore some relation to a number of tintypes showing people in fancy dress that were among the pictures in a Civil War–era family album I had bought at a flea market. In a more general way I could connect the sense of incredulous wonder the photographs in the dream produced in me to that provoked by the Nadar exhibition I had seen earlier that year—the portraits of Baudelaire and Daumier hardly seemed less miraculous than photographs of ancient Romans. And as for the James Bond knockoff, suffice it to say that my unconscious is well stocked with mid-1960s movie imagery.

Thus I could account pretty conclusively for the dream's constituent details. I could only admire its narrative architecture, with a twinge of envy at the dream state's resourcefulness and ability to compress. On the other hand, what I couldn't explain at all was its emotional force. Oh, sure, I had gotten chills reading Kapuściński's *The Emperor*, and that Borges story never failed to raise gooseflesh no matter how many times I read it. I've always been a sucker for tales of lost civilizations, pockets in time, suppressed documents. But the fear the dream left me with was not disinterested. It was not as if I had just seen a scary movie; the echo of terror was persistent, and deep, a chill of the soul. I felt as if I had looked into an abyss—and, as the saying goes, the abyss had looked back at me.

In the following days and weeks I often thought about the dream. I looked for gaps in its narrative pattern, loopholes in its internal logic, trying to find its code. The first thing to strike me was the emphasis on the destruction of goods. Nothing was said about the fate of the people, whether the decadent upper class or the enraged peasantry. I lingered, for example, on the figure who might indeed have been the emperor: he was whiskered, like Marcus Aurelius, and he stared at the camera head-on, with that expression of exhausted hostility you see in early studio portraits. There was something specific about the misty gray tone of the picture that I thought I recognized from a particular photo I had seen, not the masquerade tintypes and certainly not Nadar, but I couldn't pin it down.

I knew my Romans, or at least I had known them when I was a boy. I collected books about them, and alone or with friends played Roman soldiers—one of my prized possessions was a copper-colored hollow plastic sword, short and broad, with an imperial eagle at its hilt. What I wanted more than anything else at the age of nine or so was a helmet, a toy reproduction of the ones carried by the men in the dream, with a crest of thin red plumes and a grilled visor kept above the brow by hinges and a shape that oddly recalled a duck's ass haircut, with long sideburn-like metal tongues that reached down to the jaw and a little curl upwards at the nape of the neck. I drew pictures of Romans—I still possess a series of notebooks with black-and-white-patterned covers in which I drew scenes from Roman life when I was eight or nine, although I only got a little way into my project of depicting all the ranks of the Roman army, properly equipped and arrayed and identified by their Latin titles, beginning with *Dux,* the leader. A couple of years later, beginning to write, I made a start on a historical novel set in Rome. It was presumably meant to echo some of the massive tomes my father had on his shelves, epics such as *Quo Vadis,* by Henryk Sienkiewicz, or *The Robe,* by Lloyd C. Douglas. As far as I can recall, I hadn't gotten very far there, either. I took enormous pleasure in making up and writing down names, like Maximus Cato and Egisippus Praetor, but actually trying to imagine a story was too much for me. My Romans existed not in narratives but in tableaux.

My fixation on the Romans began in my native Belgium, where they loomed large in popular imagery. Hadn't Julius Caesar said that of all the Gauls, the Belgae were the bravest? We were constantly reminded of this in school, along with a suggestion that of all the Belgae, our putative ancestors the Eburoni were in turn the noblest and best. The Romans' appreciation of us was reciprocated, as if it took one to know one. There were no dramatic ruins lying about, but various Roman traces existed, in place names and roads and suchlike. *Spirou,* the weekly comic magazine to which I subscribed from age five or six until my late teens, featured numerous strips that dramatized ancient history or used its setting for humorous effect, and its competitor *Pilote* ran the exploits of Astérix and Obélix, a feisty Laurel-and-Hardy pair in winged helmets. And then too, my childhood coincided with the era of the vast biblical spectacle, or at least its later phase. *Ben-Hur* was supposed to be my first movie (although bad grades or misbehavior scotched this plan, and my virgin cinematic experience was reserved for *The Absent-Minded Professor*). But those movies were all around: *Spartacus, King of Kings, The Fall of the Roman Empire,* all those international co-productions with funny haircuts and stilted speech and posters on which the title appeared to have been carved out of massive blocks of stone, on and around which suggestive details of the action swirled.

Those posters, as far as I knew, showed history as it truly was, a sweeping epic pageant in which nostrils flared with passion as people wrestled horses or gathered their heaving bosoms. In America, where I arrived four times in my childhood with a differently shaded feeling of discovery every time, I learned that the epic vision of history applied with equal drama to the Civil War, another occasion for dashing uniforms, rearing horses, and gasping maidens. My first encounter with the subject came in the form of a series of bubble-gum cards, each devoted to a particular battle with a stirring name—Antietam, Cold Harbor, Spottsylvania, The Wilderness—that showed uniformed figures waving swords amid impressively spattered gore. For some years my reading—and, consequently, the continuously unfurling panorama in my imagination—alternated in half-year sequences: ancient Rome and the Civil War, Europe and America.

Then, rather abruptly, I lost interest. It was around 1966, the year before I attained puberty. The turning point, at least as it stands in my flawed memory, came when I saw *Grand Prix* at the Strand Theater in Summit, New Jersey. This John Frankenheimer movie, apparently a tremendous flop in its time, was an international co-production of a considerably different flavor. The colorful world of the racing circuits—the danger, the glamour—the daring men, the voluptuous women! Et cetera. My personal connection to this world was that my mother was born in Ster, a tiny village virtually adjacent to the Belgian Grand Prix track at Francorchamps, where one of the film's most spectacular accident sequences was shot, at the deadly Eau-Rouge hairpin. During her girlhood, my mother and her mother would take their knitting to the stands and watch the time trials; the experience failed to inspire her to take up the wheel, however. For me, the movie did more than launch an incidental and highly aesthetic interest in racing cars. It introduced me to the glamour of the modern world.

This glamour was epitomized by the film's female lead, Françoise Hardy (I could hardly tell you who the other actors were). She was lithe, had long brown hair with bangs that hooded slightly slanted eyes, proud cheekbones, full lips that approached but did not quite attain a pout. I was terribly smitten. She was a pop star in Europe, but I couldn't find her records in America, so I had to content myself with the tunes she mentioned as her favorites in an issue of the French pop magazine *Salut les copains* that had been sent me by relatives: "Take It or Leave It," by the Rolling Stones and "Don't Mess with Cupid," by Otis Redding. Those immediately became my favorite songs, too. She and I had everything in common, the age difference notwithstanding. But I couldn't very well run into her on the Canebière, take her off in my Aston-Martin to a secluded spot in the Pyrénées-Orientales, eventually get married in a ceremony conducted by the bishop of Andorra before a crowd that would include Jean Shrimpton, Salvador Dalí, David Hemmings, and Jeanne Moreau, with live music by the Yardbirds and a forty-eight-hour nude pool party afterwards, and then settle down in a seventeenth-century *hôtel particulier* on the Île Saint-Louis, now could I?

So I employed the only strategy available to me: I plunged my imagination into that world. I dug out a jacket, sent to me by my aunt and uncle, that I had avoided because it resembled nothing worn by any of my peers—it was an off-white gabardine item, with epaulettes, that resembled a cross between a trench coat and a safari jacket—and began wearing it with paisley shirts, white chinos, pointed loafers, and wraparound sunglasses. That outfit, I imagined, would undoubtedly make an impression on Françoise Hardy should I ever meet her on Springfield Avenue in Summit or at the Blue Star Shopping Center in Watchung, New Jersey. I gave less thought, perhaps, to her possible reaction to the accoutrements I carried around—she might conceivably have been impressed by the radio with hidden components that folded out to convert it into a submachine gun, had it been real, but given that it did nothing else but unfold and that it came from a boxed set of gear inspired by the television show *The Man from U.N.C.L.E.*, intended for ages eight to fourteen, she might well have looked down her pert but dignified nose.

In my mind, though, I was an international jet-setter: pop star, avant-garde poet, connoisseur of fine wines, racetrack daredevil, and, of course, spy. Spies were everywhere then, in novels by Len Deighton and John Le Carré, in television shows ranging from the slapstick *Get Smart!* to the brilliantly terse *Secret Agent*, on the radio in the latter's American theme song by Johnny Rivers (it was the British series *Danger Man*, slightly repackaged), and of course at the movies, in the adventures of James Bond and his several dozen epigones. There were spies in real life, too, but popular concern had evidently reached critical mass somewhere around the time of the U2 incident, in 1962, so that the dangerous implications of their activities had to be culturally supplanted by a suave burlesque. I effortlessly identified with spies, not only because they were glamorous but because they were all but stateless. Obviously, spies were always represented as fighting for this government or that against its opponent, the godless other, but in fact they seldom visited the mother country except to receive assignments or attend parties, they were not notably effusive of patriotic sentiments or burdened with much hometown cultural or emotional baggage, and in general they seemed to pledge their actual allegiance to sundry casinos and beachfronts, souks and palazzi, fleshpots and yacht basins, from Tangier to Macao. Spying was a game, and if along the line it carried a loftier or harsher meaning, they were indifferent to it.

I was terrifically well equipped to be a spy, I thought. I was multilingual (bilingual, really, but I imagined on the basis of stray phrases that I also spoke German and Italian), knowledgeable in various areas (I could throw around marques of sports cars, had a glancing acquaintance with Bordeaux vintages—not that I had yet tasted any—and of course I could recite prodigious lists of Roman emperors). I was fast on my feet and, above all, I was cosmopolitan. I had crossed the Atlantic seven times—three times by airplane and four by boat—had visited Brussels, Paris, Rotterdam, Montreal, and Aachen as well as Washington, D.C., Philadelphia, Ostend, Le Havre, and once a boat I had been on had put in at Southampton, which I had regarded from the deck, so that I could claim to have visited England as well. And I felt at home in all those places, or perhaps what I meant is that I felt equally homeless in all of them.

I was not American, quite literally—I possessed a green card, in those days actually green, and when traveling I carried the maroon-covered passport of Belgium. Lately, however, I had begun to realize that I was not Belgian, either. Of course I had the language, and some vestiges of the accent in my English speech, as well as the taste for fried potatoes and comics (*bandes dessinées,* that is) and evergreens and stonemasonry and train travel and leek soup and *football* and *fußball* and sitting around nursing a cup of Bovril, but none of those things made me so much Belgian as indefinably European. And I wasn't truly European at that, since I collected baseball cards and could count myself a WMCA Good Guy (I had the sweatshirt) and chewed bubble gum and ate Sugar Pops and read *Mad* and owned a Whiffle Ball and had personal knowledge of four or five places where George Washington had slept. I was something of an international co-production myself, I guessed. I knew the doings of two continents and could appreciate them lightly and without undue investment. From trying to be two things at once, I had gone on to resolve the conflict somewhere in the middle of the scale.

Being neither one thing nor the other could easily have left me feeling stranded, orphaned, outcast, but as a cosmopolite I was eligible for membership in a much fancier club. I could hover in the orbit of discothèques and après-ski lounges from Gstaad to Monte Carlo, meet up with my friends at the Whiskey à Gogo in Paris or Cheetah in New York, date starlets who had been discovered by Carlo Ponti and heiresses to Anglo-Dutch petroleum fortunes who wore paper minidresses and thigh-high white boots. I would have racing stripes, ultra-modern stereo equipment, tight houndstooth trousers and elastic-sided winklepickers, magnums of Mumm's lying casu-ally forgotten on lower shelves of refrigerators in various of my *pieds-à-terre,* invitations to weekend parties impulsively thrown by second sons of dukes on private islands off the coast of Irian Jaya to which the guests would be ferried unaware of their destination until the last minute aboard livery jets contain-ing whirlpool baths and billiard tables. I would not, of course, need any money, since my friends would have mounds of it lying around in bowls like so many combination salads at a smorgasbord. This vision fermented unseen by anyone; such friends as I actually had were still, as far as I could tell, primar-ily interested in playing dodgeball.

Pursuing this line of thought, then, and applying it to the dream, it would seem that the sequentially downtrodden, wised-up, and furiously destructive peasantry would have to be me. The decadent aristocracy, it would follow, were my par-ents. This made a certain amount of sense. I had, naturally, rebelled against my upbringing; indeed my rebellion would now be approaching its thirtieth year of continuous activity, and it might eventually be seen as permanent, fulfilling Trotsky's exhortation. But what, then, would the treasure be? What astounding, irreplaceable riches had I obliterated by my revolt, out of sheer spite and with no heed to my own profit?

The lost treasure of the Santes. The idea made me laugh. The notion was remote even from my fantasies. Like many children, I had more than once entertained the idea that my parents were stand-ins, that I had been adopted or somehow switched at birth, that I was descended from more worthy, more interesting beings. It had not, however, crossed my mind that these spectral progenitors might be rich. I had imagined them as vagabonds, mountebanks, carnies, thieves. They were everything my parents were not—adventurous, daring, roguish, *bad*—but only up to a point, since the romance did not involve money, not even fugitive sums deposited under false names in the vaults of scattered South American banks.

Maybe my father had once had a corresponding fantasy, though. Not knowing where our name came from or what it meant, he had suggested that it might represent a corrupted form of *Saint* or *Sainte.* He had gone so far as to sketch a scenario for me in which our ancestors were French aristocrats whose name was some sort of compound on the order of *Saint-Médard* or *Sainte-Euphrosine.* They had fled the guillotine during the Terror, running as far as darkest southern Belgium, where they had insinuated themselves among the populace and taken up suitably humble identities. A few generations later, their descendants did not suspect the glory that lay dormant in their bloodline. My father, who had left school at fourteen, as young people of the working class did then, nevertheless was a prodigious autodidactic reader, fascinated by the French Revolution, so I could see where the idea had in part germinated.

The rest might have been inspired by the tale of his cousin Alphonse Faniel, the son of his father's sister Bertha. This Faniel, nearly a generation older than my father, like virtually all his first cousins, had been a layabout, the despair of his parents. At length, though, he had found work in a factory, assembling bicycle frames. He was sufficiently adept at it that he proposed starting his own enterprise, and his parents had set him up in a small business in the Belgian Congo, where he imported disassembled bicycles, put them together and sold them. He hired Congolese help and kept them on by giving them bicycles as bonuses. He initially parlayed his profits into a truck, to ferry his wares from the port of Matadi to Léopoldville, the capital, and then bought another truck, and eventually a whole fleet. Then he started buying houses, which he rented out at inflated rates to American military and diplomatic personnel during the war. When he made his long-delayed visit to his native Verviers after V-E Day, he came in a late-model Buick—in that time and place, he could not have caused more of a sensation had he arrived on the back of an elephant. A few years later he retired to Spain, buying a substantial tract of land that came with a castle and a title, and lived out his days as the Marquis de Mirmas. That was the closest anyone had come to establishing a Sante fortune.

I never met Alphonse Faniel, and it is more than probable that he never knew of my existence, nor would he have cared. He existed throughout my childhood as a distant mythic figure, and I came to believe he was fictitious; indeed I conflated his title with that of the Marquis de Carabas, which Puss in Boots bestowed on his master. If his story seemed improbable even to a child, it was because money had never otherwise smiled upon the Santes, or for that matter on my mother's family, the Nandrins, nor upon the host of accessory lineages: the Hermants, the Remacles, the Éloys, the Cornets, the Sauvages, the Werners. My father's side seemed to consist entirely of factory workers—day laborers, not artisans—while my mother's family was apparently an undifferentiated mass of subsistence farmers, not even smallholders but (as it happened) tenant farmers, who might have considered themselves prosperous had they possessed a single cow. I accepted from an early age that we were just that way—*p'tites gens*—folks meant to scratch out a living by the sweat of their brows, whose every meager advance would be met with a consequent reversal.

I had concrete evidence of this within my own three-person nuclear family. My father, after leaving school, worked for the railroad for a while, as a track inspector, and briefly for a textile job-lot dealer and in a wool-carding plant. After the war, which he spent mostly hiding from the Germans, he found work in a fulling mill, then in an iron foundry that manufactured carding machines. There, around the time of my birth, he ascended from the shop floor to a position in junior management. Then the place shut down. My parents spent a year of misery, running a Bata Shoe franchise in a grimy industrial suburb. Then the foundry reopened, my father got his job back, my parents bought themselves a new house on a corner lot in a brand-new development. They hardly had time to enjoy it, however, before my father's employer shut down again, this time apparently for good, and in a severe economic climate that all but precluded other employment possibilities. Which is how we wound up emigrating to America. Where my father was back once again on the factory floor. His advances had come through hard work and application, his reversals from sheer bad luck. One step forward and one step back—this was our lot, like a curse, a mark of Cain.

Thus the dream's identification of my parents with a militant dynasty would seem particularly tendentious, on the face of it. On the other hand, my role as the repressed masses had some internal validity. I could reasonably claim to have been kept in an ahistorical bubble during part of my childhood, not that my parents themselves were particularly to blame. For every year that stretches between my current age and my early years, some sort of psychological logarithmic expansion seems to occur, so that by the time I hit my fortieth birthday my childhood felt a century removed. I didn't become aware of this curious relativistic phenomenon until my late twenties. Around that time, I developed a consuming interest in the turn of the last century, prompted in part by the place where I was living, the Lower East Side of New York City, where every hundred-year-old tenement shell, with its scalloped cornice and ornately detailed window frames ornamenting vacancy and rot, appeared on my retina accompanied by a grimly ironic caption: THE NINETEENTH CENTURY. I was haunted by those ruins, as if every one of them said, I am Ozymandias King of Kings. I wanted desperately to see them when they were newly built, convinced that such a time must have been sunnier, more humane (I was wrong).

As I immersed myself in the nineteenth century, I was struck again and again by a personal identification that verged on cryptomnesia. I *knew* that time, as if I had lived in it myself. In impressionable adolescence I had toyed with the idea of reincarnation, but I was no longer vulnerable to that sort of nonsense, I told myself. At length I realized that the haze gathering around my peripheral vision as I pawed through documents and photographs and attempted to bore my way ocularly, Superman-like, through ten decades of grit on the inner and outer surfaces of neighboring hovels was my own childhood. The distance between the atmosphere of my infancy and that of my fledgling adulthood was something measurable in epochs.

I spent my early years in factory towns and their adjacent suburbs, amid bricks and soot and smokestacks and cobbled roads. We took streetcars for short trips and trains for long ones. We bought food fresh for every meal, not because we were gourmets but because we lacked a refrigerator (less perishable substances were kept in the root cellar). My mother got up every morning in the chill and made a fire in the parlor stove. Running water came in only one temperature: frigid. We communicated by mail and got our news chiefly from newspapers (we were sufficiently modern, though, in that we owned a radio roughly the size of a filing cabinet). My early classrooms featured potbellied stoves and double desks with inkwells, into which we dipped our nibs. We boys wore short pants until the ceremony of *communion solennelle*, at age twelve. And so on. But this wasn't any undiscovered pocket of the Carpathians, it was postwar western Europe, where "postwar" was a season that stretched for nearly twenty years.

Seen from that angle, the dream's decadent aristocracy might be my parents, but it could as well stand for Belgian culture in general, although such a distinction might easily be perceived as academic by the Metaphor Central whose offices lie in my back brain. The Belgium of my youth certainly had a vacuum-sealed quality about it. Material deprivation aside, its relation to the modern world was ambiguous at best. On the one hand, it could hardly be said to lie outside history; it had, after all, recently undergone five years of rampaging, furious, deadly history. On the other, Belgium—especially, it seemed to me, the southeastern portion of the country, the provinces of Liège and Luxembourg that contained nearly all my family— was determinedly monochrome. Although this rump brushed the borders of four other countries, it only held one tribe. However much the surnames might apparently vary, French or Flemish or Walloon or German or Dutch or Luxembourgeois, the people themselves were visibly of a single stock. They followed one religion—in my mother's pious family it was said that there were two sects: Catholics and people who had had a fight with a priest. They were monolingual, or almost. The old Walloon tongue was dying out, and only a few people knew the language of their neighbors just over the border.

People generally stayed put. Rare were the ambitious youths who made it as far as Brussels; going to Paris for more than a once-in-a-lifetime holiday was unheard of, except maybe among the rich, but we didn't know any of those. In the country, people remained in their native villages unless they were driven out by misfortune. Neighboring lands were inhabited by the Other, variously indolent, mendacious, thieving, irreligious, cruel, dirty—and for that matter the next province or the nearest town might be just as foreign and unwholesome. The rest of the world was composed of heathens, who lived in huts and presumably ate each other. Of course, Belgium possessed that extraordinary appendage in Africa, but that was perceived as a job more than as a place—you'd go for a year, working for high wages under what were understood to be supremely trying circumstances, then get three to six months off at home, and a few decades of this would finance your retirement. America, of course, was a myth. It existed in the movies, but

was there more to it than that? Everyone had heard of somebody's cousin's mother's uncle who had gone there and pros-
pered, living in sultanesque luxury on a ranch on the Great
Plains, driving a Cadillac among buffalo herds when not dodging bullets in Chicago—but all such stories were legendary, un-
verifiable, and believed only wishfully.

The fact that Belgium is a monarchy, however constitutional, unquestionably lent it a Ruritanian quality. The rich
were phantoms, who wore titles and inhabited châteaux. Maybe
you'd met one—my parents had some fancy friends at whose
home they once dined with a baron—but they chiefly existed
on another plane, touching on common soil only briefly and
magnanimously. The royal family held a place in the popular
imagination akin to that of Hollywood stars. People spoke of
them, speculating on their relationships and personalities, as if
they knew them, but the materialization of one or more in the
town square, to dedicate a monument or commemorate a feast,
was clearly a sacred occasion. One would bathe in the projected
radiance even as one felt it somewhat untoward to stare directly
at those elevated beings. A pilgrimage to the gardens and
greenhouses of the royal palace at Laeken, on the week in May
when they were opened to the public, represented nearly as
much of a hajj as the trip to the miracle sites of Lourdes or
Fatima for which poor people might save their centimes for
decades. And the king—the shy, modest, bespectacled Baudouin, who assumed the throne in 1951 upon the abdication of
his rather questionable father, Leopold III—was perceived as
nearly Christlike in his humility, his wisdom, his love for his
subjects. His common touch, his lack of affect, was the very
quality that marked him most evidently as a divinely appointed
monarch. Belgians, whatever their individual opinions or atti-

tudes, were cast in the role of subjects; the delineations of class were indelibly inscribed.

I had inherited Belgian culture as a package of fragments. I had my impressionistic memories—a heap of short strips of film, blurred stills, muffled or corroded sound recordings, waxily unreliable scratch-'n'-sniff cards, as well as a box of startlingly efficient emotional triggers. I had my mother's definition of the national character, which was rural, pious, familial, severe, sentimental, and unquestioning, and came with culinary, botanical, and zoological annexes. I had my father's, likewise sentimental but otherwise urban, far less reverent, class-conscious in a somewhat feistier vein, humorous but scarred by war and striving. And I had scattered glimpses of my contemporaries and their experience, a little bit through my infrequent contact with friends over there, much more from the books and magazines that I got in the mail by subscription or courtesy of my godfather and his wife my aunt, newsagents in Lambermont. This collection of elements, of wildly uneven size and impact, accounted for perhaps three-quarters of my personality, or at least my self-definition, even in late childhood. My rebellion was a complex matter, since I wanted to break free of the influence of my parents without jettisoning what I valued, and they stood as both guardians and embodiments of everything connected with my early life.

But dump I did. Willfully, accidentally, organically, negligently, crudely, systematically, inevitably I got rid of a section of myself, a part that was once majority and shrank to accessory. I went from being the little Belgian boy, polite and diffident and possessed of a charming accent, to a loutish American adolescent. This was nothing special: I drank, I smoked, I stole, I swore, I stopped going to church. I went in for the usual extremes of hair length and took drugs and listened to abrasive music and hung (timidly enough) around various countercultural scenes, that sort of thing. I grew increasingly bored with school, cutting classes and skipping days at every possible opportunity—eventually getting myself expelled—and used the time to, among other things, read books that would have made my parents blanch, beginning with *Naked Lunch* when I was thirteen. I pursued girls, although haltingly, because I was still an awkward little Belgian boy. Otherwise, of course, none of these activities distinguished me from my contemporaries, and I would likely have engaged in them no matter where I lived, but my mother was convinced that Belgian children did not do such things, her view of Belgium becoming more idealized with every year she spent away from it. My view of Belgium became correspondingly more hostile, because it represented authority and also because I was certain its taint was what made me timid and awkward and unpopular and unattractive and solitary. I began a project to reinvent myself, acknowledge no bonds or ties or background, pass myself off as entirely self-made.

At least this is one way of looking at things; it could also be said that I subtracted nothing, but merely added. It never occurred to me to change my name or adapt its pronunciation or stop using French; I would never become one of *them*. I would never pledge allegiance to the flag—or any flag, for that matter—and I would never eat soft white bread or drink Budweiser or watch the Super Bowl or refer to my parents as Mom and Dad or refer to or even think of Americans as "we." This defiance was impelled in part by rage at the country that made me feel like a pariah—jumbled up indiscriminately with issues of taste and belief or the lack thereof—but also by a vestigial pride. And yet along the way a fundamental loss took place, something that the dream transformed into a treasure. Certainly the theme of loss is constant for exiles, even two-bit job-seekers and their offspring. My parents lost friends, lost family ties and patterns of mutual assistance, lost rituals and habits and favorite foods, lost any link to an ongoing social milieu, lost a good part of the sense they had of themselves. We lost a house, several towns, various landscapes. We lost documents and pictures and heirlooms, as well as most of our breakable belongings, smashed in the nine packing cases that we took with us to America. We lost connection to a thing larger than ourselves, and as a family failed to make any significant new connection in exchange, so that we were left aground on a sandbar barely big enough for our feet. I lost friends and relatives and stories and familiar comforts and a sense of continuity between home and outside and any sense that I was normal. I lost half a language through want of use and eventually, in my late teens, even lost French as the language of my internal monologue. And I lost a whole network of routes through life that I had just barely glimpsed.

Hastening on toward some idea of a future, I only half-realized these losses, and when I did realize I didn't disapprove, and sometimes I actively colluded. At some point, though, I was bound to notice that there was a gulf inside me, with a blanketed form on the other side that hadn't been uncovered in decades. My project of self-invention had been successful, so much so that I had become a sort of hydroponic vegetable, growing soil-free. But I had been formed in another world; everything in me that was essential was owed to immersion in that place, and that time, that I had so effectively renounced. Continuing to believe that I had just made myself up out of whole cloth was self-flattering but hollow. I once wrote a rock and roll song whose chorus went, "If I only have one life, let me live it as a lie," and I really believed it, then, at twenty-five. But later on I could no longer ignore the contradictions. Shame and pride, self-loathing and rage, arrogance and solipsism all blurred together insupportably, so that I could truly be myself only when under attack. I was in danger of being devoured by my own negativity. I took cover in nostalgia, perversely enough a nostalgia for times and places that were not my own. There was nothing wrong with that, of course, except that I was in part using it as a blind, and the details I uncovered became substitutes for my own constituent ingredients. It is fascinating and often fruitful to try on another skin, but it is ultimately meaningless if one hasn't acknowledged one's own. I already had a history, intriguingly buried. It might even be an interesting one. Eventually I came to the conclusion that if I did nothing else, I at least needed to uncover it. Maybe some of what I thought I had lost was merely hidden.

Like it or not, each of us is *made,* less by blood or genes than by a process that is largely accidental, the impact of things seen and heard and smelled and tasted and endured in those few years before our clay hardens. Offhand remarks, things glimpsed in passing, jokes and commonplaces, shop displays and climate and flickering light and textures of walls are all consumed by us and become part of our fiber, just as much as the more obvious effects of upbringing and socialization and intimacy and learning. Every human being is an archeological site. What passes for roots is actually a matter of sediment, of accretion, of chance and juxtaposition. Recent research on genetic inheritance has been deformed into legend by chatter, and made to serve old and often destructive notions of destiny, ethnic or racial or social or economic. Behavior, though, gets passed down less by encoding than by example; tendencies and inclinations and limits and the ability to surpass them are formed not in the womb but out in the air. Parents exert an overwhelming effect on their children by their words, their deeds, their omissions and concealments, but children simultaneously conduct their own education, absorbing everything that crosses their field of reception, and that is a matter over which parents have little or no control. So the damnedest bits of fugitive trivia may show up years later, recombined and inexplicable, prominent in the baggage of the adult self. The archeological detective who can trace their passage in detail does not exist and never will. I don't claim any special ability in my own case, but I do possess a circumstantial advantage. Emigration, like a natural upheaval, sheared my foundation when the ground was soft, laying open expanses of strata. Pieces of matter and machinery protruded that would otherwise have dissolved or been driven underground. Time has blunted their contours, so that identification is rarely certain, but enough remains visible to allow for guesses, at least to suggest the whereabouts of the template that cast them. I can't in any way be conclusive about what made me. All I can do is to reconstruct the site, and imagine the factory at work.

III Fait-Divers

We own our birthdays, each of us, and it amazes us when we first encounter someone who shares that singular date. Actually, it's probably best if we don't immediately meet a fellow native in the flesh, but first hear about some personage, famous or dead or both, with whom we can share the occasion without rivalry. In my case, I learned from a newspaper sometime around the time of my seventh or eighth birthday that I could blow out a candle or two in honor of Leslie Uggams, who had a lovely voice and was in addition the first and possibly the only black person ever to appear on the *Lawrence Welk Show*. That variety program always seemed to be playing when I went with my parents to visit their friend Marie-Louise Lenihan and her mother, Mme. van Hemmelrijk, bourgeois French-speaking Antwerpers who, along with two other daughters and their husbands, had inexplicably ended up living in various towns on the eastern end of Union County, New Jersey. Mme. van Hemmelrijk, who possessed the gravitas of an eighteenth-century Austrian empress, had a special fondness for Welk, whose accent so resembled the Flemings' that I thought for years he was one, too, and possibly imagined that his program was put on solely for their benefit. His bloodless tin-pan alley clichés made me writhe, but I was used to discomfort when visiting elderly Belgians. The television show was merely an American refinement of the torture, supplanting the hollow Belgian silence.

But I didn't mind Leslie Uggams, and later I added to the

list Jean Crain and Miles Davis and Ralph Waldo Emerson. We
formed a merry quintet. I was conscious of allowing the others
the right to share my birthday, and for that matter I thought I
owned the month of May. After a while, when I heard about
someone else being born in May, I felt less trespassed upon than
bound with them in a benign fellowship, which however did not
diminish my sense of ownership. Later this was all explained
for me by astrology—those born after the twenty-first, at least,
were Geminians, too, and so we all possessed exactly the same
personality. But this lay far in the future, and by that time I had
laid claim to the year 1954 as well. Eventually I was to abandon
all modesty and stake out the entire twentieth century, the fact
that it was more than half over when I came in notwithstanding. But in all the components of the date May 25, 1954, I saw
the lights of home, through the same magic of adherence by
happenstance that makes people stake their personal happiness
on the vexed fortunes of the hometown team.

By contrast, I can't take much joy in the ex post facto gener-
ational label affixed to a swath of some twenty years of which
mine falls a bit before the halfway mark. It mostly conjures up
an old chromo image, babies' heads popping out of cabbages
(with, in its postcard version, a caption such as "Utah's Finest
Crop" above). The catchphrase's other major association is
clearly non-applicable. If Belgium uttered a sound in 1954, it
was hardly a boom, maybe an intake of breath not preceded by
an exhalation, which was certainly preferable to the wounded-
stag noises that had emanated from it not all that much earlier.
The faces surrounding mine on my first appearance in the family album are not swelled by prosperity or flushed with sunny
expectation of the future. Had the pictures been taken seventy-
five years earlier, the severe countenances could be explained
by the length of the exposure and the discomfort of the pho-

tographer's studio apparatus. These are snapshots, but few of the parties pictured appear familiar with the conventions of contrived spontaneity.

My mother and father are, it is true, smiling. Just a year and a month earlier, they had suffered a stillbirth, and doctors were concerned the unhappy event might be repeated. I use the term "doctors" loosely, since it is not clear that a physician was in attendance, my birth having been overseen by a nun-midwife, who appears in the photos as a formidable presence in white, her face barely discernible at the end of a tunnel of cowl. The site was a small clinic on Rue Masson in Verviers, the Maternité Ste.-Marie, which curiosity drove me to try and find thirty-eight years later, but either its place had been usurped by the faceless new construction on the one-block street's west side, over toward Rue Thil-Lorrain, or it had moved out of one of the three-story eighteenth-century bumps across the way. The pictures, presumably taken with my parents' old Voigtländer, possibly exaggerate the darkness within. The one where my mother is sitting up in bed has all the cavelike density of an uncleaned Rembrandt, the faces of her mother and my father's mother emerging from an opaque black fog. There is no way to gauge the relative comfort of the appointments, although it is worth noting that she and I remained at the clinic for the better part of a week after my arrival, for no other reason than that was the routine.

I was, in fact, baptized in the clinic's own chapel at the age of five days. The arrangements were, per tradition, impressively compact. My maternal grandmother was my godmother, and in her honor I was given Marie as my second name. Joseph Peerboom, who married my father's sister, Armande, was my godfather, and so Joseph was inscribed as my third name. François became my fourth name as a mark of dedication to the

Franciscan order, by way of gratitude for my safe birth, and for good measure I was given Ghislain as my fifth. Just about everybody in my mother's family had Ghislain or Ghislaine tucked somewhere into their chain of names, as did a very large portion of the natives of the Ardennes region, because the saint was invoked as protection against epilepsy (Ghislain is a cognate of Vitus, as in St. Vitus's dance). My first name, meanwhile, represented a tribute to my father and his father, both named Lucien, as well as an innovation. No one in either family had ever been named Luc, but it was a popular name that year, as I was to discover when I started school, my classes never having fewer than three or four of us.

The name had been chosen well in advance. At some point during her pregnancy my mother had, in those pre-sonogram days, consulted a wise child, that is, a boy whose father had died before his birth. This youth had taken my mother's wedding ring and dangled it on a chain above her belly. The vertical path it chose for its rotation indicated that the offspring would be male. My stillborn sister had been prepared for with the name Marie-Luce, which shows that the theme was already in place. Coincidentally, my father's oldest sibling, who lived for only a few days after her birth in 1910, was named Lucienne. My parents' loss of their own eldest, which they never quite stopped mourning, echoes many earlier sad family statistics. The serial deaths of infants and children, a matter we associate with the dark past, continued well into the present century: a stillbirth here, a drowning there, scarlet fever, meningitis, poxes various. My small uncles Adelin Remacle and Alfred Stelmes look up at me from the family album, both set to die shortly after their pictures were taken and thus to remain toddlers for all eternity. Poor Adelin, his dim image cut out from some group shot and then rephotographed against white, already looks like a ghost.

I was fated to be an only child. My mother's condition was sufficiently delicate that after my birth she was advised not to attempt any more pregnancies. That honed the family tree down to a point. My parents, oddly for their time and place, each had only one living sibling, neither of whom had children. Elsewhere in the family, collections of six or eight offspring were not uncommon. If I had no first cousins, I had so many seconds and thirds I could never remember them all. But this activity took place on my mother's side, especially in her maternal lineage, among the prolific Remacles. My father's family was another story. Wide gaps separated the generations there. My father, born in 1921, was the late child of parents born in 1879 and 1881, respectively, who themselves were younger children in their families. Such first cousins as my father had tended to be his seniors by as much as thirty or so years—his Lecoq cousins had children older than he was. They were not, needless to say, close. Consequently, the only Santes I ever met were my father's sister and his mother, his father having died in 1948.

My paternal grandmother, Marie Sante, née Hermant, died when I was barely four, so my memories of her are hazy and inseparably entwined with others' accounts. She was a small, explosive package, less than five feet tall and famous in her neighborhood for having, frying pan in hand, chased a German soldier out of her kitchen in 1914. She peppered her food so intensely my mother couldn't eat it (this fondness for assertive spices skipped a generation), and shortly before her death she bought me my very first magazine subscription, to *Tintin*. That is virtually all I know about her. In the earliest photograph I have of her she is already over fifty, and in that and all the subsequent others she is robust, wry, and seamed, her jaw clamped shut in a way that suggests that her teeth may not be in good repair. Seated at my mother's bedside she wears black, in protracted mourning for her husband. She reposes her hands in her lap in that attitude of those who have done a great deal of hard work over many years and are permanently weary. Her death in 1958 was the only time my father is known to have wept.

My other grandmother, Anne-Marie Nandrin, née Remacle, sits at my mother's bedside wearing white. She looks severe, as she does in nearly all photographs, although she does not appear emaciated during this period. The 1950s were the one time in her life when she ran ever so slightly to plumpness. She was a proud and rather imperious woman, who nevertheless endured a lifetime of being known by a name she hated. She called herself Anne-Marie, her baptismal first name, but permitted everybody else to call her by her middle name, Honorine, bestowed in memory of her own godmother. By her side in nearly every picture is her husband, Édouard, always the nattiest dresser in any group. Indoors, he has removed his suit jacket to reveal his splendid striped braces. At the door of the clinic he models his gray double-breasted with the presence of a senior diplomat, an illusion further accentuated by his trim gray mustache, aquiline beak, and the pouched eyelids of a man who has seen it all. He was, in fact, an unlucky striver all his life, who attained his greatest glory around the time of the First World War, as a streetcar conductor in Liège.

In the depths of my mother's room my Aunt Armande is barely visible. It is surprising to see her with a great mop of black curls, even looking a bit like a saucy café singer in her striped dress. My album, with its patchy accretion of photographs, many of them of people who were not often photographed, contains only one earlier picture of her. In that one she is perhaps eleven, holding by the hand my father, ten years younger and in rompers. Her hair at that age was light enough that she may, like him, have begun life as a blonde, only to have it begin darkening after the first decade. I last saw her when I was twenty, so my recall is more than fleeting, but even so she drifts through my memory as a sort of cloud, a large, kind woman of few words, advancing through the kitchen bearing an enormous pot of soup or *tête de veau*, holding its blazing handles through bunched folds of her apron. She may have gotten a bit hard of hearing in old age, since the characteristic expression of hers I retain is a sweetly chirping, high-pitched *"Hein?"*

Her husband's real first name was Pieter, a fact I didn't know until I saw his obituary notice clipped from the paper in 1989. He was Dutch, a native of Vaals, a town that sits at the extreme southeasterly point of the Netherlands, virtually astride its borders with both Belgium and Germany. He was, unsurprisingly, multilingual, and came from a family of customs agents, although he himself was a landcape gardener by vocation and training. He had a creased, good-humored face beneath a steeply raked comb-over that topped his head like a saddle blanket, and usually wore a misshapen extinguished tailor-made parked in a corner of his wide mouth, the very ends of which were usually turned up in an expression of serene irony. He was a character, all piss and vinegar. His knockabout youth, retailed in scattered anecdotes, sounded to me like something out of Blaise Cendrars or Pierre MacOrlan, and he looked enough like Cendrars that I tended to conflate them. I was his chief heir; I received seven hundred dollars when he abandoned his worldly goods to enter a charity nursing home.

The only principal absent from the party attending my christening was my mother's brother, René, who was employed by the Ministry of Public Works in the Congo and had not made an appearance in Belgium for some years nor would for nearly five more, to the continuing distress of his mother, whose favorite he was. Uncompromising though my grandmother was in all matters of morality, she was prepared to forgive her son anything, whether it was his drinking or his having married a divorcée, who anyway eventually left him. There may have been other scandals, for all I know; such things were discussed out of my earshot or in Walloon, which I only understood in snatches. Uncle René's two stepchildren, Claude and Renée, *nés* Schoumacker, were my phantom first cousins, having ceased to be my relatives even before I was born; in any case I never met them. My uncle walks through my infancy in a single guise, represented by a photograph I possess: thin, hawk-nosed, with a red pencil mustache—a shady character on the edges of some French colonial film noir—wearing a solar topee, a white ensemble of many-pocketed safari jacket and pleated shorts, and white knee socks, leading a German shepherd on a leash, followed at two paces by a bare-headed, short-socked, serious-looking African gentleman whose job description was that of "boy."

Soon after the baptism my parents took me home, to 44, Rue de la Colline, a respectable address in Verviers, a town in which the measure of respectability increases with every degree that one moves south of the river, up the hill, and west of the commune of Mangombroux. The quarter of the city thus described was built serially within twenty or twenty-five years on either side of the turn of the century, the lower tiers—among which was Rue de la Colline—for the petite bourgeoisie, and the upper, known as the Quartier des Boulevards, for the upper. My parents were more prosperous than they had ever been in their lives. They both came out of relative poverty, and now my father was wearing white shirts and neckties to work, the first in his family ever to do so, as production manager at the Duesberg-Bosson foundry. My mother, who had worked ever since leaving school at sixteen, had quit her secretarial job at the family welfare office of the textile industry's Fédération Patronale to become a full-time housewife and mother.

The birth announcement they sent out was in the classic style: my parents' formal visiting card in buff, their names (Mr et Mme. L. SANTE-NANDRIN) across the center and their address at lower right, with the addition of a line below their names *(have the great joy of announcing the fortunate birth of a son)* and the maternity clinic's address at lower left. Joined by a white ribbon at upper left was a tiny card bearing my first name and birthdate. It was the baptismal announcement that was the venue for cute illustrations of babies in cribs surrounded by angels and suchlike, in several designs sufficiently standard I see them every time I visit a flea market in Belgium, and every time experience a minor jolt before I open the card lying on the heap, half-expecting it to be one of mine.

I arrived in a world of guarded optimism, of meagerness and caution, of modest ambitions and dark nondescript clothing. On May 25, the morning newspaper prognosticated a high temperature of twelve degrees (that would be fifty-three degrees Fahrenheit), partly cloudy, wind from the south, no precipitation but 70 percent humidity, with a slight possibility of storms later in the day—cool and damp, the Belgian spring. The news was minor: explosion at blast furnace in Marcinelle injures seven; four men hold up *agent de change* in Ixelles, make off with 200,000F; death of Lutunu, tribal chief who guided Henry Morton Stanley in the Congo in 1882; Belgian fishermen arrested by German maritime police for trawling off the Isle of Sylt; Anderlecht first in association football rankings; seventh provincial competition for breeding sows held in Bastogne. The advertisements are stark: "Thin men gain weight with Jessel Pastilles, in a base of cod-liver oil"; "For women—Dupuis red pills." Also "Nosta is good fresh milk" and "Côte d'Or is good chocolate" and "Top Bronnen mineral water procures health and youthfulness." For that matter "Sunil makes the whitest wash in the world" and "Ten, twenty, thirty Belga cigarettes . . . always a pleasure to smoke." But then "The beauties of the Belgian Congo: Who would imagine that this lovely beach is on the shore of Lake Tanganyika?" At the movies, more stars than there are in heaven—Richard Todd and Glynis Johns, June Allyson and Van Johnson, Vittorio Gassman and Gloria Grahame, Raf Vallone, Yvonne Sanson, John Payne, Silvana Pompanini . . . And in the actual heavens, the real stars dictate: "Children born this day will be reflective and studious; they will early on acquire a sense of duty. After some struggle against adverse circumstances, they will enjoy success and a good marriage."

That was old news, anyway, by the time I actually emerged, around 11:30 P.M., when everyone was asleep but the night shift and your stray insomniacs. The whole town was shuttered except the main waiting room of the train station and those cafés that catered particularly to night workers. The narrow streets of Verviers presented row upon row of shopfronts completely hidden behind thin-slatted wooden shutters. Street lights emanated just enough of a glow to form a yellow puddle around their bases. Obscure mechanical groans and clacks sounded from the depths of the train yards and a few round-the-clock factories, unheard by all. Cats made their way from ground-floor windowsills to the bits of woods adjoining the river on its far bank. A man in a raincoat was weaving down Crapaurue on his bicycle, singing snatches of songs to himself. Two men crossed in the darkness on the diamond-cobbled pavement of Rue Spintay and muttered clipped *saluts* as they passed. Somebody was just turning out the lights inside the poster frames heralding *Commando sur Rhodes,* with Dirk Bogarde and Akim Tamiroff, abruptly snapping their faces off twice, at the Coliséum cinema on Rue Xhavée. The last tram from Pepinster was lurching and ratcheting its way along Rue d'Ensival, with a load comprised of a staring drunk, a grandmother reading a devotional pamphlet, a disconsolate teenage girl looking at her feet, two garage mechanics reading boxing magazines, and a professorial-looking old gentleman in a three-piece suit worn shiny, his head thrown back at an unnatural angle, snoring lustily. All over town, compressed into their narrow, high beds under the two blankets adjudged adequate for the sharp nights of May, were laborers and marketwomen and trolley conductors and café waiters and cloistered nuns and magistrates and amateur painters and dealers in woollen rags and ends.

Among them would be people who had known the sepia eighties and nineties, had heard Vieuxtemps play at the Harmonie and been in attendance at the opening of the theater, had stood in the front lines during the 1896 general strike, had taken their caged finches for walks in the hills on Sunday afternoons and entered them in the annual singing contests, had slumped powerless in August 1914 when the first smug German battalions had marched through in the flush of taking their first city, had seen the canal paved over and the hillsides terraced and built upon, had joined numberless choral and dramatic and political and debating and literary and domino-playing associations, had fled on foot and bicycle in May 1940 against the dull horror of history repeating itself, had returned ashen and sixty

pounds lighter from forced-labor camps in '45, were now trying
to convince themselves that their society had resumed its normal stride for good and that the Cassandras predicting the imminent collapse of the single and omnipotent local industry
were merely blowing smoke.

The following day, as dawn broke, you could see them
bestirring themselves in their apartments, the mingled odors
of coffee and burning coal and the liquid fuel called mazout
and creosote and truck exhaust and caporal tobacco wafting
through the streets in a stream. Women emerged in floral
dresses under floral aprons of nearly the same dimensions, and
stockings and slippers, with buckets and mops in hand to wash
the sidewalks. Men set out on foot or pushed off on their bicycles or jammed the streetcars, in raincoats and suit coats, neckties and neckerchiefs, berets and fedoras, with a smoldering
butt or a pipe alive in a corner of their faces and sending up
plumes, miniatures of the ones rippling from the smokestacks
of the works whose bell they were rushing to beat, even if a
few here and there detached themselves from the ranks to stop
at a *zinc* for the essential *café arrosé*, dosed with the ginever
called *pèkèt*. They aimed for points all along the Vesdre River,
factories lined up almost shoulder to shoulder from Ensival to
the Île Adam, up Gérard-Champs to Pont Léopold, from the
Prés-Javais to Renoupré, with annexes going north to Dison
and northeast to Andrimont. They filed through the gates and
stopped in the locker room, changing into their smocks or *sa-
lopettes* of a uniform bluebird blue, some of them removing
quite respectable-looking suits to do so. Then they started their
looms and cards, attended their warping racks and dyeing vats,
as generations had before them.

The colors of Verviers are green and white, from its pun-
ning device *Vert et Vieux* (although, oddly, it didn't start out as

a pun; *"Alten grün,"* had said the archbishop of Cologne in 1418, admiring the local oaks). Its color scheme in 1954, however, was gray and brown. This could be said of nearly all Belgian cities, but Verviers was more concentrated, more emphatically gray and brown than most. My parents, stepping out onto the sidewalk from their small stoop on Rue de la Colline, saw primarily gray. Gray were the houses, the sidewalks, the streets themselves, here even more than above in the fancy neighborhood, where there might be affectations of French white or pale yellow among the houses, and bona fide green in the trees around them. On Rue de la Colline, however, vegetation was restricted to back courts; the houses were flush with the sidewalk, which itself was no wider than necessary. The houses were four-story stacks of flats, three windows per floor, the windows simply outlined, no more ornamentation than that, everything made of brick and painted gray, the mansarded roof covered with diamond-shaped dark gray tiles. Every window was hung with white curtains backed by drapes. Their sills might host a specimen or two of the ubiquitous serpent plant *(sansevieria)*, although ground-floor residents would feel compelled to put on the dog, displaying in addition to plants various hammered-brass objects, pitchers and plates and whatnot, or possibly some Delftware, and crucifixes and candles and statues if they were devout.

Rue de la Colline slants up from Rue du Palais to Rue du Centre, my parents' previous address; slanting is the course it takes both in plane geometry and in solid. Its slope is relatively gentle, because it catches Rue du Centre near its base; linking the same two streets a bit farther up, by contrast, is the Escalier de la Paix, one of the city's many arterial staircases. To head down to the center of town, to accomplish, say, the marketing, my mother would cross Rue du Palais, catching a glimpse of the huge and forbidding multispired pile of the Palais de Justice down to the right, engage the brief Rue des Ploquettes above the railroad tracks and then descend a flight of steps that forms the head of Rue de Rome. Here she would encounter definitive brown, brown in the factories looming at the river's edge beyond, brown in the somber façade of the Jesuit *collège*, St. François-Xavier, and the adjacent lump of the church of the Sacré-Coeur, in whose style the nineteenth century paid its respects to the Counter-Reformation. But the street would then issue her onto Place Verte, the very center, with its cafés and newspaper kiosks, its vast department stores and groceries, Le Grand Bazar and La Vièrge Noire, its milling crowds and clanging trolleys. Here was where fashion was made, where scandal was broadcast, where significant sums changed hands, where important people were to be seen, strolling by, hands clasped behind their backs, casual as you please.

This bustling metropolis, home to some forty thousand souls—roughly comparable to, say, Elmira, New York—on the edge of the Pays de Herve, Belgium's creamery, and the gateway to the Ardennes Mountains as well as the mysterious heaths known as the Hautes-Fagnes, was an important town, primarily for its four centuries as one of Europe's major centers for the weaving, warping, washing, carding, and dyeing of wool. It was popular with the German army for its proximity to the border—little more than twenty miles away—and the level roads between it and Aachen. Otherwise not many foreign visitors had graced its squares, for all that masses of them had descended at voguish intervals upon Spa, just a few miles south, where the concept of the mineral cure had virtually originated. Verviers was not famous for its architecture; it possessed no university; its museums were minor-league at best; its theater was adequate but distinctly provincial; its culinary specialties

were possibly delightful but hardly refined. It did have a curious sideline in the production of violin virtuosi, but those were
of course mobile and exportable. It was neither capital nor
crossroads nor port, not even a river port such as its neighbor
Liège, with its francophile pretensions. Rather, it was enclosed
and a bit solipsistic in its tight little valley. It failed to be
counted as one of the major cities of Belgium.

As my mother, *filet à provisions* in hand, negotiated her
way through the aisles of La Vièrge Noire in the direction of
the leeks, a grocer nasally trilling something about *toutes ces
fleuuûûûrs*—maybe a congealed Tino Rossi—and somebody
else just outside the door barking a mechanically repeated
phrase so elided that you could just make out the single word
tombola—lottery—and the one-two bells of the streetcars and
the deliberate deep bells of Notre-Dame des Récollets all col-
liding, my grandmother waited outside with me, half-dozing in
my pram, dressed too warmly for August, probably, but you
never knew when a sudden breeze might come up. The Virgin
that gave the shop its name—blackened, apparently, by having
been hidden in the chimney of a sacristy converted into a black-
smith's shop during the French Revolution—hovered above, affixed midway between the second and third stories, the most
enigmatic of the many competing icons of the square: the nearly
life-sized and all too bloody crucifix guarding the corner of the
café on the Pont Saint-Laurent side, the Sioux chief in full headdress smoking a Cogetama cigar, the grinning fez-topped black
face widening eyes over a cup of Banania, the silhouetted black
cat curling its tail in respect to Chat Noir coffee, the archangel
spearing a demon on behalf of St. Michel cigarettes, the cloche-
hatted and fur-collared flapper named Stella Artois coyly
acknowledging her throne as the muse of beer. My mother
emerged with vegetables lumped at the bottom and protruding

from the top of her sack, inbetween a bunch of grapes in brown paper and some kind of globular fruit in individual color-fully printed white wrappers. They walked—I rolled, almost awake—over to Pont aux Lions and looked in the windows of the Grand Bazar, where a man wearing a café waiter's long apron over his shirtsleeves was demonstrating a brand-new miracle waffle iron, passing out samples to the ragamuffins.

After a few distracted minutes they walked on, through Terre-Hollande to Place du Martyr, where they did not so much as glance at the statue of the martyr, Grégoire-Joseph Chapuis, beheaded on that site January 2, 1794, with a saw, after seven ineffectual axe blows, on orders from the prince-bishop of Liège, for among other things having conducted civil marriage ceremonies in his function as officer of the revolutionary council. Instead they headed straight for À l'Innova-tion, whose name continued to guarantee the forward thrust of its fashion sensibility despite its more than five decades on the spot. Inside they parted the hanging garments on the racks, fingered a cardigan, sighed over two or more little dresses, as I slept soundly, rocked by the rhythm of their chitchat and that of all those other pairs of women agreeing or mildly disagree-ing sotto voce. But they steeled themselves and renounced any purchase, not too difficult a decision because of the limitations of their pocketbooks and the cost of everything today, God knows. Instead they continued down the length of the square to the church, aux Récollets, stopping for a minute to look up at the statue, which as everyone knew had come alive during the earthquake of September 18, 1692, when the Infant had been about to smite the populace with his sceptre for its unabated wickedness, but his Mother had seized his arm and pointed it away, in which attitude the two had remained frozen ever after.

They lighted a pair of candles in a side chapel, praying for more money and enduring health after depositing their centimes in the slot, and then at the holy-water font crossed my somnolent form before crossing themselves.

Then came the long walk, bumpity-bump over the cobbles, down Rue du Marteau and then along the Vesdre. My mother glanced briefly to the right up the hill on the other side of the river at the neighborhood called the Dardanelle and the approximate location of Rue du Paradis, invisible behind the houses at the top, an absurdly precipitous walk from the Spintay up Hautes Mezelles, prettily green but too much huffing and puffing for anyone but young marrieds, as she and my father had been when they had lived there. They passed Pont du Chêne and crossed themselves in sight of the spire of St. Antoine on the other side, debated a minute about whether to go to the bakery also bearing the saint's name at the mouth of the Spintay, but, no, there was enough bread in both their houses, and they would forgo pastries in favor of fruit. Then Rue du Chêne (bumpity-bump) feeding into Rue David (bumpity), past Pont Dicktus, then that long, dingy stretch of ancient crumbling riverside houses, factories, garages, little machine shops, debris, and here and there a vacancy not yet filled where some building no one could quite remember had been decimated by a shell ten years earlier. Then, finally, Pont Léopold, where the river took a hard left, and across the street loomed the high banked artificial hillside that supported the tracks and yards of the Verviers-Ouest freight station. They turned onto Rue des Gérard-Champs where just a few feet away stood the *librairie*—newspapers, magazines, chocolate, *citronade,* Tiercé Colonial—that marked the head of Rue Robert Centner.

There, in an enclave of houses almost entirely surrounded

by factories, lived my Nandrin grandparents, at number 12, one of a trio of stern gray-yellow late-nineteenth-century edifices. Across the way, in a smaller and older brown brick house, number 17, my Sante grandmother had been living alone for almost six years now. Both families had, by sheerest coincidence, moved in around 1939. My mother, pretty and extremely shy and tending to look at the pavement as she walked, and my father, rather feckless and footloose in those days, had known each other by sight but little more. Her appearances in public were few and purposeful. He was just *"le fils de l'aubette"*—the son of the kiosk, metonymically—at least as of 1946, when his father retired from *chez* Voos and took over the newsstand on Place du Marché from a friend of Aunt Amélie, the boy's godmother. Then in—was it the autumn of '48?—she had gone as she often did on Sunday afternoons to the dance at Polleur with her friends Gaby and Suzanne Degotte, and had danced with this one and that one, she didn't really notice because she was too timid, but on the way home on the tram she was holding on to the pole and a hand slid down gradually but meaningfully to touch hers, and it was the Sante boy. She got off at the Harmonie and hurried, practically ran, down Rue David, hearing him rushing behind her, unavoidably toward the same destination. She softened a bit at a dance in Ensival that winter, going so far as to permit him to sit with her as they ate *oeux russes* with *frites*. But, you know, they were young, which means silly, and he was out of touch for a while and she cried, and her mother cleared her throat and shrugged and said, *"C'était pas fait pour durer,"* it wasn't meant to last. But then one day there he was again, and he went all the way to Lambermont with her when she was just going to the tailor's, and it suddenly began to look serious.

ɪᴠ Flood

In the fall of 1989 I found myself in a suffocating modern hotel off Kensington High Street in London, in a bedroom-and-bath combo I could have misplaced in a corner of my New York tenement apartment. I was in England to conduct an interview with a literary figure, which I must have dispatched because I can look up the published article in my files, but I have little memory of it. I was preoccupied with a plan that had arrived at my jet-lagged bedside at night and presented itself as an order. Ever since I had been trembling. It will sound like no big deal: I was to call the airline and change the venue of my return flight from Gatwick to Brussels. Then I was to take the boat train from Victoria Station, the Dover ferry to Ostend, and there a train to Verviers.

I had last set foot in Belgium in 1974, when I was twenty and midway through a romantically besotted summer in Paris, ostensibly studying among other things "The Vampirism of Meaning," with Félix Guattari, and "The Insistence of the Image in the Freudian Text," with Hubert Damisch, but really paying very little attention to anything as pedestrian as a lecture. My mother called then, possibly just as I was leaving for that little sweatbox of an African disco in the cellar of Le Caméléon, on Rue St. André-des-Arts, and in no uncertain terms commanded me to go and at least visit my Tante Fonsine and my godfather and Tante Armande, it doesn't have to be more than those three, but they won't be alive forever. I had protested and groaned, but the visits had actually been wonderful. Tante Fonsine—short for Alphonsine, my grandmother's sister—had given me brandy and a cigar after dinner and settled me into the big leather armchair in her little house in Ciney, to watch badly dubbed Tweety Bird cartoons, and in the morning she brought me up a bowl and a pitcher of hot water for shaving. She said my sideburns reminded her of the men of her youth, and right then I felt like one. My godfather had merrily gotten me drunk on Scotch cut with apricot schnapps and we had rolled cigarettes and talked like old cronies, sitting at the oilcloth-covered kitchen table of the house at the far end of the square in Lambermont, while Tante Armande circled and hovered and laughed and said *"Hein?"*

I kept the warm glow of those visits for a long time, but somehow it wasn't enough to make me go back there. My mother was right: all three of my favorite relatives were to die before I set foot in Belgium again. For fifteen years the country sat on a back shelf of my mind, a reproach and a question mark. During that time, of course, artistic poverty long prevented me from going anywhere farther than I could get to on the subway, and when for example my friends all went off to Berlin, the East Village of Europe before the wall fell, I could only envy them. But now I was thirty-five, and living a bit higher in the saddle, and had actually been to France, to England, to Spain and to Portugal, just in the past couple of years, and you'd think I would have had at least the curiosity to swing a mere few kilometers east or northeast or south, if only to have some *frites* and a bottle of Orval.

Furthermore, my parents, after much agonizing and debate, had taken the step of which they had so long dreamed. Upon my father's retirement from the Ethylene Corporation of Mur-

ray Hill, New Jersey, they had sold their house and car and
pared their remaining belongings down to what could fit into
the exact same nine packing cases that had transported their
household across the ocean in 1959, and had caused to be
erected a prefabricated house on the parcel of land they owned
in St. Hubert, in the heart of the Ardennes, just two plots over
from the house of my mother's cousin Nelly Wathelet. But in
the two years since their move in '87 they had been calling me
and writing letters and even coming over, taking a room in
Summit at what used to be called The Hotel Suburban, a place
they had so long thought of as being beyond their means if not
above their station, alternately pleading with me to pay them a
visit, just one little visit, and further agonizing about moving
back to America yet again. Belgium was not making them
happy. People were distant, called them "les Américains" behind their backs, would probably still call them that if they remained for thirty years, and my father didn't know what to do
with himself once he had accomplished the morning walk to
the village to buy the paper, and anyway the television pulled in
these German stations that ran commercials that were pure
smut.

But I put them off, again and again. I was afraid of my parents and afraid of Belgium, and the combination of the two was
more than I could bear to contemplate. I was an accredited
adult by then, with a domestic relationship, and assets mostly in
the form of old books, and even a profession, of sorts. Nevertheless, my separate identity, which of course I had built with
my own two hands from twigs and straw over a couple of
decades, still seemed so tenuous that I had to guard it against
the slightest stirring of breeze. "Belgium," since I had returned
from my last prolonged stay there on the threshold of nine, had

been something both more and less than a country. Didn't my mother, when I misbehaved, wield the threat of sending me back there to boarding school, so that it came to seem like the awful final punishment, much worse than your father coming home and taking off his belt? (The term for boarding school is *pension,* which happens to sound a lot like *punition.*) Wasn't I, for that matter, constantly shown how all my torts derived directly from living in America; how Belgian children were obedient, well-mannered, and clean; how if only we'd stayed there I would have been a model schoolboy and the perfect son? Instead I was a chronic liar, a thief, a sullen and willful and defiant child, who constantly incurred bad grades both academically and in the "behavior" section on the back of the report card, whose teachers were always lamenting his lack of effort and attention despite such potential, who wore unbecoming and ragged clothes and made no attempt to be neat, and who probably didn't even go to church anymore despite what he claimed.

All of this was true, of course, and the reality was rather worse than my mother feared. I was a little one-boy guerrilla army waging war against my upbringing—a covert war, naturally, since I knew my parents could have crushed me with little effort. Or maybe I was actually capable of killing *them* with my bad behavior, and then having blood on my hands and guilt staining my soul for the rest of my life. I wasn't sure which. In either case, Belgium played the role of ultimate authority, a monstrous shadow perhaps wearing a cassock that loomed behind my parents in every fight I had with them. And I had no allies, no brothers or sisters, no other relatives around, no friends who could have begun to understand my particular predicament. My parents were isolated, very much so, but at least they had each other, and they had that phantom country to turn to, which grew more mythic and embracing with every year they were away from it. I moved around in American life with more ease than they did, but I wasn't a part of it. My upbringing had taken care of that, and whatever bits it had left unattended were armor-plated by my pride. I was unassimilable in two cultures, waging a solo war on both fronts, but whereas I could negotiate and dodge America, passing through it undercover, Belgium apparently had my number, my mug shot, and my prints.

You could say that at thirty-five I was too old for that sort of nonsense, had been living on my own for far too long to be still battling the beasts that made their nests under my childhood bed. But maybe it was my avoidance that had made them thrive. Anyway, curiosity finally got the better of me in 1989. This mature undertaking was not without its perverse aspect, however, because in deciding to go and confront Belgium head-on, I was nevertheless faced with the problem of my parents, still in residence there albeit for just a few weeks longer—they had decided to move back to New Jersey. I only had three days in which to do my exploring, which was about the minimum time my parents would demand, so that I had to keep my visit secret. They would absolutely fail to understand. I had to slip into the country and creep around like a spy. My reasoning was not purely melodramatic. Belgium is a very small country, and even though I was going to Verviers and my parents were deep in the countryside, the distance was more psychological than actual— only about sixty miles. St. Hubert felt itself sufficiently remote from town bustle that on summer nights, movies were shown projected on a sheet hung from the side of a truck on the main square (as if the locals couldn't just get up and drive fifteen minutes to Marche-en-Famenne or Neufchâteau, some people grumbled). Yet my parents often came all the way to Verviers to shop. I would be expecting to see them around every corner.

So it was that, nerves ajangle, I rode to Dover through green fields dotted with sheep, then endured an absurdly lengthy crossing of the Channel aboard an apparently becalmed boat filled with Flemish soccer hooligans, then got on a train bound for Welkenraedt, its penultimate stop Verviers. As the train cleaved the little kingdom diagonally in the darkness, I grew increasingly excited as disused sensory organs twitched back to life and deep memory corridors opened one by one. In Flanders, the empty stretches that I knew represented apparently limitless flat fields alternated with brick villages tinted sticky yellow by streetlights. Nothing moved at nine o'clock in those burgs except the recurrent filmstrip of billboards: *De Standaard,* Pieter Stuyvesant, Omo, *De Morgen,* Daz, *Het Laatste Nieuws,* Maes Pils, Bru, over and over and over. The two women across the aisle were instantly familiar—sixtyish, bespectacled, wearing flowered dresses and dark blue cardigans—and I couldn't miss the drawling cadences of their Walloon-accented conversation. A seat ahead was a youth in a sweatshirt carrying a graffiti-covered skateboard, listening to a Walkman, and smoking Marlboros. He immediately stood as representative of the total Americanization I expected to find, but then he got off at Brussels-Centre and I didn't see his like again.

At the great stations—Bruges, Ghent, Brussels Nord and Centre and Midi, Louvain, Liège—I picked up little pieces of the past, in the trackside conferences of imperious conductors, the wooden benches, the unintelligible authoritative shouts, the vending machines dispensing Côte d'Or chocolates. Gone were the two-wheeled long-handled carts heaped with suitcases, the acrid diesel smoke, the great huffing sighs of the steam brakes, the men selling packages of thin oval waffles from trackside through the open windows. The train I rode was for that matter essentially a commuter conveyance, with minimal appointments, whereas my memories were principally attached to the important international expresses, with their compartments, their news vendors and coffee carts, their wood-paneled walls, their framed black-and-white photographs of alluring touristic destinations. I remembered those dramatic farewells, hands clutching through the open bottom flaps of corridor windows. I remembered the yellow light turning brown as night drew on and men with tinted glasses and cliffs of hair above high foreheads lit their seventeenth Boule Nationale while playing gin rummy on the little metal table that stuck out under the window. I remembered my mother enlisting a fellow passenger to show me the exact spot where Albert I, *le roi-chevalier,* had been killed in a freak climbing accident on the rocks above the Meuse at Marche-les-Dames in 1934. I remembered sharing a compartment with a family of Spanish migrant workers headed for the Ruhr, one of whom had a hacking cough, and my mother donated her box of Smith Brothers cough drops—this was one of the times we were coming back from America—which incredibly enough provided immediate relief, and they adopted us, sharing roast chicken and hard-boiled eggs and wine in skins you had to hold six inches above your open mouth, and communicating excitedly in sign language and pidgin and promising to keep in touch.

When the train pulled into Verviers I was alone in the coach. To the left of the field of tracks, aglow in the railroad light, stood a row of four-story houses identical to those enduring a rain of bowler-hatted men in Magritte's painting *Gol-*

conda. Above the head of the train the station loomed like a great bridge. Inside, the station felt like three o'clock in the morning, blue lights and shuttered newsstands and a single snoring drunk. It was 11:30. Outside, the town was dead, narrow gray houses huddled together under the goosenecked streetlights. As my taxi roared up the hill toward the modern hotel in the Quartier des Boulevards, I spotted on the corner of a side street the now-defunct Grand Hotel, where my parents and I had stayed during our last family visit, in 1969. We might have been the only guests; at breakfast we sat all alone in the vast, ornate, decaying dining room, like the last members of an aristocracy gone irredeemably to seed. I had felt an impatient disgust with the setting, in fact the whole town, the whole country, as I jealously read garbled Belgian newspaper accounts of the Woodstock Festival.

But that was a happy trip, anyway. We were performing the exile's grand return, in our small way and in our rented Peugeot following Alphonse Faniel coming back from the Congo in his Buick, or "Marie d'Amérique," a remote cousin of my mother's, who after a couple of decades in Argentina had similarly rolled into her native Ardennais village of Malempré in some automotive behemoth, passing out peso notes to the urchins and gems to their mothers. (Hers was a cautionary tale: Marie and her eight kids emigrated, but her husband refused to go; later he hanged himself.) We obviously weren't rich and didn't pretend to be, but were anyway accorded all the glamour of America by those for whom the movies were an exact documentary record. When I was smaller and attended school during the urgent trips back I made with my mother, my classmates would ask me about the Indian bands I had surely seen roaming the plains on their Appaloosas. On my visits even now, when I am not assuaging the fears of older relatives convinced that I live in a cop-show setting of constant riot and bloodshed, I am having my ears bent by taxi drivers telling me of their schemes to relocate to Miami and become millionaires.

In Belgium in 1969 I felt a curious dislocation, as if I were listening to a guide giving me the potted tour of my own kitchen. I was bored and restless but comfortable and eager. It went along with my age—fifteen, simultaneously enough of a kid to share my parents' hotel rooms (except at the vacant Grand, where for the first time in my life I enjoyed the sensation of turning my own key) and sufficiently adult to get a share of their bottles of wine. I was safely and meekly at home in Belgium, and I was also a seasoned and faultlessly with-it cosmopolite, suavely mediating all impressions through a New York beatnik poetic grid that fragmented them into alluring cubist shards with neon brand names darting off sideways *(Arlon CAFÉ DES SPORTS old men drinking DIEKIRCH as i/ see again yr face in walletsize photo & EDDY MEERCKX/ looks down from flickering blacknwhite tv set . . .)* and I was everywhere accompanied by a satisfyingly dramatic rock and roll sound track.

Now, as I stood at the window of my top-floor room looking toward the city represented by a mere haze of humid light rising from the depths of the valley hidden by houses and pines, I imagined I was some other kind of critter. I had arrived at night, almost nobody knew I was there, the room featured a narrow single bed—I didn't have a trench coat and I had registered under my real name, but I wore the right kind of bemused fatigue, my excitement having been hung wilted on the bathroom's suction-tipped roll-out clothesline. I tasted the luxuriously bittersweet pang of a storm-tossed fugitive in an earlier Europe, shivering in his once-smart suit and pillowing his head

on his broken shoes in some unnamed wayside while waiting
for a dubiously rumored train to the border, suddenly realizing
(the odor of wild thyme, the peeling pale yellow of the walls)
that he has accidentally alighted in the very place where a lifetime ago he ran and ran between the pillars, the stationmaster's
képi falling down over his eyes, a melting chocolate bar in his
hand, easily outfoxing his nurse's stumbling attempts to catch
him. The television lulled me to sleep with *Ceiling Zero*
(Howard Hawks, 1935).

I went down to breakfast long after the businessmen had all
stormed through, leaving me only the sports section of *La
Dernière Heure* to accompany the archetypal Belgian-hotel unbreakable roll and coffee. Instead I browsed through the available tourist literature. It boasted of Le Hall Omnisport, site of
le Grand Jogging, in June, the city's *grande activité,* with more
than two thousand participants. After that came its public
swimming pool, its Bowling Squash (eight lanes, with elec-
tronic scoring), its various convention and conference facilities.
Its many honored restaurants, which propose to your palate numerous refined dishes exceptionally served in a rustic setting.
Its up-to-date medical facilities. Its vocational training centers.
There was also a museum of archeology and history and a museum of fine arts. Upcoming local activities included a speech
on blood transfusion and a series of lectures on foreign travel,
illustrated with slides.

I set out, clumsily orienting myself with the crude photo-
copied map supplied by the front desk. The day was sunny in a
brisk, purposeful way, as if it had been set in motion by the
Syndicat d'Initiative. The city tumbled down the hillside ahead
of me and rebounded up the opposite bank. Endlessly I followed the solid residential dullness of the Chaussée de Heusy,

circling women wearing floral aprons over floral dresses washing the pavements, until something made me hang a hairpin left
onto Rue du Centre, from which I slid an easy right onto Rue
de la Colline. I paused in front of number 44, where a brass
plaque announced the presence within of a family-planning
agency. I continued down and down, on canted sidewalks and
staircases nearly but not quite monumental, past monuments
that seemed to come complete with their dedication ceremonies
in 1906 (florid speeches with heroic gesticulation by whiskered
parties in cutaways, rat-faced bank managers stifling yawns
under their umbrellas, gently snoring veterans in long beards
and Napoleon hats, a little girl dwarfed by her hair bow glumly
and vigorously rubbing slippered foot against stockinged calf
as she awaits the cue to proffer her bouquet), impasses and
courtyards, brick walls and plane trees, black squirrels and alley
cats, idling scooters and cars parked half up on the sidewalk.

Place Verte was quiet, even somnolent, almost entirely covered by parasol-topped café tables mostly unoccupied on a
weekday midmorning. At one corner rose Le Grand Bazar,
oddly vacant within, with little clots of goods here and there, as
if it had been having an unannounced fire sale. I strolled a further block to Place du Martyr, where Chapuis bobbed above a
sea of parked cars. Here and there along the square's tributaries
I was surprised to see ancient, precariously leaning wattle-and-
daub houses, which somehow hadn't at all figured in my memories. My memories were all fin-de-siècle brown, or actually
sepia. Somewhere deep in their recesses I saw something like a
railroad trestle, roofs around it, dotted hillsides beyond, everything in a smoky Sunday-afternoon light, through a scrim of
age, as in an early photograph. This image, which possibly
went back to infancy, used to occur to me in adolescence, when

I was given to playing Ravel's String Quartet and smoking what I imagined was opium residue off the copper-mesh screen of a pipe held upside down, and then it would seem to me to be evidence that I had lived before. The conceit got extended until it was fairly elaborate, and for a few months there at seventeen I was more than halfway convinced that I had been present, if not exactly at the seat-tossing premiere of the *Sacre du printemps*, then at least somewhere on the periphery of the Bateau-Lavoir. I had worn a lavalliere tie and a floppy beret, had strained absinthe with Aristide Bruant, had shared an attic room off Place Blanche in Montmartre with a family of cats who came and went through the window that opened onto the roof, had burned unsold copies of my volumes of verse for meager warmth in the terrible winters. Et cetera. It seems not to have occurred to me that the inspirational memory might be a genuine recollection of my own in my present incarnation, so remote did Belgium seem then, freshly visited but less accessible than the astral plane.

Now here I was, in the middle of all that brown, now tempered with the beige of reinforced concrete and with plate glass and chrome and bright plastic trash cans and bus-stop indicators, but resolutely Industrial Revolution brown at the core. My memories came in loosely gathered folios, oddly assorted but shelved together for convenience. There were those antediluvian impressions from earliest babyhood, specific and varyingly detailed pictures and sequences from later childhood, fuzzier tableaux that perhaps represented some imaginative montage of received tales and family snapshots run through with a thread of genuine recollection, and underlying all, here in the center of town, a sense of place sufficiently strong that I hardly needed my map anymore. I couldn't account in any systematic way for the fact that as I stood in the center of Place du Martyr I knew without prompting how to find the Hôtel de Ville, several churches, the river and its curves, most of the principal squares. As I went along, the townscape constituted itself, materializing like some Brigadoon awaiting my witness to resume existence.

But as I approached the river just past Notre-Dame des Récollets, I knew that something was off. The notion got stronger past Pont du Chêne, where I expected to be entering Rue David, only there was no more Rue David, lined with factories and stray ruins—it was now Rue Lucien Defaÿs, a broad, clean sweep with sundry gas stations and supermarkets on one side and on the other a low wall overlooking the Vesdre. It seemed discordantly modern, almost antiseptic. And I could look directly across at the lumped downhill shapes of the Hodimont district, backs of houses long only visible to their neighbors across the water. The place was so intensely familiar, without my actually having a single concrete memory—no memory at all later than 1959, certainly, not of this part of town, which fell clear off the edge of the hotel map—that the unfamiliarity had a nearly physical force to it, as if I had looked down and noticed a strange new foot on the end of my leg. The motif was to persist as I walked around, with one constant: most of the factories, dozens or—it seemed to me—hundreds of them, which had defined Verviers as much as its river or its hills, were gone. Although a few had been turned into car dealerships or office complexes or preserved for their historical value, most were simply erased. Abruptly, the whole city was called into question. I couldn't say that I felt any particular love for the factories, which had worked my ancestors and hundreds of thousands of others like dray horses, but I couldn't imagine what now went on in a town that had been utterly dependent on them. How did people survive? Did they take in one another's washing? Without its factories Verviers felt like a plinth without a statue.

Just before I turned the corner between Pont Léopold and the high embankment of the Verviers-Ouest depot, I suddenly knew exactly what I would next see. Until that moment I had no idea where I was heading, or why I was veering toward this drab section of town rather than proceeding in one of the more obvious and alluring directions. But I was guided by some sort of internal magnet. It had led me without pause or hesitation by a twisting path right to the head of Rue Robert Centner. There was the *librairie*—Kim cigarettes, Vieil Anvers beer, panels leaning up against its walls featuring blowups of tabloid covers screaming the latest dirty secrets of Johnny and Sylvie—and there were its eight or nine severe houses and its two or three factory buildings and then the river. I could see the whole thing down its one-block length, entirely preserved, the street I could thank for my existence. I walked down its middle on domed cobbles. I wanted to tell somebody I was there, but no one was around. My mother's parents' house looked untouched since 1959, and my father's parents' house looked as if it hadn't changed since the day it was built, even if the alley that ran next to it down to Rue du Gazomètre now gave onto a vacant plain. The factory buildings on either side were intact, although they now housed a sawmill and storage facilities, respectively.

The street seemed to compress the whole story of industrial Europe into a capsule, as if it had been confected from lightweight synthetic materials and run down a museum corridor between the Hall of Machines and the Age of Realism. Work-

ers in drooping mustaches and long blue smocks and wooden
shoes and high-crowned black caps seemed to drift by anamor-
phically flattened, along with the Little Match Girl and Jean
Gabin walking his bicycle and the ragged hordes from a
Steinlen cover of *L'Assiète au beurre* and the miners accompa-
nying Zola's casket shouting *"Ger-mi-nal! Ger-mi-nal!"* in unison. There were houses of the style my father had lived in, two
or three stories, bricks so dark they were nearly black, white-
framed windows, and ones like my mother's, four stories and
with an air about them, like workers in their Sunday suits. They
faced off accommodatingly across the narrow street, their
doors one step up from a pavement that had once been just a
curb, all pressed together for half the street's length. No break
separated them from the factories that occupied the second
half, stubby things that still contrived to loom within the concentrated scale. Here and there, closed off from my view, were
small courtyards that had once lodged horses, carts, various
piles of sacks. Maybe the *librairie* had a century ago been an
estaminet, a saloon, to complete the picture. Only the parked
cars served to indicate the decade.

When I had thought of the street before seeing it again,
though, bricks and soot and centuries of labor had not been uppermost in my mind. It was the street on which I had celebrated
birthdays and Christmases, had spent a lot of afternoons and
evenings cooing and gurgling, spreading my toes and waving
my arms, watched over and pampered by my grandparents. I
couldn't remember my father's parents' apartment at all, but I
thought I had an impression of my mother's: high ceilings,
massive dark furniture, lace table runners, although such items
could be found in the homes of all Belgians of their generation.
The one very precise image I thought I had preserved, of

dishes drying on a rack on a table, with a calendar over it and a single ornamental shelf above that, turned out to derive from a snapshot of my mother as a teenager, the only picture I knew for sure had been taken in the apartment. Reaching back far enough, I primarily associated the street with pleasure, with great mounds of waffles on New Year's Day, with illustrated books and Steiff animals and Dinky cars and hand-knit sweaters. I could hear its name, *Centner,* in the way I had heard it before I could read—a two-stage nasal honk—and with the overlay of homonyms a few years later: *centenaire* (centenarian) and *Sante-naire,* almost *naître,* almost born.

I walked to the end of the street and onto the footbridge that led over the Vesdre to Lambermont. There, wedged into the cliffs on the far bank, stood a massive house, with balconies and mullioned windows and eight gables topped with witch-hat roofs clustered around a central chimney proportioned like a factory smokestack. I knew that house; it had figured in my dreams. When I needed an image of a mansion around which to dispose the action of some novel I was reading, it had eagerly presented itself. Once or twice I had wondered where in life I had seen it. Now it was empty, and a six-lane-highway viaduct ran right over it, clearing its chimney by no more than a few feet. I looked down at the Vesdre, running low, ducks fighting for space in the scattered pools in the mud on its verges. From there the factories, or the shells that had once been factories, seemed to form a solid brown wall along the river, running from its sharp bend just before Pont Léopold down to a vanishing point somewhere near the Île Adam. Dust motes hung in the air in the indefinite morning sun, blurring the edges of things the way smoke does.

v House

I'm always seeing my father among the gaggles of urchins who invariably garnish old pictures of Quai de la Batte or Ruelle Bodeux or the Trô Navai. It seems that every time a postcard photographer disposed his equipment in the working-class districts of Verviers, three or eight or twenty kids would materialize and stand in front of the lens, poking each other and making faces, and he would have the task of herding them into a picturesque grouping slightly to the side. Adults are infrequent, and in the bourgeois neighborhoods there are usually no visible humans at all. My father always seems to be in those crowds of rascals, somewhere toward the middle, the smallest kid but clearly a ringleader, effortlessly exuding personality. Never mind that all the pictures I am looking at were taken fifteen or twenty years before his birth, and that Quai de la Batte and Ruelle Bodeux and the Trô Navai had all been erased by progress by the time he was old enough to run around outdoors unsupervised. The earliest pictures I have of him are in the same spirit; they are in fact mostly postcards, as are nearly all the pictures in my album between the age of the formal cabinet card and that of the snapshot, and they were taken by street photographers.

In the earliest one he is no more than a year and a half, maybe two, his blond hair in a raggedy pageboy, wearing a one-piece garment that looks like jersey but was inevitably wool, holding on to Armande's hand. She wears a flounced dress that may have been white and proclaims itself unmistakably as Sunday best, with midcalf boots, possibly buttonhooks. She's nervous and doesn't know how to pose: mouth screwed up, shoulders hunched forward, free hand pinned by the exposure in midcrawl along a flounce, resting all her weight on her left leg, which slants so far right it appears she will soon have to cross the other leg over so as not to topple. I recognize my father by his stare, already then skeptically alert, prepared for the worst, not declaring himself but maintaining reserve. He is a little waif, *un petit bout d'chou,* with the eyes of a grizzled and unflinching witness to the spectrum of human folly and deceit.

They are standing on a diamond-cobbled pavement in front of some official or at least prosperous-looking edifice with deep windowsills and, right behind Armande, a cavernous rectangle formed by the eyebrow of a basement window looking up from its underground business. It is manifestly not their house. My father grew up in a tenement on Rue de Mangombroux, a narrow thoroughfare that appears to wind endlessly, in part because for much of its length it is unencumbered by side streets. It presents a solid panorama of elderly three-story houses, cyclically unspooling like the landscape that accompanies the racing Huckleberry Hound, with the same small shop recurring at intervals, the logos of Ola ice cream and *Le Jour–La Meuse* timed to appear every four beats. Its distinction resides entirely in the old slaughterhouse (now a brewery depot) as solemn as a Victorian train station, that appears near its mouth at the site of the Porte de Heusy, the medieval gate whose dismantled stones were in 1863 used to enclose the final terrors of innumerable doomed cattle and swine.

That was my father's formative atmosphere, a working-class district that in the nineteenth century must have passed for airy and enlightened in contrast to the warren of alleys and tunnels and impasses around the Canal des Usines, where his ancestors had lived. He was baptized, ten days after birth, at St. Joseph, just up the way on Rue des Carmes. The announcement is pink—blue was for girls there and then—with a swaddled infant in relief extending an arm, hand spread, with the other crooked and ending in a fist, as if it were performing a soliloquy from the last act of *Phèdre*. His father was Lucien Louis Joseph Sante, his godfather Mathieu Lavergne, his godmother Amélie Lambrette—the name composed itself: Lucien Mathieu Amélie.

At perhaps eight years old, he is standing on a diamond-cobbled pavement outside what might be the very same self-important building that formed the backdrop for his first appearance before the lens, captured by a photographer who has, on a sunny day, chosen to frame him within the single available curtain of shade, with only the tips of his shoes taking the spotlight. He is wearing a coat and scarf and a beret pulled down to expose just the ends of his bangs, along with the short pants and tall socks that gave generations of boys all-weather knees by the time they were twelve. He is even more himself in this picture, staring guardedly through hooded eyelids under arched brows, with an apparently stern and unyielding cast to his mouth that you'd know only if you knew him well is actually a studied theatrical parody. It takes no imaginative energy on my part to hear this mouth intoning with mock gravity his favorite alexandrines from La Fontaine or Victor Hugo: *"Mon père ce héros au sourire si doux. . . ."* * Looking at the picture I know that he has begun collecting the vast stock of allusions to

* "My father, that hero, whose smile was so sweet. . . ."

obscure boulevard comedies and punch lines of forgotten vaudeville wheezes that will figure in his speech as reliably enigmatic punctuation, like the Latin tags in Sir Thomas Browne. *"'Aha!' s'écria l'ouvrière,"** he will say upon realizing that he has forgotten to shut the garage door. Having traced the cause of a clogged sink to a blob of soap choking the pipe elbow, he will assume the orotund vowels of a doctor in a farce to pronounce, *"Voilà pourquoi votre fille est muette!"*†

I also remember him exclaiming, "Yaba-daba-doo! This is America!" in English of course, when at the wheel and bearing down on one of those great swoops of unfettered highway that didn't exist in Belgium when we lived there. So that was presumably as of 1962 or so, when *The Flintstones* came on at 7:30, presented by Winston cigarettes. It would have been after the pack of Luckies disappeared from the dashboard—he quit in '61—but when the postwar G.I.-issue aviator shades still resided there next to the Virgin and the Infant of Prague, under the windshield of the '53 Buick or the two-tone '55 Chevy, the one broadsided by a drunk one autumn day at Springfield and Tulip in Summit, when the car spun like a top, the landscape revolving like a zoopraxiscope. What did he say then? After making sure we were all right—I only knocked my nose bloody against the back of their seat; my mother's whiplash didn't show up until later—did he resort to a *mot,* or to a song? It's more than likely. My father's thimble theater always came in handy in a crisis. An outrageous reversal could be parried with, for example, *"tout se paie en ce bas monde"* (everything has its cost in this fallen world, more or less), because chance and rit-

---

* " 'Aha!' cried the working woman."
† "Here is why your daughter is mute!"

ual balanced each other, and because mildewed verities revealed the footlights and prompter's box present at any scene,
and because the turn of phrase was the most elegant of life pre-
servers. After all, my father always noted, Cyrano's *panache*
was more than just his literal plume.

My father's panache was such that he could make the basketball team at the Athénée even though he was the smallest kid in
the school (or maybe the second smallest, after André Blavier,
who went on to become municipal librarian, poet, novelist, editor, etc.). This mettle is visible in the chronological third photo,
in which he is possibly nine or ten, affectionately manhandling
his friend Pol Dosquet, who looks sheepish in a Fauntleroyal
smock featuring a lace collar, of all things. My father's clothes
are rougher, and his attitude is pure Spanky. Pol has at least two
inches on him, maybe three, but you sense that the difference
would be meaningless in a tussle. My father's nickname wasn't
Spanky, though, but Tintin, after the short blond boy reporter
then making his debut in *Le Petit Vingtième,* the children's supplement of *Le Vingtième Siècle.* This right-wing Catholic paper
could find its way even into Socialist households such as my
grandparents', in the red city of Verviers. Tintin was an immediate sensation. Even in the crudely drawn and schematically
written early stories it was clear that the Belgians had at last
been given their hero, their metaphor, their twentieth-century
heraldic emblem more convincing, not to mention unifying,
than any Flemish lions or Walloon cocks rampant. In French
the adjective *"petit"* is extraordinarily versatile, festooning random nouns much the way "old" at least used to in American,
but this is a small country whose citizens hoist smallness as a
banner, calling themselves not *Belges* but *petit Belges,* so that
even some overgrown galoot, challenged by truculent Parisians

and perhaps fortified by a drink or two, might boast, *"J'suis un p'tit Belge, moi."* The boy reporter—who did no visible reporting and was only notionally ascribed an age group—embodied every wishful reflection Belgians sought in the mirror. My father, who at the height of his height attained maybe five feet two inches, always enjoyed the gravitational power of being small and tough and smart, which can make taller parties feel weedy, insubstantial; his son, unnaturally elongated by American Grade-A milk, knew well the sensation of having one's brains and one's shoes separated by half a mile of slack.

My father's *communion solennelle* pose is standard, resigned. The white gloves he carries in his left hand fool no one—he can't muster a bit of the insouciance required for the gesture. His family's financial circumstances are perhaps revealed by the announcement, which is handwritten in contrast to every other such I possess, all of them printed. Could he have written it himself? It's a schoolboy hand that gives a bend to the upper loops like poplars in the wind, and looks nothing like the penmanship of his adult life, in which flatly ovoid capitals lead strings of corrugated furrows that might be letters in some other alphabet, maybe Sumerian or Hittite. In the last picture of his childhood, he is at least twelve, old enough to be wearing his first adult suit, featuring a broadly double-breasted jacket with lapels on which you could dispose the setting for a light lunch for two, along with plus fours that plunge to his argyle ankles. He is grinning down into his collar, gazing up impishly, pointing his left leg out as if he were beginning a dance step, partnered by his mother, who is holding his arm flat-palmed. On his other side his father sways gently. They are standing in what looks like their back court—the faded sepia is stingy with details. His parents are wearing their everyday clothes, Marie in a patterned housedress with a matter-of-fact V neckline and rolled-up sleeves, Lucien Louis Joseph in a shapeless cotton jacket, white shirt, necktie, horizontally striped sweater vest and vertically striped trousers.

It is, beyond any doubt, the picture of a happy family. My grandmother gleams with love and pride, which you know is a constant even as you know that the picture-taking represented a brief interruption of her scrubbing or peeling or stirring. My grandfather looks a bit abstracted, as if he were just then thinking of how to word a phrase. He is barely taller than his wife, only about five feet. He was a handsome man, with darkly gentle eyes and a perfect triangular mustache and deep vertical creases in his cheeks. He worked as a foreman on the weaving floor *chez* Voos for at least forty years, and was the only person allowed to smoke on the premises. He acted in Walloon theater companies and was known for his singing voice. He sang at home and he sang at gatherings; he sang the Walloon standard "Mame" to his wife (*Mame c'è-st-on grand no/ Qu'a-st-on ptit gos' di låme:* "Mom is a great name that has a little taste of . . ."—the word means both "tears" and "honey") and he teased his son by making up songs about the girls the teenager had crushes on. He kept a fiercely loyal flock of chickens in that back court. He was—somehow I find this hard to register; he seems so much more ancient—an exact contemporary of the first generation of modernists. I feel an obscure but stabbing hurt that I never got to know him, although he is vivid in my father's memory and in his speech, and I grew up with a sense of him almost present in the room, and I felt especially bad when I did mean or petty things, thinking he could see them.

Since I didn't long know my grandmother, either, I can only vaguely guess how my father's inheritance of character was apportioned. It seems obvious he got from his father his show-man's turn and his fireside philosopher's love of the polished bromide, perhaps also his ear for the music of sentences. On the other hand, his humor could have come from either par-ent—you can sense his mother's sly deadpan mischief, his fa-ther's timing and benevolent sense of the ridiculous just from their faces. He could have also gotten from either of them his antlike capacity for labor, which is maybe one part duty, one part stubbornness, one part pride, and one part fatalism: a nearly biological imperative of bending to the task because that is what fate has decreed, but that could have been leached from the very air of Verviers, or transmitted through countless gen-erations of drudgery without reward. Unresolved are his diplo-macy, his compassion, his inwardness, his generosity, his adaptability, his tenderness, his suspicion, his custodianship of what must be vast and encrusted archives of emotions that have never been let out to breathe. And one other thing: his unfore-cast ability to cast off, at the age of thirty-seven, into the track-less unknown.

If my father was Tintin, my mother was Little Lulu, whom she startlingly resembles in a studio portrait taken at about age five, signed by Lucas & Bédart of Brussels, although I tend to doubt the session actually took place in the capital. She wears a cap of straight black hair with an enormous bow, knee socks and a soft wool dress in some dark shade, and a purse-lipped, droopy-lidded expression that says "Phooey." She was born and then still living in Ster, a village of no more than a couple of dozen houses that on my Taride map, published for *automo-bilistes* and *cyclistes*, is shown as having a single fine line—

meaning a path inadvisable for vehicles other than horse carts—leading through it. Since the map was printed before World War I, the German border lurks not more than three kilometers to the east, although by the time my mother burst on the scene a decade later the margin had been extended considerably. After the armistice Belgium was awarded territory that though historically linked to Wallonia was claimed by Prussia after Napoleon's defeat, largely German-speaking but including such a fortress of Walloon culture as Malmédy, the nearest substantial town. Her parents did some minor and scarcely remunerative farming in Ster (the name is a suffix, the same one that appears in Munster or Winchester or Manchester, so that the place might as well have been called Burg or Ville), where her father had moved with his brothers as a young man, later importing his bride.

Their courtship took place during the war and was unavoidably straitened by it. I possess a markedly unromantic relic of its course: a postcard sent April 14, 1915, showing a view of La Fosse Roulette in Vielsalm (a chunky two-carriage train emitting voluminous smoke struggles along an uphill track set right beside the road lined by houses, with hillsides of glum evergreens looking on), addressed to Mlle. Honorine Remacle à Fraiture-Bihain, Luxembourg (meaning the province), its entire text the name Édouard, the whole chaperoned by Germania, in her vermillion three-pfennig edition, who is nearly obliterated by the Fraktur overprint *Belgien 3 Cent.* It presumably got to its destination the following day, where she glanced at it and tucked it into the frame of her mirror. She would have had to be in love to have been charmed by it; presumably she was, since she saved it. Vielsalm was the place one went to to buy postcards or conduct official business or find work. Both came from adjacent dots a few inches to the left on the map, Édouard from Odeigne and Anne-Marie-Honorine from one of southern Belgium's three or four Fraitures, hers remaining to this day a dead-end village, with a road leading in but none leading out.

Vielsalm was where one went to be photographed, too, at G. Gillet's studio, which featured an unchanging painted backdrop of the Arch of Triumph viewed from an angle. A series of virtually identical portraits taken there at some point in the teens shows my grandmother and her sisters Alphonsine and Éva (who drowned a few years later) sharing a single dress, a complicated black satin affair with a lace collar and leg-of-mutton sleeves and a row of pearl buttons running diagonally along one breast and then down to the waist, with a long thin chain around the neck each of them has chosen to drape differently. Each rests a fist on a rather plain and scarred example of Victorian plant stand, with a rush-seated, overly architectural parlor chair idling to the side. Her brother Albert, in his army uniform, with a light spot in his ear that I used to think was a hearing aid until I realized the unlikelihood of such a thing at that time—he was stone deaf, at least in later life—presses his forefinger and thumb on a construction of twigs presumably meant to evoke a rustic fence. Édouard, perhaps on the point of graduating from suitor to husband, wears a superbly waxed mustache, a high and possibly bulletproof collar above an elaborate four-in-hand, and a watch fob of unparalleled magnificence, and rests his elbow on a higher plant stand bedecked in a fringed whatsit. All wear expressions caught halfway between dreamy and stern; their poses exude severity and importance. I have seen no earlier pictures of any of them. Given their backgrounds, of tenant farming in unvisited waysides, they may not have appeared before a camera until then.

These villages, Fraiture and Odeigne, Malempré and Sovet, Ster and Viville, among hundreds of others, were assemblies of ten or twenty or thirty houses around a church. They were made of stone whose color varied according to the predominant geological stock of the region; driving through the Ardennes you can see the shift from gray to blue to red to yellow. The houses, which could cluster along the side of a through road, or huddle in a recess, or gather in a loop described by a stream, or straggle partway up a hillside, were backed by fields, frequently owned by the inhabitant of the nearest château, and which the villagers worked on a percentage basis. The system, in sum, was not far removed from the feudal era. The church was the center of communal activity, and until the beginning of this century was also the home of the only literate resident, who thus functioned as the de facto government as well. There might also be a bakery and some sort of general store, the latter often informally worked out of someone's kitchen. Routine was fixed by the agricultural calendar and enlivened by religious feasts, whose celebrations were hardly distinguishable from the pagan rituals they had begun as. Not much outside news filtered into the villages, which were often a hard journey from the nearest railway, although matters improved somewhat in the late nineteenth century with the inauguration of the *trams vicinaux*—rural streetcar lines, which formed a web of connections. Even so, populations were less stable than you might think. The scarcity of land drove young people, who were not about to inherit anything more than a bedstead, a coffeepot, and a crucifix, from village to village in search of work and living quarters. Many of them, of course, ended up in the cities, more and more of them as the twentieth century gathered steam. My maternal grandparents, for example, accomplished this journey—from native village to other village to rural suburbs to city—over roughly twenty years, in the space between the wars.

My grandfather had briefly dipped his toe into city life during the war, when he worked as a streetcar conductor in Liège and assumed the solemnity accruing to that office, at least in pictures. My grandmother was country in the gravest sense, absorbing all the moral certitude of life ruled by God in the guise of weather. The city must always have seemed remote and savage to her. Since she was a determined traditionalist in most spheres of life, it is interesting that she was radically modern in her naming practices, eschewing allusions to the departed. René, born in 1920, and Denise, three years later, were given flashy monikers that might have hung on Parisian boulevardiers. My mother is puzzled by her name to this day, commenting recently that she still can't quite imagine it belonging to an old lady. The only cultural reference any of us can ever come up with is to Denise Darcel, née Billecard, star of *Tarzan and the Slave Girl* and *Seven Women from Hell,* but as it happens she is my mother's near-exact contemporary. In the family the choice was considered mildly scandalous, but any hard feelings were soothed by the freight train of middle names, hitching Lambertine (after her grandmother-godmother, Lambertine Éloy) to Alberte (for her godfather-uncle Albert Remacle) to Marie and Ghislaine for their protective auras. My mother makes her first photographic appearance quite nude, looking very much like a kewpie doll as she supports herself with both hands on a damask-covered pouf, or maybe a pile of boxes that when damask-covered could pass for a pouf, and looks to the right of the lens at some truly amazing phenomenon, perhaps a talking sock. The astonishment in her eyes persisted; it's still there.

She grew up in circumstances that antedate the twentieth century, in a jot of a village where there were few neighbors, and some were her relatives, and life was determined by family, church, and crops, in that order. Nevertheless, the Francorchamps racetrack, within a short walk, retailed flash, not to mention roar, and radiated dazzle. Parties of champagne-guzzling cosmopolites descended in open cars to watch the Grand Prix events and the twenty-four-hour races. My mother and her parents and her cousins were the countryfolk they may have fleetingly noticed, the local color. In a photograph taken when she was maybe five, in her Little Lulu period, she appears in a beautiful courtyard, with moss growing between the cobblestones, the old stone wall of the house to one side and vines or hedges to the other, standing shyly among a group of adults sitting on low stools drinking glasses of milk. They are city people on a walking jaunt, as is evident from the boaters and cloches they have removed and set on their leather hiking cases on the ground, and they have stopped by the house for refreshment, as people did then in the country even when the house carried no sign. They thought she was as charming as the house and the foliage and the village and the hills—*how rustic*—and maybe they took her picture in turn, artistically composed, *Une petite Ardennaise.*

Her parents gave up on the perpetual long odds of farming around the time of the worldwide crash, moving to the outskirts of Verviers and to the logical next phase in the urbanization process. They started a business of collecting milk from farmers and carting it into the city to sell, putting in arduous workdays that began around two or three in the morning. It is a quite different and somewhat less picturesque yard that appears around that time in the picture of my mother's dog Blackie—

he was light brown, but somewhere she had picked up what she thought was a good name for a dog (it was an earlier dog, however, who ate his meals out of a German helmet, fastened to the ground by its spike). The place names then succeed each other pell-mell. My mother underwent her solemn communion in 1935 in Wegnez (with the cap of her long white veil falling over one eye she looks like a befuddled child bride). Several shots taken outside an imposing suburban apartment house in 1936 are captioned "Tribomont" (my grandmother proudly displays her bicycle; Denise and René are yoked in feigned togetherness, both their hands resting on the handle of a shovel in the garden). A portrait of my grandparents identified as set in Andrimont shows them in Sunday dress, standing in a field, hunched and slack-armed and drawn-faced, like people who have never posed before and are intimidated by the box and its operator, but probably they're just exhausted. They look like subjects of an FSA picture from Alabama.

After approaching the city by degrees they succumbed to Rue Robert Centner in 1939. Both parents got jobs at the Aiglon chocolate factory, my grandfather eventually winding up in one of the textile plants. My mother, however temperamental as a tot, grew up to be a good girl, that much is clear. As time draws on in the stream of pictures she recedes from them, fulfilling a duty but swallowing her personality in the process. I recognize her in her strained formal mode, trying to oblige company by wearing a half-smile of the sort that signifies virtue rather than pleasure, not quite knowing what to do with her hands, standing meekly while attempting to guess what is required of her even as she boils inside. I can only surmise the tensions that ruled in her family, the accommodations she had to make and the drudgery she was assigned because she was the

girl. Just underneath her skin I can make out the stinging intelligence and wild humor that she has spent much of her life sup-
pressing. She is a labyrinth of serpentine hallways and false
doors and hidden staircases, easy to misconceive and difficult
to negotiate, and yet somewhere along the line she adopted the
belief that both she and life ought to be simple, with clearly
marked paths and boundaries.

She drew from her childhood a love of nature, a fear of catastrophe, a yearning for the cozy interdependency of the extended family, and an absolute submission to the laws of the
Church. Those four constants have stayed with her all her life;
she has, in other words, taken her village with her to an America she still experiences as utterly foreign after thirty-five years.
In the sad and harsh first few years abroad, her sole consolation
was watching the squirrels, because although they differed
greatly from the small, black, pinch-eared Belgian variety they
were nevertheless creatures of a woodland she could imagine as
running continuously from here to there, also because while
they looked defenseless they were tough and fast and resilient.
America was for her a puzzle of hidden correspondences.
Under the foreign skin there had to be particles of the known,
and her probing was sometimes rewarded with a bird (the swallow), a flower (the lily of the valley), a tree (the willow, the rare
poplar), a shrub (boxwood, which in Belgium served as a proxy
for the unobtainable palms of Palm Sunday), or even a whole
landscape (the Poconos at first, eventually Vermont). They became coordinates in a grid of defense she had to erect amid the
storm of confusion and fear that overtook her on the new
planet.

Catastrophe was in her blood, probably, from whatever inherited memory of failed crops and sudden frosts and famine

and epidemic, and its hold on her was reinforced by war and
job loss and deaths and the constant threat of destitution. She is
fascinated by disaster, has made a study of it. It is for her the
forbidden book she can't help looking in even as she fears to do
so. Any phone call from her will begin with an often impressive
recital of cardiac cases and suspected tumorous growths and
children born with dire conditions, not to mention sudden
deaths, matters affecting a variety of people ranging from her
New Jersey neighbors to distant collateral relations I've never
met and never will. This is not a matter of sadism, but it is not
without prurience, and above all it constitutes the only kind of
information she has ever really believed: bad news. In the family there is safety, but that is not news until it falls apart.

The family is her oasis; for her the world is a succession of
concentric rings in which our three-person nuclear unit forms
the center, her cousins and their offspring the next circle, all
Belgians the circle after that, and so forth. Her cousins who are
her contemporaries have been her friends since infancy. She has
had other friends, even close ones, but they almost require a
different word, so distinct is the difference in intimacy. She is
apparently innocent of social forms that she perceives as
"American" (even though they have now become the norm in
Belgium, perhaps even rural Belgium). Once, when I was already grown and living away from home, I mentioned that I
had gone to a party the previous evening. "Oh, whose birthday
was it?" she asked. She observes, and she analyzes, but she re-
fuses to adapt. In part this is due to fear, and in part to obsti-
nacy, but above all it is due to an idea of class that for her is an
article of faith. The relative fluidity of American life unan-
chors her. She addresses the majority of her contemporaries as
Mr. or Mrs. this or that, and when they eventually beg her to
please call them Madge or Don, she concedes with difficulty

and reluctance. Whenever she has cause to refer to a friend or colleague of mine who is superior in age to me, she says *"la dame"* or *"le monsieur,"* even if she has met them. If I happen to mention an upcoming meeting, even a casual event, she instructs me, *"Fais-toi bien propre,"* make yourself clean, because people will judge you on the shine of your shoes and the sharpness of your creases. I imagine that my life is a mystery to her, until she surprises me with her insight into some aspect I'd thought she hadn't noticed. The American system that I have grown into is for her appalling chaos, an ongoing carnival of misrule that can only end in disaster. People behave as if there were no up or down, but eventually gravity will reassert itself, and everyone will crack their skulls on the firmament.

She is desperate for order, and in the chaos of her life only the Church has ever given her any. She has no interest in theology, only in observance. She has never read any part of the Bible other than the excerpts included in the proper of the mass, but she says many hours of prayers every day, prayers printed or sometimes handwritten on the backs of holy pictures, which she keeps in a stack, many of them ragged-edged and mended with tape from decades of daily manipulation. There is a crucifix in every room in her house other than the bathrooms, and pictures of the Virgin and the Sacred Heart scattered liberally, and statuettes in the car (although the magnets will no longer stick to the dashboards, nowadays padded, so they are relegated to a tray just north of the gearshift), and a Virgin in a shrine my father built in the front yard, and scapulars between the mattresses and their box springs, and a holy-water font by the bedroom door. She wears several religious medals and so does my father; I wore a gold St. Christopher medal that had been given to me at birth until I lost it while going off the high dive at thirteen. It was probably around the same time that I finally rebelled against the little cloth sack that I wore pinned to my undershirt that contained bits of linen or paper that had touched the bones of various saints. For her these objects are immanent; they are not symbols or reminders but aspects, material forms containing an actual franchise of the divinity. She is a believer—with *la foi du charbonnier,* the faith of the coal heaver, my father will say, himself citing Pascal's wager in apologia. Doubt is a temptation to which my mother has never succumbed.

But doubt has afflicted her continually concerning every other part of life. She sometimes moves as if afraid that the floor will open under her, does not seem to know from one day to the next whether everything solid will crumble—this between bright flashes of canniness, so that I am often left wondering to what degree her meekness and hesitation constitute a pose. She is in the water, staring incredulous at the shipwreck, clutching her few constants as she would a spar—or else she is in the clutches of the secret police, protesting that she is harmless and knows nothing, hiding within herself. She once collected pictures of the royal family in a scrapbook, dreamed of playing the piano and speaking Italian and riding horseback. She taught me how to eat an orange, an apple, a banana with a knife and fork, should I someday allow her vague dream to be fulfilled vicariously—to consort with *des gens comme il faut.* Had she ever come into money and security I suspect she would have been a strict arbiter of behavior and taste; instead she feels herself relentlessly judged by others. Growing up in meager farmland and then on a sooty factory block she imagined various gilded or sordid futures for herself, extremes of fortune reconciled by immutable laws. She never figured that she would grow old in a lawless world kept in motion by dice.

VI Caesura

Nowhere in my childhood did I feel more at home than in the second of our two apartments at 7 Irving Place in Summit, New Jersey. It was a plain white stucco two-family house, the left half of which was occupied by the proprietor, the widowed Mrs. Feibush, who also owned the local stationery store, run by the younger of her two sons. Our right half had its own enclosed porch and its own peaked roof, and a space between it and the sidewalk occupied mostly by a profusion of rhododendron bushes that for a while constituted my personal jungle. The rear of the house, meanwhile, was so shaded by enormous trees—in my mind's eye they are several hundred feet tall—that no grass grew; the result was a permanently dark dirt square that for me continues to embody what is meant by the word "yard." The street was only a couple of blocks from the business district, in a small neighborhood mostly made up of sprawling houses from the beginning of the century, cut up into apartments or occupied by large families, on narrow lots, that lay wedged between the serpentine roads of the rich and the scraggly woods that adjoined the railroad tracks.

We had initially occupied the downstairs apartment, but by 1962 or so had moved up to the joined second and third floors—no one then would have thought of calling the place a duplex. The bathroom stood welcoming at the top of the stairs; off the corridor to the right ran living room, dining room, kitchen, and a glassed-in rear porch that housed the washing machine and my father's tool bench. On the top floor, at the front, was my parents' bedroom, which I rarely visited but always found enticing and a bit mysterious, with its walls that slanted in halfway up, conforming to the shape of the eaves. The rest of the floor was mine: two tiny rooms, one just big enough for my bed, the other home to my toys and my books. My friends, many of whom came from large families and shared rooms with siblings, marveled at my domain. The back room evolved, over the three years or so we lived at that address, from a simple playroom into an impressive complex: military headquarters (several years' worth of weekly twenty-five-cent allowances went toward the purchase of individually packaged British-made toy soldiers representing wars from the Punic to the Korean, each box supplying the soldier's biography, which I memorized), newspaper office (a neighbor gave me an erratic old typewriter on which for a while I strove to publish my own weekly; its circulation was restricted by the limitations of carbon paper as a means of reproduction), and library (anchored by a gift from another neighbor, the 1948 edition of *The American People's Encyclopedia*).

The apartment, with its dark hallways and stairs and its small but well-lit rooms, was almost infinitely mutable in my imagination, and in fact it continues to be—that dark yard with its twin double-decker porches has turned up in a number of movies, for example, such as Josef von Sternberg's *Blonde Venus* and at least one obscure ZaSu Pitts comedy, and the second-story corridor has enigmatically migrated to the brownstone flat in Brooklyn I now inhabit (the glass rear porch sometimes visits at night, but alas is always gone by morning). My bedroom in that apartment must have been small indeed, if it could hold only a single bed no more than five feet in length, with barely room for a chair. Its dimensions were ideal, though, for pretending that I was in a sleeping car on a train. Sometimes I'd be riding through the Simplon Pass or along the shores of Lake Baikal; sometimes I'd be a soldier, nobly if superficially wounded, being shipped home after the second battle of Bull Run. When I was sick, as I often was in those years, getting every childhood disease one after the other—I was home with chicken pox when Kennedy was shot in Dallas—I was put to bed on the sofa in the living room, where the television was, and where access was easier to the bathroom and the kitchen. This might have reserved the little upstairs bedroom exclusively for the more pleasant range of fantasies, but the room held its terrors, too.

During most of the time we lived there, Irving Place was directly under a flight path, presumably from Newark Airport just a few miles east. You might think that with so many airplanes overhead on a daily basis, I'd have simply stopped hearing them. This was true during the day—all I can remember is how the insect buzz of a single-engine light aircraft, heard from a grassy field, was an essential ingredient of summer, and I think the sound gave me my first intimation of what it was going to be like, one day, to remember. At night, though, every airplane carried a bomb, and every bomb was about to drop on us. This was no mere voluntary fantasy; it was a real, constant fear. Whenever I'd hear an engine above at night I'd start to pray, and I'd often pray from the same fear when the town's noon whistle blew. The fear maybe partly derived from the cold-war panic of the time: the U2 incident, the Bay of Pigs, the Cuban Missile Crisis. I had sat with my parents at night in the parking lot of the Blue Star Shopping Center and listened to reports of the missile crisis over the car radio, hearing them de-

bate whether to flee back to Europe, somehow identifying the
specter of nuclear war with the creatures I had just been staring
at in *Famous Monsters of Filmland* at Sav-On Drugs while my
parents shopped for bedsheets and boxes of instant minced
onion to send to relatives in Belgium. The fear of Armageddon
was also bound into the rituals of the church, with its prayers
for the conversion of Russia and its hints of apocalyptic
prophecy from the Virgin of Fatima. Such things scared me
rigid, but remained nevertheless abstract.

Much more tangible to me was the threat of the Germans,
just over the border. Whenever I heard an engine overhead I'd
see the hole in the courtyard at my Nandrin grandparents'
house on Rue Robert Centner, where a German shell had
dropped through the roof during the Von Runstedt offensive.
And then I'd play back my godfather's story about the night
he'd heard the whine of a V-2 coming straight at him, and how
he'd remembered just in time that the thing to do was to run *toward* the sound, otherwise the missile would pursue you until
your angles met. Maybe I'd also remember the story of my
mother's great-aunt Marie Nandrin, who went mad from the
tolling of the bells while hiding in the cellar of the church during the pounding of Houffalize in 1944. The war was nine years
gone when I was born, but I nevertheless grew up in its shadow.
I seem to recall seeing ruins and piles of rubble on the streets of
Verviers, and although I can't say for sure they weren't just
houses dead of old age or heaps of construction debris, I was
persuaded they were casualties of war. Even as late as 1974, I
was certain for a minute that a collapsed house I saw in Paris
had been toppled by a shell thirty years earlier. But then, if I
didn't finish all the food set in front of me, my mother would be
sure to say, *"Ce qu'il te faudrait, c'est une petite guerre"* (what

you need is a little war); even now I seldom fail to clean my plate. To this day my parents hoard stocks of canned goods on shelves in their basement; often I heard of the meals my mother and her friends made of dry peas mashed with mustard.

When the German army invaded on May 10, 1940, they came the same way they had in August 1914, by the straight road from Aachen to Verviers. It was not a surprise, and yet it was. After the occupation of the Rhineland, next door, in 1936, and the annexation of Austria, and the invasion of Czechoslovakia, and then Poland, and the strange becalmed stretch of the *drôle de guerre*, the "phony war," people had gotten so used to anxiety that it was blunted into something like disbelief. The invasion of 1940 was somehow unreal, a bad dream, a case of déjà vu for those old enough to remember 1914. There was already an expression, perhaps left over from some previous century: *s'en foutre comme de l'an 40* (to care no more about it than about '40, more or less). My father was eighteen and working for the national railways as a track inspector; my mother was sixteen and had just left the Lycée pour Jeunes Filles, where despite its sonorous name she principally studied sewing.

My father did not become eligible for military service until the Belgian army had already been mobilized and was heading northwest. He followed them by train to Binche, in Hainaut, arriving too late. He was advised to continue westward on foot into France, traveling by back roads and farm lanes to avoid being seen. He had left Verviers alone, but many others were in the same situation, and he gradually met up with hometown friends; their group grew to eight strong, then ten, then eleven. They boarded a freight train; my father left his friends in charge of the gear while he went off to look for straw to rest upon. When he returned the station was in ruins and the train had left. But he found it again, and after a long journey, interrupted by many stretches taken in reverse, and then forward again, they arrived in Arras, where they met British troops who received them graciously, poured them tea, and advised them to head for the coast. They entrained to Gravelines, on the North Sea, where they were sent on their way once more. They followed the shore "like tourists" to Boulogne-sur-Mer, only to find the Germans already there. There was no choice but to head back toward Flanders. They stopped at Dunkirk, where they learned that the Belgian army was busy piling into boats of all sizes for the trip across the Channel.

My mother and her family left Verviers right after breakfast, leaving the dirty dishes on the table, having no idea whether they'd be gone for hours or for years. They packed as much as they could into a single enormous suitcase, which René strapped onto his bicycle; my mother insisted on bringing her tennis racket, and that was strapped on top of the suitcase. The first day they went as far as Liège, where they spent the night at the house of my mother's aunt Adolphine Woos, and in the morning the aunt and her two children joined them on the trek southwest; her husband was kept in Liège by his job. On orders from the skeleton Belgian army command they kept to back roads and farm lanes, sleeping on piles of straw in the countryside, not that this kept them from being seen, since every road was clogged by long columns of refugees. They were intermittently strafed by the Germans—no accident, since it was clear that the Messerschmitts flew low enough to see that they were civilians. At one point, my mother saw the handlebars of some man's bicycle get neatly severed by machine-gun fire. When they arrived on the outskirts of Fleurus, near Charleroi, the town was being shelled. They ran to lie down in a field, my grandfather yelling, "Make your Act of Contrition!" They were picked up by the driver of a delivery truck for the Aiglon chocolate factory in Verviers, himself fleeing, who took them to the French village to which his family had fled in '14, and there they stayed for a few days in a house whose inhabitants had in turn fled to the south of France. Then they caught a train to Toulouse, where teenage boys, René included, were rounded up, presumably to be drafted into the military. The rest of the family boarded a train headed farther south. Some Belgians advised them to get off in Alaigne, a few miles from Carcassonne in the Aude department, in the southwest.

The scene in Dunkirk when my father and his friends got there was one of multifaceted chaos. The embarkation of British and Belgian troops on the beach was temporarily halted while massive aerial bombardment went on, and the confusion kept them from getting to the beach. More and more German squadrons—Stukas, for the most part—flew in; my father's group crouched in the gutter with their heads down. By chance they were very near a complex of seven enormous gas tanks, but were held in place by the strafing; "If one of those things gets hit, we'll be shot straight back to Belgium," said one of his friends. Between passes by the aircraft they looked up and saw that an adjacent statue had been decapitated. Nearby, a house front had collapsed. It was a house with a cellar entrance on the street, and thus was in use as a shelter. The Germans must have hit it deliberately, having seen people running toward it. My father and his friends jumped in to help clear away the rubble and rescue those trapped inside. When soldiers and firemen arrived, the boys tried once more to get to the beach, but were halted halfway there and told they'd be massacred for sure if they stepped out into the open strand. They slunk back to Belgium, and there were picked up by a remnant of the Belgian army, who interned them in a camp in De Panne for a few days, not knowing what else to do. After they were released, they were hailed by Wehrmacht grunts driving an empty truck. *"Wohin ist der Weg aus Lüttich?"* they asked, and so the boys caught themselves a ride to Liège, and got home via the last train to Petit-Rechain.

My mother and her parents stayed in Alaigne for three months. A postcard she brought back shows Place de la République: a dirt plot with a random grouping of plane trees, people standing around listlessly, in the center a *perron*, which is to say a fountain up three steps and surmounted by a statue, in this case what looks like a large rabbit holding an orb and a scepter. This is perhaps appropriate since rabbits caught on traplines by my grandfather constituted most of their diet during this sojourn; they didn't trust the meat in the fly-infested butcher shops. During bombings they huddled in a corner of a brick house, and the rest of the time they lived in various empty shacks occupied in season by migrant workers. There was no electricity or running water in those flea-ridden hovels, which were built of wood on a cement base; the beds were boards upholstered with straw-filled burlap sacks. The owners, who allowed them to live rent-free, supplied them with bedsheets and wine. They cooked on an open hearth and fetched water from the communal pump; in this village, as in those of past centuries, the sewers ran down the middle of the street. By and by orders came from the Germans for Belgian refugees to return to their homes, threatening reprisals against their relatives who had stayed behind should they fail to comply. René turned up, having been nowhere near the army, instead having spent the three months working in a widow's vineyard not many miles away, and so did his bicycle, which had been resting comfortably at the depot in Toulouse.

The next four years brought terror and boredom—mostly boredom, with red splashes of fear. The underground, the *armée blanche*, published clandestine newspapers, sabotaged lines of communication, blew up electrical pylons, killed the collaborationist mayor; the Germans engaged in arbitrary reprisals, house-to-house searches, volleys of arrests and disappearances and executions. They bled the city of money and metal, took over all industries, conscripted labor. My mother was assigned to a factory that manufactured bouillon cubes. My father, like all young men, was subject to deportation to a labor camp in Germany. Some of the friends with whom he had traveled to Dunkirk were so deported. André Joust, called *Jus de Prune*, died in a labor camp; another died when the labor camp he was in was hit by an American bomb; another died during a bombardment in Belgium; another died in Buchenwald. Only five of the group were still alive at the end of the war. Meanwhile, my father's best friend, Fernand Corteil, who was a bit older, had succeeded in joining the army; he died in the prisoner-of-war camp in Battice. Even in 1940, though, the odds of survival seemed slim. Boarding a train to Germany had to be a one-way ride; more than that, it represented capitulation to the enemy.

Determined not to go, my father assumed another identity. The photo-booth portrait of this phantom reveals how little the disguise strayed from the truth: he merely dyed his hair back to its original blond and assumed the eyeglasses he would not actually need until he was over fifty. "Philippe Werner" was his name, the first half possibly plucked from the air, the Teutonic second merely filched from his Luxembourgeois grandmother.

His sister and brother-in-law were living in a château on the outskirts of Pepinster, where Joseph was the gardener and Armande worked as a maid. Since the other servants had left after the invasion, they got my father hired first as the woodcutter, then as the footman. With a bit of difficulty I can see him, blond hair and eyeglasses, black cutaway and striped yellow waistcoat, being correct (of course, I've borrowed his outfit from Nestor, Captain Haddock's butler at Moulinsart in the later Tintin adventures). But for some reason this didn't last long, perhaps due to a surplus of prying eyes, and for a time he was hidden in an *entresol* there, his meals slipped to him through a slot. He gravitated back to Verviers at some point, and got black-market work repairing shoes. I know that once—this sort of thing was almost routine—when the underground announced that it had mined a stretch of train track, and the Germans rounded up random Belgians and loaded them onto a train to test the threat, my father was among the selected victims. Another of them was a very drunk old art professor who proclaimed that any fool could draw a straight line; the mark of draftsmanship was the ability to draw a perfect circle. As the train lurched toward possible imminent catastrophe, this man, who could barely stand up, drew perfect circle after perfect circle on the wall with a stub of a pencil.

Lying so close to the border, Verviers had always been full of ethnic Germans. In the nineteenth century they had had their own newspaper as well as sundry other institutions. The International Working Men's Association, for example—the First International, which found many adherents in the region in the 1870s and '80s—had among its local sections one just for germanophones. But peaceful coexistence had been sorely tested by the first war, and in the second the city was plainly divided. Overlaps, complications, and ironies were rife, though. Coming home from the factory one night, my mother was accosted by two German soldiers, each of whom took one of her arms and walked on, speaking softly in French to her as she trembled. They released her under a streetlight, and in its glow she recognized one of them; she had been friends at school with two of his sisters. After the war, when my father finally joined the army, he was for a time a guard at a P.O.W. camp, where he found he could speak Walloon with various of his charges— one had lived two blocks away from him. One of his classmates was director of the local branch of the German industrial giant Bechtel during the war; he was executed in '45. Another—not a *shleu,* as Germans were pejoratively called in Walloon, but the son of a leading figure in the Walloon fascist party, the Rexists—was appointed director of the *marché couvert,* the wholesale produce market. One day when "Philippe Werner" was riding a tram in Verviers (his family had put out word that Lucien had been deported) he found himself sharing the platform with his former classmate. Their eyes met. Anyone would know that an able-bodied twenty-two-year-old at large in town would have to be a German hireling, and any German employee would know that my father was not one himself; furthermore, here he was in transparent disguise. Terrified, the clandestine passenger got off at the next stop and lay low for a week, convinced that he had been denounced. But he hadn't. Alfred had kept mum. After the war my father got his chance to convey his thanks. The two passed on the street. My father was in uniform; his former classmate had just been released from prison. He was a pariah, and seeing my father he lowered his head. "Hello, Alfred," my father said. The other brightened, grateful to have been acknowledged as a human being.

The uniform my father wore was American—no Belgian army gear was to be had at that point. Thus it was that his picture turned up in a local storefront display devoted to "our American liberators" in 1994, the fiftieth anniversary. I don't know which picture it might have been. There he is in a street photographer's square Kodak, striding down Crapaurue in his Eisenhower jacket, cap cocked jauntily to the side, and there he is, in a couple of studio portraits printed as postcards, with crossed rifles on his lapels, the outline of his face airbrushed into a mist. Whatever the uniform, he looks no more American than Charles Trenet. What does it mean for a face to look European? Something about the mouth, the way the lips seem to be tasting something; about the eyes, some kind of upward pressure on the lower lids. Hairstyle plays its part, but the very shape of the skull seems different, more high-crowned, more elongated. Americans of European descent seldom look the least bit European, some force in the water or the language responsible for flattening the face—not aesthetically but geometrically—and drawing back the lips and scrolling back the lids. (I myself have acquired an American cast to my face by this point in my life, even though I know from having seen myself talking, in mirrors and on film, that my mouth was shaped by the requirements of French: my upper lip doesn't move at all when I am speaking English, but it naturally purses and curls and protrudes to form the globular or gourdlike native vowels.)

In my mother's contemporaneous studio portrait the lens is so swooningly romantic that while you can make out every detail of her lace collar, her right shoulder is entirely out of focus—she is emerging within a dream. The clincher, though, is that while the picture is in sepia her lips have been tinted red, her eyes—roving upward toward some heaven—blue-gray.

The result is exactly in the mode of those romance postcards that have been printed in Europe for nearly a century and that you can still buy at stationery shops in Spain and Greece. Looking at it I find it difficult to keep in mind that the subject is, or will be, my mother, instead of an idealized fiction standing in for some tongue-tied young purchaser's runny emotions. But then can I really know what hers were at the time? What was it like to be twenty-one then, romantic and weary, naïve and scarred, having been robbed by events of the most tender stretch of awakening youth while still, internally, standing on its threshold? Having witnessed death and disaster at firsthand she nevertheless managed to retain her unworldliness undented, something like a wheat stalk, shot through a wall by a tornado, that unaccountably remains intact.

The Liberation brought relief as well as a different kind of danger—that of aerial bombardment, for example. In November 1944 a bomb hit the gasworks a block away from Rue Robert Centner; the shock wave was felt for miles. During the raids my mother's father would prudently repair to the cellar, while she and her mother and brother, sick of it all, continued their daily routine as if nothing were happening. It was war and not-war at once. While Verviers was occasionally shelled, the real misery and death was going on to the east and to the south, as the Allied armies made their way toward Germany and met the Von Runstedt offensive in the protracted three-way slaughter (Allies versus Germany versus winter) called the Battle of the Bulge. (Many years later—1979—I saw REMEMBER MALMÉDY written in chalk on the black backing of an unoccupied poster frame in the Prince Street subway station in New York City, the work of ghosts.) Verviers was a provisional headquarters, which meant that life was heightened, no longer boring. Everything was suddenly outsized and theatrical. The Americans were everywhere. They requisitioned the Coliséum cinema and ran dances there with leading swing bands; Marlene Dietrich appeared on its stage and handed out slips of paper which she autographed with her red lips. The Americans distributed food and various kinds of largesse and found jobs for local people. My father was for a while hired to help unload supply trains, and then to assist a truck dispatcher, giving directions. My godfather was engaged as an interpreter, not that he spoke English, but since he had a command of French, Dutch, German, Walloon, and Plattdeutsch, he could figure it out by triangulation. (In 1969, when my parents and I were visiting, he proudly showed us his U.S. Army translator's manual, marked "Classified"; when pressed to speak some English, he thought for a while and then exclaimed, "Fuck!" My father blanched; my mother didn't understand.)

Soldiers came to dinner. One hapless Brit earned himself a place in lasting family memory by saying, in refusing more food, *"Non merci, je suis plein"* (I had heard this anecdote many times over many years before I understood the hilarity: unwittingly he was informing my grandmother that he was pregnant). My mother, like many young European women, volunteered to take charge of the tomb of a fallen G.I., in her case that of James S. Polaski of Johnsonburg, Pennsylvania, his cross among the endless field of crosses and Stars of David at the Cimetière Américain in Henri-Chapelle. The exchange of Christmas cards and snapshots with his family continued into the 1950s; I have a 1951 picture of his wife's daughter by her second marriage, reading a copy of the Elks magazine in her pajamas, violent wallpaper looming behind her.

Somehow, through war and not-war, life managed to continue. Looking at snapshots, I can't guess their dates on the basis of the business depicted. An antic shot of my mother standing in an empty wire wastebasket in the Bois de Cambre, Brussels, is marked "1942" on the back; she perches coquettishly on a rail at the La Gileppe dam in 1941, shares a rowboat with her blonde friend Gilette Biet in Tilff in '41, kneels at the entrance to an igloo in a snow-covered field in '42. And there's my father, in '44, standing at the foot of the steps of Place de la Victoire, the old Chic-Chac, theatrical posters covering the wall to his left, looking young and too cool for words, his eyes barely showing through their lids, his hair a bit longer, the collar of his polo shirt out over his jacket lapels, his hands thrust into the pockets of pants so cheap you can make out every knucklebone through the fabric. (This was the picture I looked at when I was thirty or so that made me think, *I know that guy,* as I recognized for the first time that my parents contained versions of themselves who were my contemporaries.) Within the war and outside it they contrived to go on day trips with groups of friends, clown around, sit at café tables, tell jokes, strike self-mocking poses. All of them are slender from meager diets and so look terrifically elegant whatever they are wearing.

The Liberation put the street photographers to work, using equipment that was probably American (black-and-white rather than sepia; squarish glossy prints) to produce endless series of pictures identically composed (subjects approaching from the same angle, on the same diamond-cobbled pavement, passing the same shop windows): Dad in olive drab, Mom in hourglass floral frill or belted trench coat or dark New Lookish suit with bobby sox, hair rising to peruke-like double peak and tumbling frizzed out nearly to shoulders. They are alone or with friends (sometimes friend or friends have been scissored out), shopping or heading for work—and then one day they are together, walking *bras dessus–bras dessous* in smart matching outfits of dark jackets with white pocket squares, tan trousers and skirt. Their courtship is chronicled almost exclusively by itinerant photogs working on spec, prints available tomorrow afternoon. Something about each of them has changed, but what? Still young, still shy, but somehow now purposeful, walking toward a destination instead of a mere task. My mother now looks out rather than in; my father has been tightened two full turns.

Trying to imagine my parents' youth I have little to work with—a couple of dozen pictures, a few stories I wrote down, and untrustworthy memories of others I heard once or twice and wasn't smart enough to record at the time. (Family stories are like birds; some are your blue jays or sparrows, so familiar you cease to see them, while others are rare migrants, uncanny apparitions, but when they turn up your telephoto lens is always buried in an upstairs drawer.) And then, too, stories only convey so much—they are accounts of discrete events, given shape by time and by words, and I am desperate to *see,* to fall into transient atmospheric sensation. So I mix up their lives with movies, or other people's pictures. Verviers before the war is an amalgam of images from Jean Gabin vehicles in which it is always dawn or dusk or midnight, the cobblestones are wet although the rain has stopped, the walls are black with soot or hung with giant billboards by Cassandre, the junkman's dray horse dozes in his traces, in fact the whole city is asleep except for one set of curtained windows, two parallelograms of light flung down as a doormat, behind which you can hear accordion music . . .

The Liberation and after bears the trademark of Magnum

Photos: gray daylight, breadlines composed of young women who look like starlets and old people in the rusted black of 1910, congeries of alley cats, one or two incongruous automobiles, walls plastered with public announcements, cinemas transformed into clinics and bridge clubs into rationing centers and banquet rooms into cinemas. Everything is ad hoc and makeshift and impermanent; although everybody has been practicing improvisation for four years, now spontaneity is finally possible. Life is simultaneously constrained and giddy. From one day to the next anything can seem possible, briefly. You understand how revolutions are made in such interstices, although not here and not now, because not enough has been lost. The future stretches limitlessly ahead, but the past urges caution. Your immediate task is to build a rope bridge over the chasm, connecting your last memory of security with the highway of tomorrow still at the blueprint stage.

My parents marry in 1950, in February. They kneel at the altar rail in their overcoats. My mother doesn't wear white— far too expensive for frippery that will never be worn again. Afterward they go home to 170, Rue du Paradis, which sounds like the title of a thriller. My mother has never lived apart from her parents, my father only did so during his military service. But they live within covenient walking distance of Rue Robert Centner, of their jobs, of shops and cinemas. They have three or four small rooms, which look out over the valley of the Vesdre toward the distant heights of Stembert and Heusy. Their budget is meager, but they deploy it with taste. Their wardrobes are limited but stylish and of high quality. Wedding presents assure the elegance of their table: they have a crystal ashtray and a cut-glass cigarette box and a full cream-colored dinner setting for twelve made in Occupied Germany and ivory knife-rests from the Congo and a contraption for picking up sugar cubes that has a three-prong claw at one end and a syringe depressor at the other. They are headed for a life far richer than any their parents could have imagined. On the wall of their bedroom they hang an enlarged snapshot of a house they spotted on a bank of the Ourthe or the Aine, a pretty half-timbered house with trees around it and a real lawn sloping down to the river. It is the house they dream of inhabiting.

VII Escutcheon

For years I read avidly anything I could find that might give me some idea of my hereditary ingredients and what they could mean. I might as well have been looking for a verifiable horoscope. I was an exile with little to measure myself by. I only knew my parents, whom I greatly resembled in certain ways and not at all in others. I had no real sense of the rest of my family, who were either distant or dead. I had no letters, no journals, no memoirs, not even any names beyond my parents' grandparents. I didn't know what my family name signified or where it had come from. I rejected my father's exiled-aristocrats scenario out of hand as a wishful projection, along the lines of those concocted by people who believe they have been reincarnated, who invariably clocked time as priestesses in Atlantis before going on to serve as Marie Antoinette. I knew perfectly well that my name did not mean "health," and had spent as much time correcting francophones who pronounced it *Santé* as I did Americans who said *Santy* or *Sahntay* (my parents, less arrogant, let Americans pronounce it every which way).

I had no illusions about genealogy, a pathetic hobby that combined the bold passion of stamp collecting with the modest sobriety of medieval reenactments. The bloodline of every newly elected American president was instantly traced by Debrett's to one or more of the lesser Plantagenet monarchs. Retirees spent their sunset years documenting their descent from

Charlemagne or Cleopatra or Kublai Khan. There was (according to Alex Shoumatoff's fascinating inquiry, *The Mountain of Names*) a Levantine family that claimed descent from the house of David and whose dowager wore mourning on the day of the Ascension, and there were Mormons who had built astounding lineages going back to Adam and Eve. For my part, I knew with complete certainty that my veins ran with the blood of serfs. I squatted with Rimbaud, who wrote (in "Bad Blood," *A Season in Hell*): "If only I had a stake somewhere in the history of France! But no, nothing. It is plain to me that I have always been of inferior stock. I could never conceive of rebellion. My people rose up only to pillage, wolves falling on the cadaver of the beast they did not kill."

But curiosity drove me anyway. I suppose I was looking for a story. During college I found an obscure and since-discarded book in the university library that contained a list of the *bourgmestres* of the next-door village of Stembert; the first one recorded, in 1661, was named Sante, and so were a number of his successors. This allowed me to feel a bit less alone. I consulted heraldic lists and directories of proper names and any sort of large catalogue of people, without success except for finding a certain Paul Sante enumerated in the record of Napoleonic army conscripts kept in the museum at Waterloo. Whenever I traveled to a new city the first thing I did was to open the local phone book to *S*; I occasionally found a Sante or two but could never summon the courage to dial. I launched various colorful theories regarding the name's distant origins, almost always starring immigrants—from Italy, Spain, the Netherlands—who had adapted the spelling of their handles. I tried to imagine a specific day, equipped with weather, in a recorded century, when some hunched peasant formerly known by one monosyllabic tag, like a dog, suddenly devised or received a second unit of denomination. How was it made? It wasn't an occupational name like Meunier or Boulanger or a descriptive one like Leroux or Lenain. It might have been southern and thus saintly, or perhaps northern and arising from the sand, the dirt itself.

Eventually I got down to business. I began biweekly visits to a building across from Lincoln Center that houses the principal New York branch of the Church of Jesus Christ of Latter-Day Saints, its third floor devoted to the facilities of the Utah Genealogical Society. Mormons believe in the baptism of the dead. The devout trace their ancestry back as far as possible and retroactively convert every name they can establish; when they are done with that they begin baptizing randomly selected persons from all times and places, as a sort of mitzvah. To this end they have microfilmed and consolidated records of birth and marriage and death from every corner of the planet. Aiming for exhaustiveness, their archives include bureaucratic tallies, parish registers, spoken and sung and painted pedigrees—millions upon millions of names, even if fire and flood and the interdictions of other religions, not to mention simple lack of records, restricts the total to a small fraction of human history. Their zeal is such that the institutions of many countries, including all the branches of the Belgian Archives de l'État, owe their microfilm collections entirely to the Utah Genealogical Society, each meticulously catalogued reel the work of Mormon missionaries.

It became a ritual: I would cross Columbus Avenue from the subway station, sign the register in the businesslike lobby crowded with freshly barbered young elders in white shirts and dark neckties, ride two stories on the elevator hung with framed citations from the Book of Lehi, admire the corridor decorated with paintings of the revelation of the angel Moroni, and enter the library staffed with unfailingly pleasant retired ranchers and schoolteachers and sheriff's deputies, the most exotic people to be found in Manhattan. In this setting, as spotless and well oiled as the vault of a suburban bank branch, shielded by thick draperies from the impieties of the street, I would scroll through microfilm copies of handwritten ledgers, sometimes in barely legible scrawl, sometimes in corrupt ecclesiastical Latin, sometimes stained with the evidence of antique lunches, looking for traces of the passage of my ancestral ghosts.

At length, and after many wrong turns and dead ends, I had summoned an assembly of shades, who stood in tiers that faded off into mist and regarded me skeptically. They were hard to see through the gauze of centuries. The facts of their lives had gone the way of their clothing and their kitchens. I was denied a portrait gallery of the kind that sweeps across the mezzanines of haunted houses, and so I could not satisfyingly follow the evolution of my chin or pin blame for my male-pattern baldness on a union consummated during the reign of Charles V. What I had was a load of names and some dates, occasionally embellished with an address or a stray detail of circumstance. The documentation made available by the Mormons stops at around 1880 in order to preserve the privacy of the living, and literacy did not become general among the Belgian working class until a decade or two later, so I could only look upon the signatures of two of my antecedents. The *X*s of the remainder did not allow for much variation, and so the *punctum* of the evidence was fairly abstract. At best I could satisfy myself that maybe the original of the page I was inspecting had been eye-

balled across a table by this or that millhand or plowboy standing hat in fist, in smock and leggings and wooden shoes, a little
intimidated by the ceremony, watching the quill scratch lines
and curls the significance of which could only be taken on faith,
the glyphs by which the upper estates spoke to one another at a
distance, perhaps imparting scandal, perhaps nonsense.

The Santes, whose existence was first recorded in 1221 in a
census conducted by the friars of the abbey of Val-Dieu, which
is still in operation a dozen miles from Verviers, were once a
populous clan. They owed their name to an otherwise unsung
wraith called Alexandre, who in Walloon would have been
called Zande. Consistency in the spelling of proper names—
not to mention that of Walloon—lying far in the future, his
descendants were variously known as Alexandre, Alexandré,
Alsand, Alsande, Alsandre, Xandre, Sainte, Sand, Sande, San-
dre, Sandt, Sant, Sante, Santt, Santte, Sente, Zande, Zandre,
Zandt, and Zante. By the eighteenth century, though, "Sante"
had established itself as the preference of the majority of
scribes (the other variants nearly vanish from the records), and
by that time there were hundreds of Santes in Verviers and surrounding villages. Municipal censuses were not taken until the
end of the sixteenth century; the earliest direct ancestor I could
find was a certain Léonard Zante, born at an uncertain date
before 1600. I know, however, that he was born in Verviers
proper, as was every single bead in the chain. My maternity
ward on Rue Masson, a block from the Vesdre, lay within the
limits of the old city, a few blocks from its poor quarter, and so
within half a mile of the probable birthplaces of all the previous bearers of my family name, excepting only my father, who
was born in the Pré de Mangombroux, about a mile away.

Details accrue baldly and in specks. Léonard's son Paul

Zante (b. ca. 1630) had nine children. His grandson Paul Sante (1692–1760) married Élisabeth Gilet (d. 1774), whose name appears in the records sometimes as Sante, sometimes as Gilet, sometimes as Jacobi because her father's first name was Jacques, and sometimes as Lejeune because her husband, the third Paul in a row, was referred to as *le jeune*. Their son Jean-Joseph (1738–1794) died in the hospital on Rue de Limbourg. His son Michel-Joseph (b. 1791) lived on Quai de la Batte (a redundancy, since *"batte"* is Walloon for *"quai"*), the bank of the industrial canal built in the Middle Ages to serve the textile industry and paved over in 1906. He was himself a spinner; his wife, Marie-Magdelaine Herman (b. 1790 in Goé), whose father was a weaver, was a knotter, a worker whose task was to tie the ends of the longitudinal threads to the frame before the weaving process (it was said that the best knotters, all women, could tie as many as twelve hundred knots an hour). Their son Jean-François (b. 1819), who was able to write his name, was a wool drier; his wife, Catherine Vanguers (b. 1824), was born illegitimate. They lived on Rue Sécheval, a block from the canal.

Their son Armand (1851–1900), my great-grandfather, lived a block farther, on Rue Liguy, although by 1879, when my grandfather was born, he had moved a block nearer, to Place Sommeleville. He was illiterate, a stoker by trade (he worked for the Simonis factory, and so, tradition had it, did all his forebears going back to the establishment of the works); his wife, Marie-Thérèse Sauvage (b. 1847), was a wool sorter. Her father was born in 1780, meaning that I am only four generations removed from the eighteenth century. I have Armand's death certificate, sent to my father by his cousin Yvonne Lecoq (daughter of Armand's older son, also named Armand) shortly before her own death at the age of ninety-four. My great-grandfather died at forty-nine of pulmonary gangrene in Ben-

rath, Germany, now a suburb of Düsseldorf. I have no idea
what he might have been doing there. I have a single photograph of Armand, a *carte de visite* taken when he was probably
in his thirties; the rest of the family documents were kept by my
aunt Armande, and she burned them all for unknown reasons
shortly before her death in 1988.

All but the last two of these generations are included in the
consolidated records of the city of Verviers, compiled in 1875
from the earlier registers. There are 370 births of Santes and
variants listed altogether, over about 250 years with lacunae, of
whom only four show up anywhere in the historical chronicles
of the municipality: a widow who briefly owned a textile factory at the end of the eighteenth century, a dealer in wool remnants indicted for improper trade practices, a tax collector, and
a fire chief. Today there remain only about a hundred Santes in
all of Belgium, of whose possible relationship to me I have no
clue. Laid into the pages of the consolidated record are the
death certificates of citizens who tried their luck abroad and
never came back, expiring in such places as Guatemala and Mo-
rocco. This caused me to wonder whether collateral relatives
might have made their way to the United States before my own
family did. One day I got a piece of junk mail from an address
in Colorado promising me the history of the Santes in America
since the Civil War. I taped it to my refrigerator door and
laughed about it for a while, but then I succumbed and sent off
a check. What I got was a computer-generated list of names
and dates of death and social security numbers, a bunch of dis-
connected entries with no apparent narrative outline. By then I
was determined, though, and so I collected the addresses of the
hundred or so American residents with my last name and sent
each a questionnaire.

I got answers from about forty, which after establishing

family ties accounted for nearly the whole lot. At least half were of Italian ancestry. One, Chandler Sante, lived a few blocks away from me, and his father had attended the same New York City high school as I did—my father had written to his years ago after spotting the name in a school publication, although it turned out that the name had been bestowed on his father in turn at Ellis Island. Lisa Marie Sante, of Buffalo, wrote that her name had originally been Santasiero; it was abbreviated at Ellis Island. So it was with Lisa Sante, of Seattle, and Geraldine Sante, of Connellsville, Pennsylvania, who may or may not be related; their names had in any event both once been Santangelo. Similar operations had been performed on the original names of Rita A. Sante, of Port Richey, Florida, who is of Romanian ancestry (Santeiu), and Ralph Sante, of Trenton, New Jersey, who is Polish (Szantoie). Ruth Tompkins Sante, of Miami, was certain that her father-in-law had been baptized Affredo Sante in Italy. An extended and very friendly coast-to-coast clan of Cubans, of Galician and French ancestry, was in touch with relatives in Spain whose name is Santé. Michael Sante called me from Philadelphia to say that his grandfather was born in Germany, but he knew little else. I thought that we could conceivably be related, but could not trace the matter any farther. Mrs. S. Sante called me from Lihue, Hawaii. She and her husband, recent immigrants from the Philippines, thought it entirely possible that their name might have come down from some traveling Belgian ancestor; I agreed, but again the issue could not be settled. Finally I heard almost simultaneously from (the late) Jan Sante, of Novato, California, and Yvonne Patty (née Sante) of Walnut Creek in the same state, who it turned out were related to each other, although they had been out of touch since before their respective emigrations from In-

donesia. They both could document descent from one Pierre
Séverin Sante, born in Verviers, who had enlisted in the Dutch
army and shipped out from Texel, the Netherlands, aboard the
Henrietta Klazina in 1829. His presence in Indonesia was officially recorded as of 1836, and the following year his wife gave
birth. The Californian Santes could actually be my sixth or seventh cousins.

Whether or not this is so, they carry a genetic trace of the
valley of the Vesdre. It is impossible to establish whether all the
Belgian Santes are descended from a common ancestor, or
whether several Alexandres bred several simultaneous lines of
succession, but there is no question that early appearances of
the name are restricted to a single small region. The valley has
been inhabited since the Paleolithic era; the city took its name
from a Gallo-Roman villa owned by one Virovius. It was long
an unimportant town, completely outside major political and
economic currents, a minor station on the road from Maastricht
to Trier. Besides being located on a narrow and bending stream
not much good for transport, it was a hundred meters higher
and possessed of a much rougher climate than its neighbor
Liège, which early on became the center of the wider region.
Nearly surrounded by the sterile heaths called the Hautes-
Fagnes, Verviers made no wine, possessed no guilds, imported
most of its vegetables from Liège, its grains from the Condroz,
its dairy products from the Pays de Herve. Its inhabitants
fished, cut wood, mined some iron ore. From the early Middle
Ages on it was, along with Theux, Sart, Spa, and Jalhay, one of
the areas called *bans* that comprised the Marquisat de Franchimont. Although Franchimont was annexed by the Principality-
Bishopric of Liège in the eleventh century and remained its
property until that city's sovereignty ended in 1795, Verviers

was nearly always separated from its ruler by some spit of land—the Duchy of Limbourg, which was Dutch; the town of Olne, a small enclave subject to the Netherlands; and the village and countryside of Louveigné, which belonged to the Abbatial Principality of Stavelot-Malmédy. In that time of shifting borders and variable alliances, most people thought of themselves in local terms, as citizens of their city and perhaps their marquisate, and were only intermittently cognizant of the larger powers that reigned above: the Holy Roman Empire, Lotharingia, Burgundy, Spain, Austria. Those entities made their presence felt by war, repression, taxation, pillage, famine. Otherwise they remained abstract.

Verviers owes what significance or prosperity it ever enjoyed entirely to the textile industry. This began in some very small way around the year 1000, but did not really become substantial until about 1450. Liège's textile works began around the same time, and would have eclipsed Verviers's were it not that the Meuse, a major fluvial highway, was thought better used for heavy transport, and so Liège became a center of the iron industry instead. (The relationship between Liège and Verviers has an almost exact parallel in that between Leeds and Bradford in England; to expand the analogy, Ghent would be Manchester.) The wool industry of the Vesdre in its early days stretched as much as four hundred square miles, from Wegnez in the west to Charneux in the north, Eupen in the east and Theux in the south; by and by it became concentrated in its center city. But Verviers took a long time to become a city in the modern sense. Engravings from as late as the mid-nineteenth century show factories with belching smokestacks ensconced in bucolic settings, surrounded by grazing cattle. The region did not provide its own wool, though; what little was sheared from local sheep made a coarse cloth, and by the eighteenth century 90 percent of the wool used was imported, from as far away as Italy and Spain (by the nineteenth century it would mostly come from Argentina, Australia, and the Cape Colony).

When the wool arrived it was washed in a solution consisting of four parts hot water to one part urine, the urine collected every morning by women in the poor neighborhoods around the canal (urine, aseptic and alkaline, functioned as a purifying agent). The wool was then rewashed in the river, its water advantageously low in calcium, using a container, called a *bot de spåneu,* that resembled a small wooden backhoe. Then it was greased, then carded, that is, untangled with a large brush whose bristles were nails. Spinning wheels were employed to stretch and combine the fibers into threads. Dyeing came after that, in a solution of water, urine, potash, and coloring agents, and then warping, the alignment of the threads. Then the cloth could be woven, on a frame with a shuttle thrown back and forth by two weavers. The cloth was immediately washed for fifteen to eighteen hours in running water with soap and urine, and then beaten with hammers, the process called fulling. After drying, the cloth was combed to restore its nap, then scraped with heavy scissors to highlight different parts of the nap (this process, called *tondage,* shearing, was so arduous that it often invalided its workers by the age of forty). The beating, drying, combing, and scraping could be repeated in sequence three or four times, depending on the desired quality. Finally the cloth was pressed, for luster.

The industry was exceedingly labor-intensive. Before the Industrial Revolution each individual weaving job needed more than thirty laborers in different aspects; the spinning process required sixteen. In any operation of the cloth-making sequence an individual worker could turn out only a few pieces per week, from ten or twelve in the case of the *tondeur* up to forty-eight for the presser. Consequently, the cloth that had passed through the entire process was extremely expensive, although the quality justified the price. But the workforce was used hard and paid little, badly housed and meagerly fed—the rates of malnutrition, overwork, exhaustion, anemia, and rickets were notably high. Skeletal deformations caused by the work were widespread. Even though a law was passed in the early nineteenth century restricting child labor to the day shift, which ran from 5 A.M. to 7 P.M., employers were known to keep children (who went to work at the age of seven) on the job at night for decades afterward. Manufacturers often paid their employees in goods, sometimes at double their actual value, and sometimes the goods were defective lots they had picked up through barter at trade fairs; eventual laws forbidding this practice were widely flouted. Salaries were frozen for very long stretches, for example the whole of the eighteenth century, which in effect meant that laborers did not benefit from prosperity, although they were subject to wage cuts in bad times. Workers began to organize for higher wages and better conditions in the early eighteenth century; the first strike, by *tondeurs* at twenty-four plants, took place in 1759. Nevertheless, progress was slow. Even though an industrywide contract, covering wages, hours, overtime, and apprenticeship, was enacted in 1789, it does not seem to have been terribly stringent. In a one-industry town, the manufacturers could dictate their own terms. They could simply fire their entire workforce and import foreign laborers, for example. For all that a labor movement began in Verviers nearly a century before the French Revolution, and that its Francs-Ouvriers (free workers) joined the First International in 1868, and that the city went on to become a Socialist stronghold, no union was legally established there until 1905.

Year to year the track of the condition of life in Verviers resembles a fever chart. From the sixteenth through the eighteenth centuries, war was nearly continuous; although the city itself remained resolutely neutral, it sat on a battlefield. Soldiers—Spanish, French, Austrian—came through, took or were given whatever food was available, were billeted in every house, looted and pillaged and raped. Between 1640 and 1705 foreign armies occupied Verviers in fifty-three years out of a possible sixty-six. Wars furthermore caused distant rulers to levy crushing taxes and to seal off trade routes; in times of peace they imposed export tariffs and manipulated prices—high prices resulted in famine, and low prices often resulted in famine as well. Famine was also caused by meager harvests and bad weather, on a regular basis. There were frequent floods and epidemics. Every prosperous year was immediately succeeded by a protracted period of misery. The city somehow held its own and even thrived through the revolution of 1789 and the French invasion of 1792, but two years later the factory owners, fearing the guillotine, fled en masse. With no money to buy raw materials or to ship goods to market, the industry came to a halt. By the time the owners returned, a year after that, four thousand people in the region were dead from hunger and associated causes.

In 1798 an Irishman named William Cockerill arrived in Verviers. Defying Britain's ban on the export of technology, he had first tried to establish mills in Sweden and in Hamburg, but had failed. In Verviers, to which he was lured by a roving agent of the manufacturer Iwan Simonis, he completely transformed local industry. One of his spinning jennies, operated by three people, could do the work of 300 (the fully automatic spinner introduced in 1857 permitted five people to do the work of 1800). The flying shuttle halved the number of weavers needed; the carding machine assumed the work of 24. The result was hugely profitable to the industry as a whole, but it also cut the workforce drastically. Before Cockerill's arrival, the woolen trade had employed 18,392 people in the Verviers region; not long afterward the number had dropped to 7801. As orders increased, more people were hired—the regional force grew to 13,000 by 1846, to nearly 19,000 by 1896, but in the same period the city's population jumped from about 20,000 to 54,000.

In 1827 three "men of letters" from Brussels, in a book surveying the country (it was called *L'Hermite en Belgique,* although published three years before the nation was constituted), wrote of Verviers: "This small but rather pretty town has a population of more than 18,000, of whom half, dependent on day-labor, are sunk in the most profound misery. There are fewer than 200 well-to-do families. . . . The city is founded on commerce and manufacture, and its spirit of commerce tends to shrink ideas, to stifle noble and generous sentiments, and to cast all relations between people in a purely venal light." There was, they noted, not one free school, no public library, no classes for workers. Meanwhile, just a few years earlier, Alexandre Dumas had professed himself unable to find a fresh egg in the entire province of Liège. The death rate stood at 40 percent, breaking even with the birthrate; half the deaths were of children under five. In 1843 the city possessed fourteen physicians and one public bath. For a twelve- and one-half-hour day, a skilled man's salary could buy a kilo of chocolate, an unskilled man's a kilo of meat, an adolescent's a kilo of rice, a woman's a loaf of rye bread, a child's a loaf of black bread. A woman's salary could not quite purchase a third-class entry to the bath. A child's salary could buy nearly a liter of ginever, or six liters of beer. A woman could buy a kippered herring for every two buckets of urine she collected.

In the same period, the canal water ran clear. There were farms right in town, cattle barns on major streets. Pigs, in fact, were butchered in the street, even after the municipal slaughter-house was erected. Although the water used to wash wool was dumped into the river, people successfully fished. There were seven marketplaces, one for fresh fruit and vegetables; three for potatoes, cabbages, and other sorts of groceries that could be stored; two for manufactured goods; and one for old clothes, old books, old kitchenware, old junk. There were numerous itinerant tradespeople: women with baskets on their heads sold cherries, red currants, gooseberries, plums, nuts, green cab-bage, herbs, the farmer's cheese called *makèye;* men sold char-coal, sand, hats, almanacs, rabbit pelts, rags, and scrap iron; they mended umbrellas, mended dishes, mended cooking pots, sharpened scissors, told fortunes, displayed dancing bears, played one-man-band contraptions, played the hurdy-gurdy. Umbrellas, actually, were only owned by the rich, who passed them along from father to son and only used them on Sundays.

There were dozens upon dozens of places to drink: cafés, *cabarets, estaminets,* grog shops. Surveys conducted in 1848 and 1860 found that one house in seven was so employed, one boozer for every eighty inhabitants. By law they were open from 4 A.M. to midnight in summer, from 5 A.M. to 11 P.M. in winter; if they featured singing and dancing they were forced to close an hour sooner. They opened early so that workers could fortify themselves before hitting the factory gates. To get drunk was called *se mettre une perruque,* to put on a wig (the consumption of beer was 50 percent higher in Belgium than in any other European country). Prostitution was tolerated in brothels and *hôtels de passe* and *maisons de rendezvous,* which were however not permitted to display a sign. Carnival, on Mardi Gras, was as everywhere an enfeebled survival of the medieval feast of misrule. Its tenor can be gauged by the relevant laws: carrying a weapon as part of a costume was forbidden; priests' cassocks, military uniforms, and lawyers' and judges' robes were not permitted to be worn as costumes; shouting insults, invading shops and houses, and throwing flour or bran at spectators were prohibited. The entire month of September was given over to the kermesse, an emplacement on four of the town's squares of carousels, performance stages, shooting galleries and the like, and booths selling food and drink. Working-class families took their routine pleasures on Sundays and holidays. The Epiphany on January 6, St. Antoine on January 17, Ste. Brigitte (patron saint of cattle) on February 1, Candlemas the following day, Ste. Appoline (patron saint of teeth) on February 9, St. Nicolas on December 6 were not days off, but special pastries were made and sold only on occasions of that sort, such as the S-shaped biscuits called *mirous,* the spectacle-shaped ones called *lunettes,* the apple pies called *vôtions,* the towering brioches called *charmoules.* On Sundays families went walking in the countryside around the city, where open-air cafés such as the Frascati and the Tivoli awaited them. Workers raced their pigeons or trained their songbirds for the annual contests, engaging in the latter by hiking in the hills cage in hand, chaffinch or linnet within, a canteen filled with *pèkèt* slung from a shoulder, encouraging with whistles the music called *radjatrwèdistruwîtch.* After the contest, held on Rue des Grandes-Rames (big drying-racks) in late spring, the losers were usually strangled.

The railroad came through in 1843, linking Liège and points west with Aachen and points east. It was good for business, needless to say. In *Le Rhin* (1838), Victor Hugo describes in awed tones the astounding job of blasting tunnels and constructing embankments necessary to run the line around and through the steep surrounding hills, at the same time that he laments the violence this work has visited on the beautiful landscape. Verviers he calls "an insignificant town, divided into three sections: the Chick-Chack, the Basse-Crotte, and the Dardanelle." He goes on: "I noticed a little six-year-old boy, sitting on the steps of his house, magisterially smoking his pipe. Seeing me pass, the smoking tyke burst out laughing. I inferred that he thought I was pretty ridiculous." That is all he has to say of the place. "Basse-Crotte" can be translated as "lower turd"; the town actually could boast of as many as nine distinct neighborhoods. The Verviétois nursed a satirical cosmopolitanism: Rue Coronmeuse, right in the center, was called *Podrî l'Rhin* (over the Rhine), while Hodimont, across the river, was known as Faubourg d'Espagne—although, paradoxically, to go there was termed *aller en Prusse*. Other Walloons called the Verviétois *matchèts* (dyers) or *rats d'êwe* (water rats) or *magneûs d'pèlote* (potato-peel eaters) or *râyeûs d'ohê* (bone pickers) or sometimes *crås cous* (fat asses, because when out of town they liked to pretend they were rich). It was in 1872 that the calligrapher Corneille Gomzé finally gave the city its anthem, the "Barcarolle verviétoise":

> *Ah! Por mi dju so fîr,*
> *Qwand dj'so-st-a l'ètrandjîr,*

D'aveûr sutu hossî
Èn on trô come a Vervî! *

Social reforms were slow and niggling. In 1886, a commemoration in Liège of the fifteenth anniversary of the Paris Commune turned into a riot, and the rioting spread to Verviers and throughout Wallonia. After the uprising was suppressed, the government hastily convened a committee to investigate industrial conditions. A year later it prohibited paying workers' salaries in drinking places, and two years after that forbade factory employment of children under twelve. The Socialists' largest and most pressing demand, however, was for universal suffrage, which was not instituted until 1893, again in emergency conditions, after that year's national strike. Even so, the term "universal" had a rather relative ring to it. Plural voting—the granting of multiple votes to the rich and powerful†—was not abolished until 1921, the same year that women were finally given the right to vote. (For decades the rallying cry of Belgian women had been "Wyoming!" after the American territory that recognized women's votes in 1860.) On the question of voting rights as on all others, however, Verviétois radicals refused to toe the line, arguing that universal suffrage was a distraction concocted by the ruling class and calling for revolution, an opinion not terribly popular elsewhere in a country whose working class was markedly more conservative than that of, say, France.

---

* I'm so proud of myself/ Whenever I'm abroad/ That I was born and raised (literally: rocked in the cradle) / In a hole like Verviers.

† The constitution of 1831 only granted suffrage to certain landowners, comprising a bare 1 percent of the population. The 1893 compromise allocated one or more additional votes to landowners and certain members of the professional classes.

Throughout Europe, weaving was the trade that traditionally harbored the greatest number of rebels and malcontents.
Weavers were prominent in the various millennial heresies of
the Middle Ages as well as in the revolutionary phases of the
Protestant Reformation (the Protestants of Verviers had dese-
crated several churches before the local movement was suppressed in 1568 and its survivors exiled to the Palatinate).
Verviétois workers began in the early eighteenth century to
form mutual-aid societies, build strike funds and defense funds
and insurance funds (accident insurance was only rarely provided by factory owners). The weavers, the spinners, the
warpers, the carders, the dyers, the washers all had established
sociétés de résistance by the mid-nineteenth century, as had the
smelters, the mechanics, and the cabinetmakers. A consumer
cooperative called La Prévoyance (Foresight) began in the
1860s, to some degree of resistance by shopkeepers—when its
committee purchased a cow to supply milk for the members,
they found it difficult to transport it to Verviers because other
wholesale dealers would not allow them a place in the cattle car.
When the Francs-Ouvriers were constituted in 1867, one of
their first acts was to start their own cooperative, and they ad-
vertised its specials in their newspaper, *Le Mirabeau:* good deals
on coffee, sugar, prunes, matches, wax, soap, and tobacco. The
Francs-Ouvriers joined the International the following year,
the second Belgian group to do so (the first was an association
of farmhands in the province of Namur). Soon there were
fourteen sections of the International's regional federation; in
1873 a fifteenth was started—a women's section, the first in the
International. The most vocal Socialists were artisans. In *Le
Mirabeau,* letters to the editor tended to be signed by occupation rather than name for fear of reprisal; weavers are repre-

sented, but most are jewelers, painters, carpenters, cobblers, ty-
pographers, paperhangers, tailors, mechanics. Laborers were
few because, of course, they couldn't read.

In 1877 Verviers played host to the ninth congress of the International, which turned out to be the last. By that time the
Marxists were gone, the break five years earlier between Marx
and Bakunin having proved conclusive, and the organization
was now wholly anarchist. The vast majority of Verviétois radicals were anarchists: anti-authoritarian, antimilitarist, antipo-
litical. This fact a partisan observer, the veteran Bruxellois
Socialist leader Louis Bertrand, attributed to the success of the
textile trade, which he claimed had given them privileges, such
as education, unavailable to common workers, who became
Democratic Socialists. At the congress, however, speeches were
given in or translated into Walloon, the language of the illiterate majority of local attendees. Among the visiting delegates
was Peter Alexeievitch Kropotkin, traveling under the incognito of Levashóff, who wrote in his memoirs that "these cloth-
iers were one of the most sympathetic populations that I have
ever met with in Western Europe." Entertainment was provided by a choral group called Les Socialistes Réunis. James
Guillaume, of the Swiss Jurassian Federation, outlined his program in seven basic theses for dismantling the state and replacing it with a purely economic distributive apparatus. Paul
Brousse and Andrea Costa argued for the duty of promoting
revolution in all lands. Guillaume protested, citing the need to
preserve the autonomy of the local sections. A fissure appeared
between theory and action. All this was debated, and variously
applauded, by professorial types in cutaways, and men with
clay pipes and stiff silk caps and squared-off beards, and thin
women with aprons and blazing eyes like Louise Michel. They

believed in the future, the dawn, progress, reason, science. The revolution would make all men equal, it would sweep away superstition and injustice and ignorance and forelock-tugging and pointless encrusted ritual. It would usher in shorter days, equal work done by all, freely given mutual assistance, recitals of good music in the evenings, study groups devoted to Darwin and Galileo and Élisée Reclus, healthful exercise in wooded settings, cooperative child care, model housing, sanitation. They didn't want much, just a civilization that lived up to its name.

But whatever glowing images they took home that day got worn to a nub. The International, irreconcilably split between the partisans of propaganda by word and those of propaganda by deed, soon foundered. By 1880 *Le Mirabeau* had ceased publication, and its various socialist and anarchist successors, though numerous, were invariably short-lived owing to censorship and seizures by the police. Most of the leading Verviétois radicals of the late nineteenth and early twentieth centuries wound up emigrating, to Canada or Argentina or Australia, where perhaps they earned a living shipping wool to their erstwhile comrades. Change crawled so painfully slowly that only desperation could keep people believing. Every increment of technological improvement was exploited by factory owners to the detriment of the workers; the flying shuttle, for example, only briefly lightened weavers' tasks—soon they were required to work two machines simultaneously. The great strikes, from the national upheaval of 1893 to the endless and frequently bloody series of local walkouts, and consequent lockouts, from 1896 to 1906, achieved mere crumbs of reform, bit by bit, at a staggering price in privation and beatings and killings and prison time. The great revolutionary visions of the previous century faded into wistful memory. Idealists became pragmatic syndicalists, or else they gravitated to Brussels or Paris and became illegalist desperadoes, and more often than not wound up rotting in jail.

The cycle was to recur in the 1930s, when factory owners joined forces to break the back of the union. My father can clearly recall the riots following the general lockout in the terrible year 1934: gendarmes imported from distant provinces turning hoses on the workers and driving their horses into the crowd, aiming their clubs at random heads, dodging bricks and stones, and soda-water bottles thrown at horses' hooves to make them rear and toss their riders. Only war could calm class rage, and wars occurred efficiently. Changes for the better could be little more than cosmetic in a place where all power flowed from a single source, even a city where the *députés* were all Socialist—except one from the Catholic Party and one from the Communist, who canceled one another out. Verviers continued to be a one-industry town until the 1950s, when it began turning into a no-industry town.

At the same time, though, it was a city noted for the stubborn independence of its inhabitants, and for a belief in culture that cut across class lines. My grandfather, with his devotion to theater and music and the music of language, despite just a few years' schooling, was hardly exceptional. By the end of the nineteenth century, workers' acting troupes and choral groups were as numerous as pigeon-racing clubs. People who could barely read were among the audience for concerts by the great violinists Henri Vieuxtemps and the Ysaye brothers, and by the town's own spectacular prodigy, the composer Guillaume Lekeu, who would surely have rivaled the Liégeois César Franck, who was his teacher, maybe even Brahms, it was said, had he not died of typhoid fever at twenty-four. Working-class families filled the cheap seats at the theater, the city's great white marvel that arose like a ship just over the crest from the train station, taking in boulevard comedies and poetic melodramas and operas and operettas of all distinctions (my father's musical taste, running heavily to Johann Strauss and Offenbach and Massenet, derives directly from the institution's perennial fare). There were laborers who were amateur scholars, linguists and historians and archeologists, and in the town's learned societies class affiliation and formal educational attainment were ignored. The name of the great historian Henri Pirenne, arguably the city's most famous native, was known even to those incapable of reading him; his imprisonment by the Germans during World War I provoked as much popular outrage as more egregious injustices. Before the municipal public library was instituted, private lending libraries served the function, and they did not deal in frivolity—I have a copy of the 1851 edition of Lamartine's *Histoire des Girondins* bearing the stamp of the biggest of these, the *Soirées Populaires* (*"populaire"* is the common French euphemism for "working-class"); it shows evidence of heavy traffic across its 936 closely set pages.

Somehow, through misery and ambition, idealism and rage, the city made itself a singular identity, one composed of stubborn and even perverse independence, brawling and scholarship, anarchy and aesthetic detachment. At least a shadow of this ornery reputation remains even in the present, when regional differences have been ironed smooth by transport and communication. As I scan the past the city becomes a creature, a coherent assemblage of contradictory impulses. At the same time I try to spot ancestral faces in the crowd of strikers and revelers, but don't know what to look for beyond superficialities of hairline and eye color. What did they do, say, hear, understand, and does it matter? I want to know where my forebears stood even though I am perfectly aware that genes cannot transmit decisions. I never will know any specifics, but I really don't need to. I can claim the city itself as my progenitor. I feel it in my bones.

Even so, I am three-quarters peasant. It's much harder for me to insert my imagination into that world of fields and forests. From the New York City tenements I've lived in to the tenements of Verviers is not much of a stretch: streets equal streets, crowds equal crowds, bricks equal bricks. In the countryside I'm far less oriented. But it's really not so far away, either. I can just drive three hours to the western foothills of the Catskills and there I can see the Ardennes, if I take the trouble to place a steeple every few feet along the horizon. To further the versimilitude, I go on: I triple the population, dispense with isolated farms and put villages in their stead, reduce each herd of livestock by two-thirds or more but multiply the number of herds, remove most of the deciduous trees—nearly eliminated by invading Germans—and replace them with conifers, add various single-lane roads and unpave many of the ones existing, turn wooden houses to stone and convert trailers into either shacks or pre-fab units depending on which historical era I'm aiming for. But I don't have to alter the hills, which are old and low, and the valleys steep, and the rain and fog plentiful.

The Ardennes is by western European standards a vast tract of forest, although it was once much greater, stretching from the Rhine to the western limit of the Meuse and running north to south a distance of five hundred Roman miles, according to Caesar, or four thousand stadia according to the geographer Strabo. It has been cut down by degrees, urbanized here and

there, agricultured in spots that now make up the fertile
plateaux of the Condroz and Hesbaye and Famenne. What remains intact is on poor soil for planting, good only for potatoes,
and some oats, rye, buckwheat, barley, spelt, strictly for local
consumption. Its inhabitants have otherwise kept body and soul
together by logging, quarrying slate, forging nails, smuggling
tobacco. It is the home of the stag and the boar and until fairly
recently the wolf. And it is an ancient locus of mystery, the domain of the Celtic goddess Arduinna, the personification of the
forest, and of the antlered Gallic god Cernunnos. Arduinna
was seamlessly syncretized into the Roman hunt goddess
Diana, and Cernunnos a bit later into Odin, and eventually
many of their attributes were assumed by St. Hubert, whose
life was changed by a vision of a stag with a cross between its
antlers. Christianity was both profound and diaphanous. It did
not chase away the *dames blanches*—incarnations of the white
goddess—or the fairies or witches or elves or imps resembling
little old men, or the werewolves or the weregoats, or the *feux
follets,* the will-o'-the-wisps. Shakespeare, after all, located the
kingdom of the fairies in the forest of Arden, the very same. It
is a land largely without history, remote from politics and
progress until the most recent wars, preserving the pace of neolithic times well into the Middle Ages, and of the medieval era
almost until our own. Its life has changed more within my lifetime than in the previous thousand years.

Let's visit the aborigines. Here's the typical house: gray or
blue or red or yellow stone, perhaps stacked slate, perhaps covered with whitewash, thatched or tiled or slate roof, tiny windows, plank door. Inside is the main room, kitchen and parlor
at once. Prominent is the stove, wood- or coal-burning, cast-
iron, maybe with blue-and-white tiles, its pipe leading out

through a sealed hearth, pot racks on its sides, a blackened copper kettle *(coukemar)* and two or three hand irons sitting on top. Occupying center stage is a large wooden table, covered with a checked cloth and surrounded by at least six wooden chairs, which can either be so simple they resemble a child's drawing or factory-made ornate, with ball-and-claw feet and woven rattan panels and graduated finials. Going back a few decades there might have been two chairs in the middle and long rough benches along the walls. The floor, depending on era and level of prosperity, can be wooden or tiled or covered with linoleum, perhaps a medley of linoleum patches in violently clashing patterns. The windows are curtained. Pegs hold hats and aprons and perhaps an umbrella, the latter more status symbol than convenience. The walls are whitewashed and so is the ceiling between the dark brown wooden beams. There will not be a sink until recent times; drinking water is fetched from the communal pump and washing of all sorts is done at the *lavoir*. There is a tallish cabinet with a coffee mill resting on top. A pendulum clock is possible in the nineteenth century, inevitable afterward. If there is a clock there will also be a calendar, a gift from the postman.

Conceivably there could be a book or two prominently displayed for effect, maybe a popular occult manual such as *Le Grand Albert*. In all eras there will be a large crucifix dominating the spread at top center, on mantel or wall. There are also a number of holy pictures of various sizes, framed or not, perhaps the popular duo in matching frames of Jésus and Marie each displaying their hearts, thorn-ringed and flaming, and perhaps images or statuettes of one or more saints in iconic pose: Hubert kneeling before the cross-bearing stag, Appoline holding a pair of pliers, Roch on a crutch and accompanied by a dog who is licking the open sores on his legs,* Lucie proffering eye-balls on a tray, Michel the archangel lancing a demon, Jean Vianney in shovel hat and soutane with long lace collar, An-toine the hermit cloaked and hooded, Remacle in bishop's miter and robe, Expédit underscored with the word *"Cras"* (Latin for "tomorrow").

There will also be a pipe rack, hung with clay or wood or meerschaum specimens, and from these each male will have se-lected one to stick in his face, the minimum age for this activity increasing over the decades from maybe fourteen a century ago to seventy or so nowadays. At least one spittoon sits on the floor between chairs. People might be playing cards, something like whist or tarot (an actual game), or, at least, one is playing solitaire. Chances are they won't be reading the newspaper, not until more recent times. There is a radio on in the recent past, dead silence earlier, or maybe just the murmuring of prayers by the senior female in her corner perch. Conceivably there is some sort of conversation, laconic and dry, with the Walloon keynote of half-humorous complaint, with long spaces between sentences.

There are three competing clouds of odorous smoke aloft: tobacco, fuel, cooking. Potatoes, always and without exception, are roasting or boiling or frying, and another vegetable sim-mering, perhaps white beans or endive or escarole. On Sunday or in flush times there will also be a chicken or a rabbit or a flank of colt *(poulain)* or a quantity of smoked ham *(jambon d'Ardenne)*; on a major feast there could be venison or young wild boar *(marcassin)*. In harder times there might be eggs. This is the midday meal. Breakfast and supper primarily fea-

---

* In other cultures this figure is called St. Lazarus.

ture bread. The bread might be wheat or rye or oat, white or gray or black depending, again, on the level of prosperity, in enormous round loaves which the male head of the household pinches between shoulder and chin and saws into slices with a posture and motion like a fiddler's. The bread is always buttered (the eternal *tartine*) and always accompanied, or rather it always accompanies—you eat bread with your apple, with your chocolate, with your cheese, with your onion. You wouldn't eat any of those things by themselves because it would not then constitute a meal, and the concept of the sandwich lies somewhere in the future. Washing it all down will be coffee—children get increasing doses in their hot unhomogenized milk beginning as young as five or six years of age—or beer (*bière de table* at 3.2 alcohol content in many families), or *pèkèt* among the hard-living.

The bedroom is in the rear; as of the late nineteenth century there may be plural chambers, and they might even be up a flight of stairs. Each of them contains an armoire, as they do to this day, the idea of built-in closets never having quite penetrated, and one or more massive, narrow beds. Country people tend to cover them with eiderdowns; city folk for some reason prefer piles of blankets. Under the beds are chamber pots, even if the house in more recent times has acquired indoor plumbing, since the midnight trip to the loo remains an arctic expedition in winter. In a corner is a copper vessel on a pole, which is filled with glowing coals and then raked over the sheets to warm them up. On the walls are, again, a crucifix, maybe a fancy one, with silver tips on the cross, backed with crimson satin in an oval frame, and selected holy pictures, and by the late nineteenth century photographs of departed forebears so heavily retouched they look waxen. (These scared the living daylights out of me when I was a child, and rightly so, because they were death images; given the expense of photography, no one had his or her picture taken until the reaper's scythe could be heard dragging in the dust outside.) By that period the walls will be papered, in complex patterns usually against dark backgrounds, which are good at concealing stains and wear.

Downstairs is the root cellar, dominated by potatoes. Outside, the house probably faces on some kind of street or square and is flanked by neighbors; isolated dwellings are extremely rare, there not being enough land to fool around with. (The farms of the rich are an exception; these are like little forts, stone buildings built in a square around a central courtyard.) The pump, or *perron*, marks the center of the village. Among the clustered buildings is the inevitable church, and one or more barns and stables, perhaps collectively employed. Horses and oxen stand in their traces, pigs and chickens wander around. The fields might be in the rear, or they might lie some distance away. The scenes there, until well into the 1950s and '60s, might have come from paintings by Millet. People are raking hay with wooden rakes, beating straw with flails, winnowing grain in cribs, picking vegetables by hand, loading bundles onto horse carts. Hay and straw are gathered into piles that are cinctured with wire and peaked at the top, looking like so many tropical huts. Between house and field is a yard, strewn with carts and pieces of carts and populated by a random scattering of chickens. By the back door stands a stripped sapling, about three feet high, on whose truncated branches galvanized milk jugs are stuck neck-first to dry. Just outside the door is a row of wooden shoes. Indoors everybody wears carpet slippers, maybe brown corduroy. The fields are never so far away—or, needless to say, so large—as to prevent anyone from coming home for *diner*, served at high noon.

Given sufficient wealth the house of the mid-nineteenth century might well have a parlor, a dizzying accumulation of wallpaper patterns and fringed runners and overwrought chairs and indescribable lamps and overlapping carpets and bibelots of every sort. Such a room might, as a country parlor I once visited did, actually possess two hearths, on opposite walls. Two hearths in one room are useless, of course, but then so is everything else in the room. The country parlor is purely ceremonial and almost never used—perhaps for a wedding reception, more certainly for laying out the dead. A parlor in addition cries out for a hallway, a vestibule, a grand staircase—and by then you have brought the city to the country (it is understood that you are exceptionally prosperous) and are living in a three-story brick edifice with colored glass and steps leading up to the front door and all the rest of it, and you are probably the *bourgmestre* of your hamlet and wear a stiff collar and four-in-hand when going out to inspect your swine.

That was not the fate of my ancestors, although my Hermant great-great-grandfather, my father's mother's grandfather, may have approached it. All I know of him is that he was an Ardennais farmer and sufficiently well-to-do that he left substantial legacies to each of his children. His son François, born circa 1837, took his lot and squandered it in Paris. That would presumably have been in the 1860s or '70s, so naturally I imagine him as some rakehell out of Maupassant, with pomaded curls on his temples and his collar askew, a Havana in his kisser and his opera hat all accordioned, a *danseuse* on either knee and fallen bottles of Krug gurgling their contents out onto the parquet beneath the potted palms, to the sounds of a string orchestra playing a *galop*. Eventually, broke and chastened, he returned to native soil, but not to his own village. (I don't know where he was born, or when, or how long it took him to dissipate his inheritance.) He settled in a *bourgade* called Froidthier, large enough to possess a church but small enough to be entirely administered by the next town over, Clermont-sur-Berwinne, about fifteen miles northeast of Verviers. He found work as a navvy *(terrassier)*. He married Anna-Katherina Werner, said to have been born in Wiltz, Luxembourg, at an uncertain date toward the middle of the century (she fails to appear in that town's birth records, which like all Luxembourgeois documents of that era are mildly interesting by virtue of having been kept alternately in French and in German in five-year sequences). They had four children, François, Lambertine, Amélie (my father's godmother), and my grandmother, Marie, born in 1881. All of them were tiny and tough, so my father tells me, all but my grandmother having died before my birth.

The only real glimpse of the deep rural past I got in my childhood was provided by my maternal grandfather, Édouard Nandrin, and his brothers Joseph and Achille, who both had settled in Pepinster, the town to which my parents and I moved in 1956, when I was two. When we left for the United States a bare three years later, my mother's parents moved from Verviers into our house, and lived there until their deaths in the early 1960s. When my mother and I returned in 1962 my grandmother was dying of breast cancer; she passed away a week or so after our arrival. (She was laid out in the vestibule for a day or two—I would see her on my way out to school—and the funeral procession, led by the hearse, proceeded on foot from our house to the church.) During and after the ordeal Joseph and Achille spent a great deal of their time at our house. The three brothers would sit in our kitchen, silently smoking their pipes, from midday into evening, not turning on lights as night fell and deepened. I was scared of them, of their hardness and taciturnity, of their deep-set eyes and thin aquiline beaks (especially Achille's, which was bent halfway to the right). I knew without knowing that these men had lived in a world more elemental than any I would be likely to experience, a world of privation and struggle and failure and bloody chance and consequent fatalism. They never laughed, and spoke in proverbs, harsh ones that predicated a bad end to all enterprises. Through them I came to endow the countryside with unspoken horror, as if they had been full of tales of squalor, disease, accident, famine, and death, but whether or not they told such stories is now beyond my reach.

I can see all of this reflected now in the face of their father, Eugène, who stares out from a tattered photograph taken when he was over sixty, with hollow cheeks, jug ears, a vast white mustache, and piercing eyes that may not really have been as cruel as they seem. Eugène was born in 1854 in Odeigne. In 1885 he married Marie-Rose Lambertine Éloy (1860–1941), of the same parish, and there they produced six children, in order Antoine Joseph (called Joseph), Marie-Antoinette (who went mad in 1944 during the bombing of Houffalize), Achille, Édouard, Adolphine, and Léopoldine, who became a nun. He seems to have spent his entire life in the village of Odeigne, where other Nandrins married other Éloys. (This in itself is evidence of nothing, though, considering that in my grandmother's adjacent and smaller village of Fraiture there are Remacles buried in the churchyard who are not directly related to *her* Remacle family.) While the Éloy clan lived continuously in Odeigne for centuries, the Nandrins had a long history of migration, between the northern extreme of the province of Liège and that of the province of Luxembourg, following meager opportunity.

The earliest image I have of my mother's maternal grandfather, Alphonse Remacle, shows him short-haired, slightly distracted, in military uniform of dark jacket and white breeches, with a saber by his right hand. The image was cut out and rephotographed, and so only part of the inscription is legible: the year 1886 and the back end of the word *"artillerie."* Born twenty years before the picture was taken, he moved once in his life, three or four miles from Malempré to Fraiture. He married Marie-Hortense Cornet and they raised four children: Albert, Alphonsine, my grandmother Anne-Marie Honorine, and Éva, who was barely out of her teens when she drowned. Marie-Hortense died in 1903, when the eldest was not quite ten, and Alphonse soon after married Élise Coulon. He himself died in 1912, at the age of forty-five. The children never stopped mourning their mother, but they were nonetheless devoted to their stepmother, who eventually remarried and lived until 1932. As a child I would flip through the black-bordered *souvenirs pieux,* the death cards from all these bereavements, avoiding the frightening crucifixion scenes on their fronts but reciting the prayers on their backs, totting up the various indulgences from Purgatory: seven years here, three hundred days there. The cards were emblematic of my principal psychic inheritance from the rural side of the family: suffering, judgment, death.

The Lord God lived in those hills, and terrible were his ways, because the devil lived there, too. The Ardennes give or at least gave the lie to the map that appears in the Time-Life book *The Low Countries,* apportioning the trio according to religion: the Netherlands appears as Protestant, Flanders as Catholic, and Wallonia as anticlerical. The latter designation certainly did not apply to anyone on my mother's side of the family (I don't know enough about my father's), and although the region had its share of Easter Catholics and people who had had a fight with a priest, Catholicism was present in every hamlet and on every road, literally so in the form of innumerable wayside shrines and chapels and crucifixes. Walloon Catholicism is very much like Sicilian or Irish or Polish Catholicism: it incorporates large and only partly digested gobs of pre-Christian animism, consists mostly of ritual and image-worship with little that could be termed theology, minimizes the Bible, selectively deploys some elements of the occult while condemning others, and derives its major emotional thrust from fear— rather than, say, pentecostal ecstasy.

Today the Church has hit a bad pass in southern Belgium. Masses are mostly attended by old people; the young have gotten worldly. Many of the trappings of the faith of my fathers have been relegated to museums. At the Musée de la Vie Wallonne in Liège you can see a portion of the bark of an ancient linden tree from Soleimont. Before it was felled by lightning in 1921 an estimated seventy thousand pious nails had been driven into it, pleading for money, love, cures, decent weather, feasible crops. It isn't necessary to be an anthropologist to see how this practice directly derives from the tree worship of the Druids (the tree also bears an unmistakable resemblance to those Central African devotional objects called nail-dogs, whose physical presence is immanent to the point of striking terror in the hearts of the most skeptical viewers, or maybe I just mean in mine). There are luck objects of all sorts: horseshoes, garlic-bulb necklaces, pieces of flint, scapulars, *chapelles de poche* (tiny churches the size and shape of a bullet, carved from bone), *milagros* of molded tin (Ste. Appoline's, for example, in the shape of a set of dentures), and garishly painted crucifixes that look strikingly Mexican. There are also amulets, little cloth bags like gris-gris, enclosing all sorts of objects—sometimes live worms were sewn in, specific to the cure of certain illnesses—but usually pieces of cloth that had touched the remains of various saints.

Until I rebelled at thirteen or so I wore such an amulet pinned to my undershirt, over the heart (winter and summer, since wearing an undershirt under a T-shirt is as Belgian as buttering bread before spreading jam on it). My mother assembled the relics and sewed the bag. I never had a look at its contents, but I can conjecture, since other items of the sort lay around the house: tiny squares of linen or paper bearing labels reading *"Étoffe ayant touché les ossements de* [name of saint]." Undressing in public, such as at the CYO day camp in Springfield, New Jersey, that I attended every summer for five or six years, I was embarrassed by the bag (which actually inspired puzzlement rather than derision in American kids), but for most of my childhood I was plain scared of it. I might as well have been wearing the bones themselves around my neck. (At least I had been spared the old custom called *taillage à St.-Hubert:* a small incision is made in the forehead and a miniscule cloth fragment having touched the remains of St. Hubert is introduced; this confers protection against rabies.)

If fear was the main object of the old religion, then I was indeed devout as a child. My terror extended everywhere. I was scared in church: scared by the scraping of the chairs on the marble floor of St. Antoine in Pepinster when parishioners turned them around to change from sitting to kneeling, scared of the life-sized crucifix that stood on a rafter high overhead, scared of the priest delivering the sermon from the raised columnar perch called *la chaire de vérité,* scared of the Gregorian chants and the frankincense, of the stations of the cross, of the stained-glass windows, of the interior dimensions of the nineteenth-century Gothic-revival church, scared even in America, in the Gothic-revival St. Teresa's, in Summit, New Jersey, where I would regularly faint during Sunday Mass. My maternal grandmother gave me some devotional booklets for children that dated back to her own youth (*Le Jardin des Merveilles*, for example, oddly enough by someone calling him- or herself "Granny"), and their illustrations scared me silly: an angel holding an enormous key appearing at the bedside of a little girl, for example, but even the unremarkable costumes in the period engravings, even the halos in the pictures of saints (to my eye they now all look like raw materials for collages by Max Ernst).

My greatest terror was that someday I would awaken in the middle of the night to see a glowing Virgin in the corner of my bedroom. Since I thought that this could happen if I were sufficiently pious, perhaps it ironically hastened my unbelief. The Walloon countryside is dense with miracle sites. On Sundays my parents and I would often take a walk up the hill across the Hoëgne river behind our house in Pepinster. It was a demandingly steep trek on a narrow paved road past fields and birch woods. In its course we would pass the local cemetery, in which my maternal grandparents would eventually be buried, then a wayside crucifix backed by a Belgian army artillery range, then, after five kilometers or so, we would arrive in the hamlet of Tancrémont. An archetypal Belgian village, its signpost next to a field of woolly light-brown cows and calves, it is centered around its chapel, at the time smaller than your kitchen (it has recently been replaced by a larger and more streamlined edifice), which features a stark but rather graceful thousand-year-old crucifix, its mournful linden-wood Christ in a stiff robe. The story I grew up hearing was that it had been dug up by a farmer at some unspecified point in the past, and that he had repeatedly attempted to paint it, but that every time the paint had slid off. (This tale is nowhere alluded to in the chapel's devotional or historical literature, which in fact points to the remnants of nine layers of paint applied to the figure over as many centuries.) The tiny chapel was filled with crutches and canes and with brown ex-voto tiles, inscribed with testimonials to the curative powers of the figure. The place scared me, but my fears were soothed by a slice of *tarte au riz* or *tarte au sucre* at the café across the road, followed by the pleasantly heady downhill canter home.

Sometimes, though, we would continue another eight kilometers to Banneux, where in 1933 the Virgin had appeared on nine or ten occasions to a little girl, Mariette Becco, my mother's exact contemporary. The miracle followed the drill established by the one at Lourdes pretty much to the letter: a request for prayers, an exhortation to the Catholics of the world, a message from the Son, a blessing of water from some local spring, a request for a small chapel at the site, a few baleful portents. Like Fatima in 1912, the occasion was well-timed; its portents, concerning war, were destined for fulfillment within a few years. For the Vatican, Banneux falls into that theological gray area of tolerance without acknowledgment. While not officially recognized and not much publicized outside Europe, it has steadily grown in importance over the decades; there are substantial hotels on the premises, and caravans of motor coaches pull in daily, bearing thousands of pilgrims, many from Germany and the Netherlands. As at miracle sites the world over, from Lourdes and Fatima to Guadeloupe in Mexico and

Ste. Anne de Beaupré in Canada and Medjugorje in Croatia, the grounds are dense with the severely ill, ashen and rigid, wheeled around on gurneys.

Banneux was and remains a power center in my mother's cosmology. She could effortlessly identify with Mariette Becco, her coeval. (A few years ago I chanced to overhear a conversation among a group of old-timers in a Verviers bookstore. The subject was the Becco family, who were regarded locally as the equivalent of white trash; of their numerous scams the one success was the miracle of Banneux, and what a success it was! Standing there listening while pretending to read, I could imagine my mother's horror and pain.) I can easily imagine my mother's girlhood wish that such a thing would happen to her. On one of our stays in Belgium during the early 1960s she acquired a stack of pamphlets in English translation, explaining the miracle and proselytizing for its recognition. Upon our return to New Jersey she began distributing them (how? I have in mind that she went door-to-door, but could this have been so?) and giving each recipient a short speech in her halting English. The pamphlet bore on its cover a milky white Virgin glowing against a field of stars, the icon of Banneux. To this day I am unable to see that image without experiencing a stab of terror. It was so real to me as a child: the night sky in the country, silence, breeze, then an unearthly music, a faint odor of roses, then that shape appearing slowly, indistinct at first and then gradually—like a photographic image in a tray of printing solution—coming into relief, a pencil-sharp halo over its head, its form surrounded by a fluctuating corona, on its lips that thin serene unfathomable smile in which I saw menace, the threat of the sealed third prophecy of Fatima, the destruction of the world.

The fear ruled my life. Its effect resembled certain symptoms of obsessive-compulsive disorder: I couldn't enter or leave my bedroom without crossing myself at the holy-water font, even if I was going in and out rapidly, fetching something. There were prayers for everything, morning, noon, night, the daily rosary, the appeals to heaven when I heard bombers overhead or the sirens of fire trucks rushing toward our burning house or the town's noon whistle announcing Armageddon every day. I made myself attend mass on the first Friday of every month, follow the stations of the cross, fulfill novenas. And I was a craven, wretched sinner, perhaps not much in deed, but my mind was a nest of vipers. When I first thought of or heard spoken the palindrome "god-dog" I knew that I had mentally blasphemed, and tried not to think of it but couldn't stop, and the enormity of it was such that I couldn't even confess my sin, but had to administer my own punishment, depriving myself of whatever pleasure I most anticipated that day, and every day, since it happened all the time. I might try bargaining with the deity, giving up a pleasure for a necessity, forsaking birthday presents, say, for a decent report card, but my chances were slim, since I was a sinner and so bargaining from a position of weakness. It was sufficient that the heavens were allowing me to continue living, and I should be grateful for that alone.

At the vital center of Ardennais Catholicism was a fear and hatred of sex. If liberals, socialists, freemasons, and readers of proscribed literature were all anathema, unwed mothers were equally so, and divorcés and divorcées were beyond the pale. Divorce was an institution designed solely to assist licentiousness, and libertinism was the ultimate abomination, worse than murder. The body was the instrument of the devil; it required mortification, contempt, concealment—even the Saturday bath was a potential occasion of evil, and urination and defecation were evils by association. Procreation, while necessary, had to be rapid and as fully clothed as feasible. The word covering this attitude toward the physical was *"pudeur,"* which more generally means "modesty" but leaning toward "shame," and with overtones of hellfire, of the divine reprisal that would ensue from its lack (its homonymic resemblance to "puberty," a word I never heard uttered in French— *"puberté"*—was not lost on me). This belief did not deny that sex was natural; therein, in fact, lay its great danger, that it was a natural evil, a constant temptation dangled before all of us by the clever one. In the religion of the hills good and evil were absolute, unshaded, jansenistically opposed forever and ever, *per omnia saecula saeculorum.* I knew that I quite literally had an angel sitting on my right shoulder and a demon on my left; the cacophony produced by their competing voices threatened to drive me mad.

Somehow, fairly abruptly, when I was about thirteen, I lost my faith. Its bottom simply fell out. I went from attending mass as much as two or three times a week (and relentlessly chiding myself for not going every day) to not attending at all. I would tell my parents I was going to the 11:15 service (they went at 10) and instead go drink coffee at the diner next door. This charade continued for years. I was persuaded that knowledge of my loss of faith would cause my mother to suffer something gravely physical, like an apoplectic seizure, and so I could not admit to her that I was no longer a believer. I evaded questions or made things up. The pattern reinforced itself over the years, all through the many phases I underwent, until my getting divorced at the age of thirty-five made the question and its answer unavoidable (my mother did not take it well, but she didn't die, either). My parents must have suspected that something was amiss with me in early adolescence, though, because they sent me off for counseling. The version of this my mother came up with was utterly in the tradition, however. On several occasions my parents drove me to a Benedictine monastery in northwestern New Jersey and deposited me with an aged German-born monk, who talked to me for hours, not about doubt or confusion or (heaven knows) puberty, but about miracles. He spoke of the holy blood that coursed once a year in, I think, Milan, and showed me pictures of the shroud of Turin, and pieces of cloth that had touched the bones of sundry saints. In all fairness, I have to recognize that I might have been the one to broach the subject. At the time I had begun to transfer my fascination with the unexplainable onto more secular or simply non-Catholic objects of immanence: flying saucers, Atlantis, magic spells, reincarnation, ESP. Maybe the monk would have been perfectly happy to discuss doubt with me, but I turned the conversation toward an area I knew something about, and that would at least reward me with fodder for my imagination and a dose of gooseflesh. In any case, what I remember best about those days was the fear I brought home, which would make me repent for a day or two, imagining the eternity of pain that awaited me otherwise. But then the spell would lift. I could always believe in fear, but fear is everywhere, and does not require dogma.

I know that my ancestors preferred this sacred fear, which promised an eventual dividend in the beyond, to the never-ending and coldly unanswerable fear of the elements, disease, ruin, war. All fears could be consolidated into that one conveniently central fear, which permitted some alleviation through good works and mortification of the flesh. It ruled the seasons, explained chance, accounted for anomalies. And then it dispensed its amenities, most of them appropriated from the religion of

the earth that had preceded it, with light adjustments: Christmas, Easter, Pentecost, the Ascension, the Rogations, All
Saints. It provided occasions of release barely Christian in
form, just before Lent and around harvest time. There was the
immense bonfire called Le Grand Feu, the ritualized madness of
occasions such as the feast of St. Martin and especially Mardi
Gras, when people in ancient costume—the *blancs moussîs* of
Stavelot, for example—would taunt the crowd with flour-filled
pig bladders or pieces of fruit thrown hard, while license was
given to drink. It even sanctioned barbaric localized survivals
of the cult of Ceres, in which a blindfolded subject wielding a
sword would have to try and behead a rooster hung upside
down or a goose buried up to its neck, to general hilarity. And
in devotional guise it could purvey a genuinely transporting
trance state such as that induced by the litany of the saints, the
entire calendar sung in Latin, each name succeeded by *ora pro
nobis*—two notes ascending, three notes level—an exercise that
would occupy an entire afternoon as the priest and acolytes cir-
culated through the fields, blessing the crops (an early exposure
to this ritual forever determined my taste in music and the
rhythm of my prose). Most of all, in harsh and elemental lives,
the faith represented the only door leading out, even if that
door was marked *Death*.

On my mother's side nearly every male was a tenant farmer
(cultivateur), nearly every female a housewife *(ménagère)*, the
only exceptions a couple of cobblers and a straw hatter. Their
peregrinations were as circumscribed as their lives; the territory
containing the villages inhabited by five generations of all the
branches over two hundred years would fit handily into the area
of New York City. Some of these villages have become towns
of relative substance in our time, others are *lieux-dits* barely

even referred to anymore: Odeigne, Fraiture, Malempré, Mormont, Dochamps, Lamorménil, Clerheid, Erezée, Briscol, Comblain-au-Pont, Plainevaux, Glons, Theux. The first nine of these lie in a tight cluster covering less than fifty square miles. Some were never much more than crossroads, some were viable communities that time passed by, some were extinguished by the decline of agriculture, some saw their entire populations die or move away and be replaced by people from the city who made their houses into summer retreats or ski chalets. My mother gave me a recent picture of the house where she was born, in Ster, sent by her cousin Ghislaine Marquet, who still lives in that village. It is a handsome expanse of brown stone, with an enormous window now replacing the arched doorway, and skylights cut into the new roof. You can imagine the newly renovated interior; you can imagine it in a shelter magazine—you can imagine the caption. Now I sit on the porch of an 1829 Greek Revival farmhouse in upstate New York where generations lived and died from subsistence farming in the stony soil, and know no more about them than skiers from Brussels do about my ancestors who once shivered in one or another stone cottage now furnished in blond wood, with a CD player and a satellite dish, that overlooks the Bois de Groumont or the valley of the Ourthe.

But how much do I really know about the history of my own forebears? The generations pass in an endless parade of hunched women in kerchiefs and hunched men in caps, weighed down by the loads of sticks on their backs, without much to differentiate the centuries. The Nandrins must originally have come from Nandrin, a town between Liège and Huy not far from the Meuse, which in turn took its name from a Gallo-Roman villa that was the property of one Andarinus.

The place names among the families of my antecedents are strictly local: the Dispa clan surely originated in Spa, just as the Lansivals must have begun in Lansival, the Marennes in Marenne. The majority of names in my tree, though, like the one I bear, are derived from first names: Remacle, Éloy, Hermant, Herman, Louis, Géoris, Rémy, Hubert (twice), Mathieu, Orban, Baras, Colard, Gilet, Pacquay, Baltus, Balthazar. These can't be anything but peasant names, not that Legros or Lenoir or Dupont or Durand would indicate any higher standing, but at least such names involved a degree of figurative thinking. Naming a clan after the baptismal cognomen of the founder— or whoever the paterfamilias happened to be on the day custom dictated the need for a collective appellation—sounds like an expeditious choice. Other names unaccounted for by those two principles of nomenclature: Cornet, Sauvage, Dechesne, Larondelle, Verdcourt, Vanguers, Moisset, Rasquint, Maloir, Lognai, Pirson.*

I can go back from four to nine generations, depending on the specific line, and can imagine the great fan of names (that as we know becomes diamond-shaped beyond a certain point, owing to pedigree collapse caused by cousin-marriage and the like, especially in the wake of devastations such as the Plague) spreading across the centuries. That my own family label happens to be Sante begins to appear accidental, a mere manifestation of a certain colonizing male prerogative. I can try on those other names like hats, imagining each in turn as the sticker pasted across my life, borne into the new world and mispronounced and parodied, and printed and hastily signed and

---

* This last, that of a five-greats grandmother on the Nandrin end of things, is weirdly close to my wife's name, Pierson. I don't know whether, like hers which is Anglo-Saxon, it means "son of Peter."

spelled out on the telephone. There is some kind of vestige of each of the bearers of those names within me, some genetic fillip, curve of the ears or shape of the jaw or disposition of the pituitary gland. Before I undertook my research in the Mormon vaults I had no idea that my heritage was so ethnically homogenous, so geographically restricted. As an American resident since childhood, I know almost nobody else with this sort of background. My spouse is half Greek and half Anglo-Saxon— a designation that usually means some combination of English, Scottish, Irish, Welsh, French, and American Indian—and all my friends are similarly admixtures of ethnic strains. Even many Belgians I know, even cousins of mine, bear some trace of migration in their makeup. I do have that Luxembourgeois tinge, but Wiltz is half an hour's drive from Odeigne, no farther than Verviers. The language might be different there, but the culture is virtually the same.

I don't know what this homogeneity means in practice. Does it make me a sort of inverse aristocrat? Am I monochrome and seamless, unlike all those who incorporate a dense weave of far-flung constituent strands? Have I inherited certain racial characteristics not found elsewhere? Do I tack to one side or another owing to an oversupply of a certain Mendelian nutrient? Would I instinctively know how to quarry stone or hunt wild pigs if I were set the task? Will I revert in time to a condition of bland fatalism encoded in my cells? Would some eighth cousin sharing four lines of descent recognize me as kin? Do I owe a debt in blood to the soil that starved my forebears? Does the notion of roots mean anything at all to a member of the animal kingdom?

IX White Flag

One after the other: Rue Large, Rue Haute, Grand'Rue, Rue Neuve; Place d'Armes, Place du Marché, Place de la Victoire, Place Léopold; Rue Léopold, Rue Astrid, Pont Albert-1ᵉ, Boulevard de la Constitution. One after the other: Rue de l'Église, Rue de la Gare, Rue de la Poste, Rue de la Cité; Rue des Martyrs, Place des Fusillés, Rue des Combattants, Rue des Déportés; Rue Jules-Destrée, Rue Frère-Orban, Rue Zénobe-Gramme, Avenue Paul-Henri-Spaak. One after the other: church, café, *librairie,* bakery, café, *night-shop,* pharmacy, *traiteur,* café, post office, church, bank, *mercerie,* tobacconist, *friterie,* bakery, *lav-o-mat,* café. One after the other: courtyard, impasse, alley, wall, wall, steps, crucifix, bus stop, gate, fountain, wall, alley, monument, *quai,* steps, impasse, *perron.* One after the other: whitewashed houses with deep roofs and small windows, brick houses with windows outlined thickly in white, brick houses with yellowish window frames, brick houses black with age, half-timbered houses with no right angles left in them, house doors two steps up from the pavement, massive double courtyard doors, wooden shop-front shutters, striped canvas awnings, stone walls with stone buttresses, tiny second-story balconies, slightly larger third-story balconies, pyramidal roofs with knobs on top, pitched roofs with curved red tiles, pitched roofs with dark gray diamond-shaped tiles, nests of idle chimneys, plane trees, linden trees, poplars. One after the other, they fly past your window, past your ears, collect briefly in your peripheral vision, are succeeded by more of the same, more and more, become a solid and undifferentiated mass, a clot of Belgium.

It is a country where you can turn a corner in a town and find yourself without preamble in a planted field, where you enter a forest only to find that the trees have been planted in straight lines, where a substantial farm can measure all of a dozen acres, where the towns have no outskirts but mostly just slide into one another, but where you are nearly everywhere within walking distance of a cow. It is a country slightly larger than Maryland that incorporates three language groups and three political regions, which do not share the same sets of boundaries. It is a country of fewer than ten million inhabitants that can boast of some seventy-three cabinet ministers. It is a country whose principal French-language newspaper regularly runs a rubric that points out colorful native idiomatic expressions so that readers can learn to avoid them. It is an accidental country, a nation by default, a haphazard assemblage of dissonant and sometimes warring elements. Its hallmarks are ambivalence, invisibility, secretiveness, self-doubt, passivity, irony, and derision.

It is 7:30. Your mother shakes you gently and with considerable reluctance you slide out from under the towering heap of blankets, aiming your feet at the slippers positioned so as to avoid the contact of bare foot with tile floor. After a rapid ablution with cold water you dress quickly and walk downstairs, where it is ten or twenty degrees (Fahrenheit) warmer, since the mazout fire, going for half an hour, has not yet had a chance to penetrate beyond the kitchen and the *salon*. You consume a slice of bread with butter and jam and a cup of sweet-and-sour hot milk (in this household it will not be spiked with coffee; you

have never tasted coffee, but you are smelling it right now and
feel deprived). A droning baritone emanates from the massive
kitchen radio. You ignore it because it makes you feel sleepy.
You put on your anorak and grab your *mallette* and head outside. It is snowing lightly. You walk east on Rue des Jardins,
past the Detiffes' house, past the vacant lot, past the Athénée
with its ten-foot karyatids, past the office of Maître Jacques the
notaire, past the confectioner's. You hang a right on Rue Neuve,
which is permeated by the odor of chocolate, thanks to the factory a couple of doors down. The larger building next to the
small chocolate factory looks even more like a factory, a particularly grim Victorian model with dark brown brick walls, but it
is the Institut Saint-Lambert. You pass through the gates and
into the courtyard, where the snow has been piled into a moun-
tainous heap and water poured around it. Boys and masters
alike are sliding around on this path. You recognize the brothers and lay faculty not only because they are taller but because
they clasp their hands behind their backs as they slide, whereas
the boys hold their arms outstretched, to try to keep their balance or deprive others of theirs.

The bell rings. You converge into groups, each heading up
one of the separate sets of stairs leading up to the classrooms
laid out in a row with separate doors like motel units. The boy
appointed monitor has been stoking the stove, and it is glowing
red. You take your seat, nodding to your assigned seatmate,
Pierre or Paul or Jean-Mathieu, and pull out your pens, your
nibs, your hard eraser, your blotting paper, your notebook. The
teacher stands behind his desk, his arms crossed, a long gray
smock over his shirt and tie and V-neck sweater. Perhaps it is
Monsieur Schyns (you are uncertain of his first name), and you
note as you do nearly every day how much, if he only wore

eyeglasses, he would resemble the king whose portrait hangs above the blackboard to the right of the teacher's desk. It is the same portrait that appears on postage stamps. The image of his consort, with her suffering eyes and insouciant flip, hangs to the left; a crucifix separates them. The teacher makes a nearly imperceptible motion with his hand, and you all stand and recite the Notre Père and the Je vous salue Marie in unison. You sit, and the teacher tugs on a ring attached to a cylinder above the blackboard and pulls down a map.

Detailed in several colors is a bulbous diagonal shape that looks vaguely like a wig, or maybe a marmot. At the upper left, just below the sea, are "flood plain" and "swamps"; top right is "sandy plain," labeled Campinne. The center is taken up by "plains" and "plateaux," the latter specified as "very fertile soil." At the bottom is l'Ardenne, "great forests." Other, more mysterious words are scattered across the map in red, and these the teacher proceeds to explain. They are the five principal tribes of our primeval forerunners, the Belgae: the Menapii, who resided in East Flanders and the province of Antwerp; the Nervii, in West Flanders, Brabant, and Hainaut; the Aduatics, in the province of Namur; the Treviri, in the province of Luxembourg; and your own ancestors, the Eburoni, who dwelt in the future provinces of Liège and Limbourg and part of Brabant.

They were robust warriors, courageous and intrepid, lovers of combat and war—the corresponding illustration in your schoolbook shows a hulking specimen adorned with a huge blond mustache and a winged helmet. They worshiped freedom, these archaic versions of yourselves, and were dedicated to their fatherland. Unfortunately, the teacher goes on, they abandoned themselves to drunkenness and violent games, and left the work to their women. Now you are looking at an artist's conception of a Belgic village, a cluster of thatched huts that look like so many toadstools, specifically the toadstools inhabited by *les Schtroumpfs,* the small blue elvish folk in white caps whose misadventures you follow weekly in *Spirou* and who will one day many years hence invade American popular culture, obligingly anglicized as Smurfs. You imagine small blue drunken louts with yards of yellow hair growing from their nostrils. You imagine your classmates, the teacher, your parents, the neighbors as they would look with blue skin, under winged helmets.

They cultivated oats, barley, and rye, continues the teacher, and held fields and woods as common property. They were, alas, pagans—their priests, called Druids, made much (unspecified) use of mistletoe—but (a strongly emphasized *but*) they believed in the immortality of the soul. At this point Jean-Mathieu raises his hand. "Did they speak French or Flemish?" Ah, an excellent question. In fact, they spoke a Celtic tongue. You see, they were themselves invaders, having come from the east and conquered the earlier Neolithic population, who were small and dark in contrast to the tall, blond Belgae. You think about this: everybody in your family is dark except for a single pale-skinned redhead per generation, and everyone but yourself is small. Perhaps you are half Neolith, half Eburon. The next picture shows the toadstool village encircled by a high brick wall. This is an *oppidum,* a fortification built during the struggle they waged for several centuries, before and after the birth of Christ, against the Romans. *"De Galli Belgae fortissimi sunt,"* said Julius Caesar after subjugating them, not without spirited resistance from the blond-mustached, winged-helmeted Ambiorix, king of the Eburoni. This means you are braver than the French, which of course you are. The scene darkens in your imagination. They stand around their bonfires and raise their broadswords, swearing oaths of resistance, these leather-jerkined Belgae, so unlike their descendants. Their world was large: huge oaks, immense night sky. Their actions were decisive: beheading Romans, burning camps. They were dangerous and dramatic. They did not wear gray overcoats or turn their chairs around in church to kneel during the ordinary of the Mass. They drank *cervoise* from ladles and casks, and their games often resulted in death. Was it Ambiorix or someone else who threw his sword onto the scales, shouting, *"Vae Victis!"*? You like the drama of this scene—playing with your friends you will shout *"Vae Victis!"* whenever possible, despite not knowing what it means—but you are getting dreamy. Maybe you are thinking of Alaric and the fall of Rome.

We profited from the Roman conquest, insists the teacher. Not only did Latin deteriorate into Walloon, which later refined itself into French, but the Romans also brought us Christianity, the greatest of all gifts. And as for the Flemish, Jean-Mathieu, they are very much like us but not quite. When the Roman Empire began its decline into decadence and chaos, the legions were called back to Rome from the provinces, and in the resulting vacuum a tribe called the Salians, who had been farming in a small way on the left bank of the Rhine, invaded the flat northern half of our country and imposed on the population their customs and their Germanic language. The Flemings resulted from the intermarriage of these peoples. Next year, *en quatrième*, we will begin studying the tongue of our compatriots. The teacher then utters a sentence in the sandpaper tones we have only heard in snatches, in beach towns or when playing around with the radio dial. None of us understands what he has said. In tomorrow's lesson we will discuss Charlemagne, who was born in Jupille—unless he was born in Herstal, or Tirlemont.

As it turned out, I didn't stick around long enough to study any Flemish—or Dutch, really, since "Flemish," as a linguistic designation, refers to an aggregate of Dutch-related dialects which, like Walloon, are not taught in any school. None of my relatives knew a word of Dutch (excepting, of course, my Dutch uncle), or I should say they knew but one single word, *witloof,* used interchangeably with *chicon* and *chicorée de Bruxelles* to mean Belgian endive, my least favorite vegetable but significant enough in the culture to merit not just synonyms but a loanword. Unlike us, the enterprising Flemings were often bilingual. They apparently thought of us as layabouts of a nearly Mediterranean indolence; we apparently thought of them as humorless Teutons. G. de Waële, in his 1917 pamphlet *Flamands et Wallons,* summarized the leading view of the differences: "Whereas the Fleming is a silent and obstinate worker, of a virile race whose taciturn soul perhaps cedes to the vigor of its body, the Walloon is no less endowed with qualities: He has a soldierly manner, a bright eye, an open face, a ready wit. He is more cheerful than the Fleming, maybe less serious, but also less bitter; he may show less application in his work but his motion is livelier. The Walloon may be less headstrong than the Fleming, but he is also more of a hothead and a grumbler." Reading this sort of sketch I both concede its broad truths and simultaneously feel as though I'm being instructed on the distinctions between Aries and Taurus.

To have been born Belgian is to have been cast, as if by the zodiac, under the sign of ambivalence. The name Belgium may date back to the distant past, but the nation itself was not founded until 1830. Only four of my sixteen great-great-grandparents, for instance, were born Belgian. Of the remaining twelve, at least five came into the world as Dutch citizens and perhaps as many as six (including the parents of my Luxembourgeoise great-grandmother) were born before 1815 and thus inscribed as French—except Antoine Sauvage, who was born in 1780 and was therefore Austrian. Today, Belgians think of themselves as Belgian when abroad or challenged or both, but at home it is often a different matter. There Belgium can sometimes be perceived as a bureaucratic entity and Belgianness as a sort of negative designation, a way of indicating that one is not Dutch or French or German. Some people, younger ones in particular, think of themselves as European above all; some older citizens still feel a primary allegiance to their city, or their province, or their region. The specificity can be nearly microscopic. Residents of the Gaume, for example, a strip hardly more than twelve kilometers wide at the country's southern extreme, are culturally tied more to French Lorraine than to any of their compatriots; their patois is entirely distinct, and as in France their villages are governed by *maires* (mayors) rather than by *bourgmestres*. The German-speaking region in the east of Wallonia may have its separateness affirmed by governmental institutions, but between it and the francophone sector lies a band of villages—Plombières, Montzen, Baelen, and on south—whose inhabitants are both or neither. They speak a German dialect, but were not ceded to Prussia in 1814 and have always been tied to the Walloons. Then there are the Flemish communes of Baarle-Hertog and Baarle-Nassau, which form an island entirely surrounded by the Netherlands. It is not much of an exaggeration to suggest that every Belgian town has a political and cultural history unique to itself.

The Flemish-Walloon border, an undulating line that divides the country more or less in half horizontally, has remained in place largely unaltered since the fourth century A.D. It forms part of a continuous boundary between Latinate and Germanic language groups that extends from Dunkirk in France to the west to Maastricht in the Netherlands to the east, and then plunges south all the way through Switzerland, following in its vertical course the edge of the dense primeval forest that acted as a natural frontier between different Germanic tribes in the age of barbarian invasions. The Walloons were permanently affected by the Romans; the Walloon language can be traced directly back to the corrupted soldiers' Latin of the legions. The word itself derives from the Indo-European root *wal* or *walh*, which might have been a catchall designation meaning "foreigner" or "other," and likewise can be found in such dispersed toponyms as Gaul, Wales, Galicia, and Wallachia (as well as in the word "walnut," a strange nut). "Walloon" originally signified Celtic populations and languages, then Celtic populations speaking Latinate dialects, then Celto-Germanic populations speaking Latinate dialects. As opposed to its linguistic application, which soon became extremely specific, the term's ethnic designation remained rather indeterminate. The Walloons who are credited with being the first European settlers of Manhattan island, for example, were—historians now say—not Walloons at all in the current sense of the term, but Picards, from the Aisne in what is now France, who because they were Huguenots sailed under Dutch colors. There are, to be sure, Picards among the residents of Belgian Wallonia, namely the population of the western reaches of the province of Hainaut, around Mons and Ath and Tournai.

The Flemish-Walloon divide, however ancient, remains

contentious. There is a Walloon island between West Flanders and the French border, part of although not contiguous with Hainaut, and there is a Flemish island between the province of Liège and the Dutch border, part of although not contiguous with the province of Limburg. The latter islet, called Fourons in French and Veuren in Dutch, has a linguistically mixed population, and thus has been the scene of intermittent bloody fighting between factions for more than two decades, with brawlers sometimes being shipped in by the busload from Antwerp or Namur. Notice that I said a *linguistically* mixed population. The entire country is *ethnically* mixed. Over the centuries, Walloon shopkeepers established themselves in Flanders; Flemish laborers headed for the factories and mines of the south. Flemish nationalists *(flamingants)* with French surnames are common—one was named Vervier—just as their opposite numbers *(wallingants)* often bear Dutch surnames. For centuries before the establishment of the Belgian state, people living within its future borders were indiscriminately referred to by outsiders as Flemish in matters of culture (not all the Flemish painters were native Dutch speakers, for instance; Rogier van der Weyden was born Roger de la Pasture in Tournai) and as Walloons in matters of war. In part these designations reflected the relative levels of prosperity of the two regions. Flanders was rich, known abroad for its great ports, its powerful merchants, its extraordinary artisans, while Wallonia was primarily agricultural, poor, and backward. The Flemish were perceived as bourgeois; the Walloons were cannon fodder.

Belgium is an accident. There is little logic of any sort underpinning its shape and its boundaries. Its only natural borders are the small coast on the North Sea and a few bits of rivers—a section of the Meuse and some incidental miles of the

Houille, the Lys, the Our. Otherwise, the plains of Flanders stretch unchecked into France and the Netherlands, and the Ardennes Mountains likewise spill over into France on the one side and into Germany—where they invisibly become the Eifel —on the other. The territory called Belgium by the Romans was seven times larger than the current political entity; when the term was revived by scholars during the Renaissance they used it in its classical sense, to refer to a loosely defined region that also included present-day Luxembourg, the Netherlands, and a significant part of France. Modern Belgium has its misty origins in the division of Charlemagne's empire by the treaty of Verdun in 843. Charles the Bald was awarded the territory west of the Rhône and the Saône, Louis the German got everything east of the Rhine, and Lothar was given dominion over the middle stretch, which became known as Lotharingia. This territory did not approach the conditions of a modern state; rather, it was a loosely defined entity containing a variety of semi-autonomous units—dukedoms, principalities, walled cities—many of which warred amongst themselves.

Over the course of the Middle Ages, the Flemish cities of Ghent, Bruges, and Ypres grew in power and wealth, their easy access to the sea permitting them to import the finest in raw materials and to export the results of their transformation by artisans; the Walloon cities of Liège and Dinant, both on the Meuse, were nearly but not quite as successful. The stewardship of the counts of Flanders ended with the death of Louis de Maele in the fourteenth century, but his daughter had fortuitously married Philip the Bold of Burgundy a few years earlier, and the region passed into the care of the Burgundian dynasty, later linked with the Holy Roman Empire. Under Charles V, king of Spain and emperor of Germany, the Low

Countries—seventeen provinces considered as a unit called the Burgundian Circle—entered an even more exalted period, when lacemaking, tapestry weaving, the metalwork called *dinanterie,* and, of course, Flemish painting achieved their respective summits of artistic and commercial success. The towns managed to retain their independence, which had been negotiated with earlier rulers and codified under such charters as Brabant's Joyeuse Entrée of 1356, which essentially allowed citizens—landowners, naturally—the power of referendum over such matters as wars, alliances, taxes, and tariffs.

In 1555, three years before Charles abdicated his throne, he ceded the Burgundian Circle to his son Philip II of Spain. Philip attempted to squelch the independence of the towns; in concert with increasing tensions between Catholics and Protestants, this led to a revolt in 1577. Two years later the Walloon provinces, jealous of the privileges of the north, signed the league of Arras, which asserted their loyalty to Philip and to the Church. The seven northernmost provinces became first the United Provinces and then, under the terms of the Peace of Westphalia in 1648, the Dutch Republic. The Flemish and Walloon provinces, retained by Spain, were yoked together by religion (although the Netherlands had and still has a substantial Catholic minority) and even more by geography. The Dutch Republic was protected by its waterways, while the south, the future Belgium, was open land easily overrun. The Peace of Westphalia was a disaster for Flanders, cut off from the Netherlands with whom it shared language, culture, and customs, and the barrier was reinforced by the strictures of the Counter-Reformation, which also inflicted enormous losses in trade. Massive emigration resulted, to England, the Netherlands, America, Sweden, Bohemia. The great cities of Flanders and Brabant were silenced and nearly emptied. Bruges, for one, never did recover; it was something of a ghost town (*Bruges-la-morte* in the title of Georges Rodenbach's 1892 novel) until English travelers of the early nineteenth century, on their way to visit the battlefield at Waterloo, came upon and revived it, if only for the nascent tourist trade.

The Flemish and Walloon provinces suffered under repeated invasions by Louis XIV, as well as the ravages of the War of the Spanish Succession. In 1713 the Peace of Utrecht, which settled that war, transfered Belgium to the Austrian Hapsburgs. The Austrians, too, set about trying to undo the power of the semi-autonomous towns and settle the provinces into their empire, resulting in predictable friction. When, during the reign of Maria Theresa (1741–1780), they decided to leave well enough alone, the result was a fairly lengthy peace, but subsequent meddling by her son Joseph II caused snowballing local upheavals. These came to a head, coincident with the French Revolution, in 1789. First Brussels, then the rest of Brabant, then the remaining provinces revolted against the Austrian military; in January 1790 they declared themselves the United States of Belgium, under the banner of black, yellow, and red. This entity lasted only a few months before capitulating to a large Austrian force, but Austrian rule itself lasted only two years after that. In 1792 the revolutionary French army invaded and won the Walloon provinces at the battle of Jemappes, and in 1794 took the rest of the country as a result of the battle of Fleurus. The French succeeded where all previous conquerors had failed. In place of a separate legal and economic structure for each province, as had been the case for centuries, the French imposed unity; the Napoleonic Code remains the basis for the Belgian legal system.

Belgium was French until the fall of Napoleon. The Congress of Vienna of 1815, whose principal task was to break up his empire and prevent any recurrence of French power, awarded the provinces to the Kingdom of the Netherlands. The Dutch and Flemish provinces were reunited at last, but nearly 250 years had passed, and the social and cultural fissures that had opened in the meantime proved deep. William I made Dutch the official language, which not only alienated the Walloons but failed to satisfy the Flemings, who were militantly Catholic and feared the move as presaging a Dutch imposition of Calvinism. The Catholics had only just recovered from the closing of churches and seminaries under the French revolutionaries; when the Dutch began similar maneuvers in 1824, they found themselves arming an alliance between the conservative Flemish and the liberal Walloons, ironically accomplishing a task long thought impossible.

The revolution came in August 1830, its first spark occurring at the Théâtre de la Monnaie in Brussels, at a performance of Esprit Auber's opera *La Muette de Portici,* the plot of which concerns a revolution in Naples. The setting of the disturbance not only echoed the previous month's riot at the Paris premiere of Victor Hugo's *Hernani,* which set off the July Revolution there, but also underscored the essentially bourgeois nature of the upheaval—or so it was in the cities of Flanders and Brabant. In Liège, by contrast, the revolution was more in earnest, just as the events of 1789 had there been more in keeping with the spirit of concurrent events in France; the insurgents of Liège had among other things completely demolished the Cathedral of St. Lambert, the third largest in the world, mourned to this day by the Belgian Catholic right. Forty years later it was Liégeois militants who flooded into Brussels and expanded the list of demands to the point where secession from the Netherlands was the only possible outcome. In Verviers, the Englishman J. Emerson Tennent wrote in his *Belgium* (1841),

> the revolutionary mania . . . exhibited itself in a still more savage form. . . . The town has neither fortress nor garrison, and for two days it was the scene of the most disgusting and uncontrolled excesses. The people assembled in tumultuous masses, and with shouts of "liberty," tore down the royal insignia of the Netherlands, and razed to the ground the houses of the government officials; factories were destroyed, machinery demolished, and the whole property of the flourishing valley seemed destined to destruction from the freaks of this drunken revolution.

The fighters at the barricades in Brussels routed a Dutch force of fourteen thousand troops, but political power was quickly seized by the nobles and the bourgeoisie. A national congress, elected by property owners, proclaimed independence on November 18. To gain international recognition, the new nation submitted its case to a conference of European powers held in London that same month. The English, who might have been expected to uphold the decision of the Congress of Vienna and insist that Belgium be returned to the Netherlands, somehow got the impression that the Dutch were just as eager to be rid of their troublesome breakaway provinces, and supported a French-backed move to install a constitutional monarchy. They drew the line, however, at a French-born ruler. But no one opposed the nomination of Prince Leopold of Saxe-Coburg-Gotha, an intelligent and politically unthreatening German noble connected by marriage to virtually every house in Europe. He was crowned Leopold I the following year on July 21, a date that continues to stand as the Belgian national holiday.

Belgium was then, as it is now, the pressurized container for a volatile and overlapping set of oppositions: between Flemish and Walloon, Catholic and anticlerical, noble and bourgeois, capital and labor, rural and urban. The Church was kept in its place by the power of the anticlerical Liberal Party, which enjoyed a strong base among the nobility and the educated bourgeoisie, particularly in the south. The Walloon south prevailed over the Flemish north in part because the court now spoke French—the lingua franca of the international aristocracy—and in part because of the south's recent and unprecedented economic growth. The cities grew rich, but the labor force was kept poor as well as ignorant, public education being all but nonexistent. Peasants in the countryside lived in a manner not much changed since the Middle Ages; on the other hand, they represented the principal base of support for the Church, and were granted certain social advantages not available to their urban counterparts. Migration across the linguistic frontier reached its summit during this period, as Walloon entrepreneurs moved north to establish themselves in less competitive surroundings, and Flemish peasants and workers went south to find jobs in the mines and steel mills and glassworks and textile and armament factories of Wallonia.

At the same time, the mutual resentment and incomprehension between Flemings and Walloons, which had been simmering for many centuries, began to increase exponentially. Cases abounded of, say, Flemings being tried, convicted, and sentenced for crimes they did not commit, unable to defend themselves in court because the proceedings were held entirely in French, which they did not understand, being unable to communicate even with their own attorneys. Of course, the largely illiterate populations of workers and peasants in both north and south were similarly excluded from the discourse of power. The average Fleming and Walloon of the working class knew only the subdialect specific to his or her locality, although the Walloon possessed the advantage of having at least a basic comprehension of French. And while the country was de jure bilingual, few Walloons of any class knew Dutch, let alone Flemish dialects, while in Flanders the ruling families tended to be francophonic. All the country's universities conducted their courses in French; the major newspapers of Flanders were printed in French; the leadership of the Church throughout the country was monolingual; many of the greatest Flemish writers of the period—Émile Verhaeren, Maurice Maeterlinck, Georges Eekhoud—wrote in French exclusively.

Flemish nationalism began to take shape in the middle of the century in intellectual circles, such as that of the novelist Henri Conscience. His *De Leeuw van Vlaenderen* (The Lion of Flanders, 1838), a semihistorical contrivance executed in the broad strokes of Sir Walter Scott, evoked the Battle of the Golden Spurs, a victory of the Flemish over the invading French in 1302; despite its conspicuous lack of literary merit it established Flemish literature. In 1846 Conscience and others founded the Heilig Verbond (Holy Union), which deployed pageantry and quasi-mystical rituals borrowed from Freemasonry on behalf of the Flemish cause. Among other things it attempted to institute a separate Flemish calendar that would establish 1302 as year one and count up from there. However idle—or, viewed from another angle, proto-fascist—this all

might sound, there is no question the *flamingants* had a point.
The pace of reform only illustrates their frustration: the use of
Flemish did not become legal in lower courts until 1873, and
not until 1883 in the lower stages of secondary education. By
1914 radicals were beginning to call for the administrative separation of Flanders and Wallonia.

The Germans who invaded later that year were not slow to
seize upon the division and exploit it for their own ends. Their
invitation to Flemish nationalists to join them in an alliance of
Teutonic peoples found numerous takers, who became known
as the Activists. Many German initiatives, undone after the
armistice, were eventually reestablished by the Belgian government itself: the conversion of the University of Ghent into a
Flemish-speaking institution, the separation of various min-
istries into Flemish and Walloon components, the later administrative separation of the whole country, the nomination of
Brussels as the capital of Flanders and of Namur as the capital
of Wallonia. The Activists were a minority, but a larger percentage of Flemings who disapproved of collaboration with
the invader were no less nationalistic. The element of treason,
however, permanently colored Flemish nationalism in the eyes
of most Walloons, resentful to begin with. Nevertheless, Léon
Degrelle's fascist Rexist movement of the 1930s was among
other things an attempt to claim Teutonic affiliation for the
Walloons. The Wehrmacht reached out in 1944, when it was
desperately in need of cannon fodder, by inaugurating a "Wallonie" legion. Indeed more Walloons, Rexist or not, were im-
plicated for collaborationist activities in the Second World War
than were Flemings. The only lesson to be derived is that while
self-interest and thuggery often find nationalism a convenient
cover, they can also thrive independently of it. In any event,
Flanders and Wallonia, like partners in a bad marriage, have al-

ways each been ready to pick on any perceived failings of the other as ammunition in a passive-aggressive war of petty digs.

The unity of Belgium, always feeble, has been eroding throughout the century, and the pace of this erosion has lately been increasing. When I was a child, a nominal bilingualism still prevailed. That is, public institutions—railroad stations, post offices, and the like—posted bilingual signs, even in the most remote nooks of either half. Large restaurants printed bilingual menus as a matter of course. In the south, movie posters would prominently feature the film's French title, while the Flemish name ran in smaller type beneath, and vice versa in the north; in addition, the films themselves often had a sound track in one language and subtitles in the other. You got used to seeing that other language appearing everywhere in a sort of visual undertone. It may not have taught anybody more than a few words of the other tongue, but it made for a certain unconscious balance, so that every time you saw the name of your country, *Belgique,* your back brain supplied *België* whether it was actually present or not.

When my parents and I returned in 1969, though, not having been in Belgium for six years, we were shocked to see this nicety being forcibly undone. As we drove, jet-lagged and in scorching August heat, from Zaventem airport to the little Flemish town of Geel, where my mother wished to call at the shrine of St. Dymphna, patron saint of nervous disorders, we immediately noticed that highway signs had been painted out. Formerly they had displayed city names, for example, in both languages: Antwerpen-Anvers, Liège-Luik, Ieper-Ypres, Mons-Bergen. We came to realize that in every part of the country but the center of Brussels, the sole place in the country more than nominally bilingual, every word of the other tongue had been effaced by nationalists. Eventually new monolingual signs went up, and railroad stations posted arrivals and departures—as well as the locations of the baggage check and the toilets—in only one language, and although stamps remain bilingual, post offices themselves are no longer so.

With every passing year new cracks appear in the Belgian foundation. The traditional nine provinces recently became ten, as Brabant was split into its Flemish and Walloon halves (on the highway from Brussels to Liège, which passes through undulating provincial boundaries, the language of signs and billboards changes five times in no more than thirty miles). The city of Brussels is ever more a bone of contention, since it is both the capital of Flanders and (although no official linguistic census of its inhabitants exists) at least 70 percent francophone. Brussels is the Jerusalem of the Flemish nationalists, who at regular intervals make a move to, for instance, suppress French-language signage. (It is unfortunate that the ancient Brussels patois has been allowed to become nearly extinct; it is roughly 45 percent French and 45 percent Dutch, the remaining 10 percent consisting of Spanish words and phrases held over from the seventeenth century.) The Flemish-Walloon friction is exacerbated by the contrast in prosperity between the halves. The Flemish economy, with its emphasis on high technology and information enterprises, appears to be on a continual rise, while its Walloon counterpart, still apparently unable to find a workable substitute for the obsolete heavy industries, seems to decline correspondingly. A color-coordinated economic map of Europe shows Flanders on an equal footing with Île-de-France, Lombardy, and the northern provinces of the Netherlands, while Wallonia shares the plight of southern Italy and most of Spain.

So what makes it a country, apart from tangled history?

Baked goods. Churches. Weather. The habit of discretion. Fried potatoes. Shrubbery. The color gray. The elaborate mandarin ritual that attends commercial transactions, or even just stepping into a shop for a minute and a half. Compactness, miniaturization. Cleanliness. The cross of modesty and prudishness called *pudeur* in French. Brickwork. Class consciousness. Women of all ages suffering in skirts and stockings in the dead of winter. Reserve, aloofness, judgment. Varnished wood. Silent children, well-bred dogs, unassertive houseplants. The fear of God, the god of fear. Wallpaper. Comic strips. *"Il faut cultiver notre jardin."* The art of the display window, of undertaking parlors or cordwainers' shops, for example. A taste for scandal, especially morbid scandal. Kitsch Africana. Flaccid pop music piped everywhere, including bookshops, hospitals, government offices. Leeks, chervil, gherkins, pickled onions. The ability to sit for long hours. White linen tablecloths, fanned linen napkins. Hammered brass. Tinted house windows. Symmetry. Monuments. The perpetual imminence of rage, blasphemy, running amok. Trees like fists. Rheumy eyes. Pale yellow, brick red, black.

x Spleen and Ideal

Yellow and black make the Flemish flag (lion rampant), red and yellow the Walloon (cock rampant). The three colors, singly or by twos or all together, show up everywhere in satisfying graphic deployment, on posters and architectural trim and old trams and packages of tobacco and in interior decor, the national allusion little more than subliminal. At least this is so in the enduring work of the past, now that the replacement of pale yellow with unmitigated canary and of brick red with scarlet signifies forward-thrusting modernity, the way the use of business-school pidgin American does in commercial language. Likewise, gray has been subject to a takeover by beige, even if it cannot be expunged from the sky. You can appreciate the full weight of Belgian gray in the grisaille backs of the door panels of Flemish triptychs: a saint in his lair with attributes and familiars, all apparently made of stone. Magritte took up this theme in the 1950s, when he painted a world entirely made of gray stone—figures, background, and sky. Magritte's grisaille, like that of the triptychs, is less fantastic than observed, a true record of Belgian air. But then, Magritte was a realist, the way you could say all Belgian painters have been realists.

Although art history connects Magritte's juxtapositions with de Chirico's migraines and Ernst's willed hallucinations, they lie closer to the stifling interiors and vacant haunted streetscapes of Maurice Pirenne (brother of the historian Henri). Both Magritte and Pirenne were visionaries of boredom, the peculiarly Belgian overcast Sunday-afternoon bore-dom, the murderous boredom of the civil servant at home, reading the obituary notices in the local bugle sitting in his club chair, an antimacassar on each of its arms and one on the head rest, bowler on the hat rack, fringed bureau scarf under unac-countable knickknacks, retouched photographs of the dead in oval frames, three nameless flowers wilting in a gratuitous vase. Magritte is never more a realist than when he makes the pocket comb as large as the bed, or shows the breasts hung within the dress in the armoire, or shatters the landscape along with the window glass on which it is fixed. It is night on Magritte's street and in his house, however blue the sky above, and in Pirenne's *salon* the heavy drapes, the heavy chairs, the chandelier, the carved mantel, the lace, the carpets stop time from penetrating.

Magritte, famous throughout the world, and Pirenne, barely known outside Belgium (quite unjustly so), are the two artists who immediately come to my mind as exemplifying the essence of Belgianness. Their point of intersection is the veneer of civilization, that gray surface stretched like a skin over the chasm. Magritte's bowler-hatted man is the Little Bourgeois to Chaplin's Little Tramp. He placidly strolls through chaos and collapse, maintaining his reserve in the face of horror and tran-scendence alike. *La Grande Guerre* is merely a green apple that blocks his view. Botticelli's Primavera, appearing on his back, is nothing more than *Le Bouquet tout fait*. Pirenne's pedestrian strolls through the empty, ghost-ridden streets of Verviers with equal aplomb. Those two walkers are neither blind nor igno-rant, but armored and imperturbable. They have in fact seen it all, and have filed the data in alphabetical order. Belgium is hardly the only country in the world to have served for cen-turies as a convenient field for others' battles, but it might be the only one to have survived such ravages by dint of studious application of decorum and order.

Belgian art, the id of the nation, manages to be extravagant and tight-lipped at once, and to counterweight its extreme subject matter, hallucinations and mystical ecstasy and anomie and galloping death, with a deadpan and often bitter humor, all of it depicted with precision of line and detail.* It is tempting to antedate this generality back to the early Nederlandisch painters, to see local characteristics in the work of Hieronymous Bosch, despite his having spent his entire life in 's Hertogenbosch, firmly in the Netherlands. His *Garden of Earthly Delights,* with its right panel of impossible couplings and anal delirium and torture-by-music, might stand as a panoramic view of the northern subconscious. At the same time, the sobriety in the face of agony that distinguishes the subjects of Rogier van der Weyden's several Crucifixions and Descents from the Cross seems somehow Belgian, when contrasted with the theatrical attitudes struck by the figures in tableaux depicting the same scenes by, say, Italian painters. None of the painters of the Nederlandisch tradition would even have recognized the word "Belgium," of course, except perhaps in its classical sense, possessing all the faded allure of a name like Scythia or Parthia. Then, too, when the Netherlands became the United Provinces in 1579 and the distinction came to be made between Dutch and Flemish artists, it was by and large the Dutch who turned out to be sober (Fabritius, Saerendam, De Hoogh, Vermeer, for in-

---

* Frank Huggett, author of one of the very few postwar studies of Belgium in English (*Modern Belgium,* 1969), asserts that "it would appear to be no coincidence that the Belgians should be drawn to surrealism and expressionism. The absence of an integral national culture has prevented the growth of a hard inner core of reality; the vision stops short at the outer mask. . . . All of it lacks much depth."

stance) and the Flemish unbridled (Rubens, Jordaens). But national distinctions, however murky they might be in our own day, are barely defensible when applied to the past. Not only were the borders different, but painters were defined by the milieu in which they worked, so that, say, Joos van Wassenhove, who was born in Ghent, lived and flourished in Urbino, and Gérard de Lairesse, a product of Liège, settled in Amsterdam and became known as "the Dutch Poussin."

Pieter Brueghel the elder, with his densely populated village scenes, has a greater claim on the local. He is certainly a national icon, as witness the inscription on the plaque that marks his house on Rue Haute in Brussels: "To the painter from his people" (the French word is *"peuple,"* which might be translated as "subjects," in both senses of the term). Brueghel's world is crowded but contained, rowdy but peaceable, subject to extremes but never without humor. The large-spirited Brueghel was equally capable of staging the Nativity in a Flemish village and of situating his Flemish villages in such topographies as the Alps (his great *Hunters in the Snow*) and the shores of the Mediterranean *(The Fall of Icarus)*. In his vision the local is global, and the village is the cosmos. A friend of mine who was a teenager living on the edge of the front in 1944 remembers an American sergeant musing to him that Belgium was "one big village," and to some degree it remains so. This can be a stifling condition, but the village as a molecular unit can also be seen underlying the fabric of the world. In Jacques Feyder's 1935 film *La Kermesse héroique,* Brueghel's village is the bastion of resistance to tyranny; it is inclusive and tolerant, a symbol of collective strength.

Brueghel's village would also stand ever afterward as the dream of an impossible lost past, the fundament of Belgium's version of traditional values, source of all virtue and yardstick against which the decadence of modernity could be measured and found wanting. This vision haunts a good deal of the art produced after the Industrial Revolution. Brueghel's peasants turn up in new guises in the naturalist paintings of Léon Frédéric (1856–1940)—as chalk vendors, as scavengers of cinders, as corpses. Anto Carte (1886–1954) and the Flemish mystics refracted Brueghel's world through the glass of Gaugin, aiming for transcendence but frequently missing. Constantin Meunier (1831–1905) showed what had become of many of those peasants in the modern world: they were in the mines, and their pasturelands had become open sores, and none of the heroic poses in which he cast their labor could quite disguise the rampant misery.

And behind the pastoral landscape, behind the delusion of progress, lay a death's-head grin. The Bruxellois eccentric Antoine Wiertz (1806–1865) spent a lifetime painting a thesaurus of baroque possibilities for gruesome death, selling none of his canvases but accumulating them in his house like pornography. Félicien Rops (1833–1898) devoted his piercing eye and meticulous engraving skills to a wild panoply of erotic nose-thumbing, from winged penises and crucified penises to elaborately choreographed sexual circuses; his emblematic figure is a pig leading a blindfolded naked woman (at the Rops Museum in Namur I saw a woman showing this picture to her small son: *"Regarde, fifi, le Pornokrate!"*). Fernand Khnopff's (1858–1921) most famous picture is *Des Caresses/ L'Art/Les Caresses*, from 1896, which shows a disturbingly carnal leopard with the head of a woman rubbing ecstatically against a somewhat less plausible epicene youth. And then there was James Ensor (1860–1949), for whom the rictus was literal.

His *Squelettes se disputant un hareng-saur* (1891), two skeletons in hussars' uniforms each tugging with its teeth at an end of a kippered herring, is an eloquently encapsulated summary of his century and prediction of the one to come. Ensor is perhaps the most deadly cynic in the entire history of art, bitter and funny and carnivalesque. When he had tenderness to dispense, he was likely to lavish it on a skate (*La Raie*, undated), pleading pathetically in its death throes.

The other Surrealist painter of note besides Magritte was Paul Delvaux, whose work seems like a single endlessly protracted scene of somnambulistic women, nude or classically semidraped, wandering through a landscape that weaves between ruined porticoes and columnades and the minor suburbs of Brussels. Delvaux's work is sensual and somehow primal, and thus stands apart from that of Magritte and the majority of Belgian artists since the 1920s, which is intellectual and extremely verbal. A fascination with puns, riddles, cryptograms, neologisms, allusions, as well as with the visual properties of words, unites the whole disparate assembly running from Magritte, and some other Surrealists more known for their writings (E. L. T. Mesens, Paul Nougé, Marcel Mariën), through Pierre Alechinsky, Christian Dotremont, and other Belgian members of the CoBrA (Copenhagen-Brussels-Amsterdam) group of the 1950s, to Marcel Broodthaers, arguably the most influential Belgian artist since the sixties, whose manufacture of objects imprinted with texts elegantly bottled one vintage from the great Duchamp vineyard. This verbal preoccupation also extends to the calligraphic drawings of Henri Michaux, the poet and very concrete mystic who is in most ways a case apart.

In this century, and especially since the war, distinctions between high and low in Belgian art have been nearly obliterated by the genius of the cartoonists. The Hokusai-influenced clear-line drawings of Hergé (Georges Rémy), father of Tintin, are known everywhere, but the English-speaking world remains largely ignorant of the no less brilliant—and more daring and pungent—work of the wild Franquin *(Spirou, Gaston Lagaffe)*, the sardonic Morris *(Lucky Luke)*, the impish Peyo *(Johan et Pirlouit, Les Schtroumpfs, Benoît Brisefer)*, as well as Jidéhem, Roba, Remacle, Macherot, and on and on, a very long list. What has prevented this complex imaginative work from reaching anglophone audiences is its crucial verbal content, agile and slippery. In English the Smurfs are wanly cute, while in French their humor is biting; much of it is entirely lost in translation, such as that the vocabulary of their language is nine-tenths composed of the word *schtroumpf,* a joke on the Franco-Belgian tendency to populate entire sentences with catchall substitute-words like *"truc,"* *"chose,"* and *"machin"* (all of them translatable as "thing"), which forces the auditor to act as cryptographer. Such fairly sophisticated lexical humor is a feature of nearly all comic strips, or at least the funny ones, and they are read by adults as well as children. Even in *Tintin,* far from the cleverest of them, character is conveyed by language, by verbal idiosyncrasies—for example, Dupont and Dupond (in English the Thompson twins) parrot each other's phrases synonymically; Captain Haddock's cursing torrents are composed of archaisms, recondite technical terms, and so on. By the time they are equal to the task of reading books without pictures, Belgians have received an education in linguistic extravagance.

Most of twentieth-century Belgian literature is unknown to foreign readers; much of it, especially the avant-garde variety, is defiantly untranslatable. This is no accident, but a natural result of Belgians' having been told so often that their native idiom is crude, provincial, barely literate; the cottage industry in manuals and newspaper columns devoted to purging Belgian French of its local expressions and tendencies is nearly two hundred years old. Cast in the role of stepchild of French letters, francophone Belgian literature has either been assimilated into the mainstream without a trace or else it has been marginalized and disdained. Belgians often cite an analogy to the relationship between English and Irish literature. While it may not have produced an equivalent to Swift or Joyce, Belgium has issued an impressive range of literary tricksters, wild-eyed punsters, deadpan devisers of triple-entendre aphorisms, one-person movements of all stripes.

Any representative anthology of French-language Belgian writing over the past two centuries will inevitably seem like a random lineup of strays and misfits. The first notable writer of Belgian nationality was Charles de Coster (1827–1879), whose *Legend of Til Eulenspiegel* (1867) collects and retells a body of tales that originated in local resistance to Spanish rule in the sixteenth century; the titular hero is a sort of Reynard the Fox with a hint of Schweik, whose mission is to create chaos. Most brief accounts of Belgian literature in foreign reference works begin and end with Émile Verhaeren (1855–1916), a poet of haunted, ruined landscapes whose Symbolist work has survived rather well, and Maurice Maeterlinck (1862–1949), who remains the only Belgian to have won a Nobel Prize in literature (in 1911). His verse and verse dramas (notably *Pélléas and Mélisande*, 1892, and *The Bluebird*, 1909) partake of a rarefied artificiality that makes them only intermittently digestible nowadays; his excursions into natural history, such as *The Life of the Bee,* were a sensation in their day (earning him a trip to Hollywood, preserved in folklore by Samuel Goldwyn's reaction to his film treatment: "My God, the hero is a bee!") but have grown musty with time and the advances of science. An accounting of the nineteenth century would also include Camille Lemonnier, Belgium's somewhat stranger Zola, the mournful Symbolist novelist Georges Rodenbach, the Jeune-Belgique poets (more notable for their unearthing of the works of Lautréamont than for anything they themselves wrote), and the bristling incidental writings of Rops and Ensor.

The Belgian Surrealists were an ornery lot, unimpressed with the dictates of André Breton and so generally independent of the Parisian mainstream of the movement. They also tended to be miniaturists, masters of the one-line poem and the subverted proverb; this, along with their implacable combination of the urbane and the anarchic, has perhaps adversely affected their standing abroad. It is a shame, though, that the writings of Clément Pansaers, Paul Nougé, Achille Chavée, and especially Louis Scutenaire have been so seldom translated (much of it patently cannot be, but then the same could be said of such French poets as Robert Desnos and Benjamin Peret, who have been). The best work of the poet Norge (Georges Mogin; 1898–1990), especially *La Langue verte* (1954), cannot be approximated in translation. The mystical, hermetic, angry, often surprisingly funny Henri Michaux (1899–1984) left Belgium at an early age, for Asia and Paris, and as a result he is seldom thought of as Belgian, except by Belgians.

That is probably the only quality he shares with Georges Simenon (1903–1989), who took off from Liège at the age of nineteen and never returned to Belgium to live. In the United States he is thought of as a mystery writer, the creator of Inspector Maigret, as well as a prodigious serial consumer of women and pipes. On home ground he is sometimes called "the Balzac of the twentieth century." The difference has to do with the relative neglect abroad of his *romans noirs,* those novels that, although they often involve crime, do not feature Maigret, are less concerned with mystery than with psychology, and above all are marked by his eerily effective, effortlessly cinematic scene-setting. Simenon's astonishingly prolific output—400-odd titles, of which 173 are early pulp works written under various pseudonyms, 76 are Maigret stories, about 120 fall under the heading of *noir,* and 25 or so are autobiographical—has tended to obfuscate perception of his best work. It is hard to figure that such haunting and powerful novels as *Le Voyageur de la Toussaint* (1941; translated as *Strange Inheritance*), *L'Aîné des Ferchaux* (1945; *The First-born*), and *La Neige était sale* (1948; *The Stain on the Snow*) were hatched and written in Simenon's usual fourteen days—two spent meditating and thereafter a chapter a day.

If there is such a thing as a Great Belgian Novel, the leading contender for the title, at least on the Walloon end of things, has got to be Simenon's first attempt at autobiography, the 1948 novel *Pedigree.* This barely fictionalized account of his childhood, from his birth in the middle of a bloody strike to his early adolescence during and after the catastrophic German occupation in World War I, is a minutely observed zoological study of the provincial petite bourgeoisie as represented by one family. The father is a sweet man who desires nothing more from life than familiarity and small comforts; the ambitious mother strives, yearns, simmers, decrees, takes in lodgers who disrupt the insularity of the family circle. Since Liège is a university town, the boarders are students, and most of them are Jews from Russia and eastern Europe, who educate the son, the young Roger, helping him burst his confinement to a life bounded by the Church on one side and the military on the other. The book is uncomfortably definitive in its rendition of the claustrophobic patterns of behavior among the Walloons: the verbal tics, the social rituals, the class-bound judgments and insecurities, the obsession with death, with illness, with *pudeur,* with *mauvais instincts,* the endless graveyard visits, the simultaneously stoic and passive-aggressive management of pains and fears, the suspicion and rancor and small-time paranoia and petty spitefulness that poison families. Roger responds to his lot with despair, rage, rebellion—by drinking, by stealing, by reading, by chasing girls, and even, at one point, by assuming the clothes and manner of the working class from which his family has studiously detached itself, as he longs for a return to a liberating messiness now bulldozed by progress:

> Roger wishes that the houses could be even narrower, more irregular, divided by dizzy angles and odd corridors, dense with mysterious nooks and crannies. He likes people who wear the garb of their trade and call to each other from doorway to doorway, people who still live in the houses where they were born and who have always known each other, who even as old granddads still squabble with each other the way they did when they were schoolboys or served at mass in the local parish.

There are other works by Simenon that provide sharp views of Belgian manners and mores, but then he provided equal service concerning French, Dutch, Italian, North African, English, and Central and North American milieux. He also wrote many other autobiographical works, including twenty-two volumes of repetitive and terminally dull "Dictations" at the end of his life, but apart from the extraordinary, punishing *Lettre à ma mère* (1974; *Letter to My Mother*), he could have saved himself the trouble. In Belgium he is a monument, although not everyone venerates it. His anti-Semitic writings, however youthfully ignorant (as well as bizarrely ironic, given those very real Jewish student boarders), and his collaborationist activities during the war, however passive in nature, will not be forgiven anytime soon. But then Simenon, as wildly inconsistent in his conduct as he was consistent in his writing, can often seem like an idiot savant who channeled his work from some source in the ether. He will remain an enigma.

Belgian letters in recent times have, true to form, been the province of eccentrics and loners (probably the most famous Belgian writer of the second half of the century is Marguerite Yourcenar, who was at once a member of the Académie Française and a resident of Mount Desert Island, Maine). Nevertheless, the most interesting products of the immediate postwar decades have occurred within or on the margins of groups, however loosely defined, that were all products of the fallout from Surrealism. Although Belgians had been hacking away at the ropes that tied them to the Surrealist Vatican on Rue Fontaine in Paris since the 1930s, Breton's increasing postwar tendency toward mysticism and the occult positively outraged them. A fecund activity occurred in reaction. Groups coalesced around magazines: the *Daily-Bul* of La Louvière, which went for a madcap neo-Dada; André Blavier's *Temps Mêlés,* of Verviers, has been a Pataphysical outpost since 1952 (as of the last decade it has been entirely devoted to the works of Raymond Queneau); and Marcel Mariën's *Les Lèvres Nues* (Naked lips), of Brussels, which espoused a radical schismatic version of Surrealism, along the way publishing texts by members of the Lettrist International. This group evolved into the Situationist International, which had a number of Belgian adherents, among them Raoul Vaneigem, who wrote the *Traité de savoir-vivre à l'usage des jeunes générations* (1967; *The Revolution of Everyday Life*), a lyrically hectoring, elegantly wayward manifesto for the liberation of the individual, and of the world as composed of myriad individuals, in the grand tradition of Sade and Lautréamont. Vaneigem has continued in this line of thought as a historian, editor, and archivist, his mission to rescue from historical oblivion the Western anti-authoritarian tradition that extends from medieval heresies to the visionary anarchists of the nineteenth century.

Belgian writers have had a funny way not only of passing as other species, but of leaving the country for good. André Blavier cites a partial catalogue—Jacques Brel, Michaux, Simenon, Maeterlinck, Norge, and the major present-day Flemish novelist, Hugo Claus*—and quotes Mariën: *"Les gens estimables n'ont pas de patrie"* (admirable people have no fatherland—I couldn't have said it better myself). Blavier, who besides editing *Temps Mêlés,* in existence for an amazing forty-five years, has edited Magritte's letters and an anthology of works by marginal literary eccentrics ("outsider literature," if you will), and written several collections of poems as well as a dizzyingly bibliomaniacal, Tristram-Shandian novel, *Occupe-toi d'homélies* (1976; even the title is an untranslatable pun), has himself never lived outside Verviers, where he spent many years as municipal librarian. Blavier also lists a few of

* I have omitted other Flemish writers from this account only out of ignorance.

the many foreign writers who at one time or another sought refuge in Belgium, such as Victor Hugo and Baudelaire; he might also have included the Brontë sisters, and Rimbaud and Verlaine, who holed up for some months in Brussels prior to the famous shooting incident, and Apollinaire, who spent a whole two months of his adolescence in Stavelot, as a consequence of which he has been adopted by Walloons as one of their own.

Of these, the one most affected by the place was Baudelaire, whose *Amoenitates Belgicae* (1866; Belgian amenities) has for more than a century given offense to sensitive Belgians and caused embarrassment among the right-thinking French. This suite of twenty-one short poems is an extended libel of such hysterical virulence that it achieves humor, perhaps despite itself. The *histoire belge,* the Belgian joke, a staple in France, Germany, and the Netherlands, is in its crudest form simply the equivalent of the Polish (or fill in the ethnic group of your choice) joke in America, with many of the exact same punch lines. Baudelaire attempts to elevate the *histoire belge* to lyrical expression. "Belgium believes itself replete with charm;/ It sleeps. Traveler, do not disturb": a delicate sample. By contrast: " 'Let no one touch me! I am inviolable!'/ Says Belgium.— Alas, it is incontestable./ To touch it would in fact be a trick,/ Because it is a shit-covered stick."* And so on in the same vein, with a number of couplets worthy of their author. He later went so far as to propose a book on Belgium in thirty-three chapters, which never came close to realization, although a substantial outline has survived in which he systematically exhibits,

---

* Blavier traces the allusion to a *mot* by the Marquis d'Argenson: "The Queen of Spain is a shit-covered stick [*bâton merdeux*]; one doesn't know which end to take hold of."

strips, and flogs every aspect of Belgian life, from the beer to the water, fine arts to politics, sex life to hygiene, piety to anti-clericalism. Belgium is a nation of conformity, vulgarity, vanity, avarice, hypocrisy, arriviste pretension accompanied by toilet humor, and so on. The *Amoenitates* may have a prankish spirit about it, but this work, also composed at the very end of his life, is plain overkill. It seems to have been intended as revenge for the abject failure with which he met when, in 1864, he arrived in Brussels in flight from creditors and hoping to find a publisher and to make some money lecturing. However banal the explanation, a slur coming from no less a figure than Baudelaire could not fail to contribute to the national inferiority complex.

Belgians love to poke fun at their country; today self-satire has become an entire industry, with products ranging from postcards and bumper stickers to television commercials and feature films. To some degree this represents a healthy iconoclasm, but it is also a classic strategy for pre-empting assaults by outsiders. Poor Belgium gets itself trashed consistently. In its reduced size and central location it has long provided a convenient target; it is an awkward child wearing a kick-me sign on its back. For the most part the slurs are harmless, just dumb jokes. In his *Dictionary of Received Ideas*, Flaubert notes that "Belgians must be called 'counterfeit Frenchmen'; that always gets a laugh." A typical joke told by a Dutchman: A Belgian is planning a trip to England. "Be careful," his friends warn him, "they drive on the wrong side of the road over there." A few days later he staggers into his café on a crutch, his leg encased in plaster, his head bandaged. "Julot! What happened?" everybody asks. "I thought I needed some practice," he says, "so I tried it out on the road from Herstal to Visé." Belgium is a more esoteric butt for American jokes, but the old *National Lampoon* trotted it out with some regularity ("the world's leading producer of lampblack") and David Letterman devoted a Top Ten list to the possible duties of the Belgian astronaut who rode on one of the Space Shuttle missions ("3. Pretend to drive with colorful toy steering wheel").

Sometimes the jokes do uncover a larger truth. When Ring Lardner observed of a character in his story "Carmen" that "she looked about as comf'table as a Belgium," he was alluding to the international misery prize status accorded the country in the course of the Great War (based on awful fact, of course, but grossly inflated by the press, especially in the United States, where people actually believed that the Huns were boiling Belgian babies to make soap; no, all they did was exterminate whole villages on a whim). And we find an echo of Baudelaire's portrait in Karl Marx's dubbing Brussels "the paradise of capitalism," which was all too true. The city in the nineteenth century was a fortress of self-satisfied philistine burghers shiny with new money, much as it is today the paradise of Eurocrats and corporate spear-carriers who could just as well be living in Riyadh or Singapore or Bloomington, Indiana, for all they know or care.

Belgium, home of excellent beer, cheese, and chocolate, is a generic continental stopover (*If It's Tuesday, This Must Be Belgium*, 1969). It is small, neat, and feisty: Hercule Poirot (Agatha Christie apparently based her character on Adolphe Max, heroic mayor of Brussels during World War I). It produces expensive shoes, which for a while at least were de rigueur among fashion editors, as well as concrete blocks and, of course, waffles (still highlighted as New! on truck-stop menus from coast to coast, this confection, the regular old waffle topped with fruit and whipped cream and ice cream, was apparently devised for the "Belgian Village" at the 1964 New York World's Fair; it can now be found in Belgium itself). It is the birthplace of a kick boxer who has implausibly become a star of interchangeable action features popular the world over; he is familiar to tabloid readers as "the muscles from Brussels."* It is the Peoria of the world, at least if it exists in fact; perhaps it's a rumor: the Podunk. The noun is *Belgium*; the adjectival form is *Belgium*; the inhabitants are *Belgiums*; they speak *Belgium*. A substitute teacher, who presided over my American fourth-grade class for a day, upon hearing that I was Belgian informed the students that my country was divided: half Communist and half Free.

I often wonder whether Belgium is any more substantial to its own citizens. Perhaps Belgium is indeed a shimmering mist that only takes on mass and weight in times of trouble. The country certainly never makes it into international news coverage until a major catastrophe occurs there. Perhaps as a result, Belgians themselves never quite succeed in imagining a place for themselves among the pageant of nations, fixating strictly on the local. Belgians who never give a passing thought from one day to the next about whether they possess a nationality do suddenly become fiercely patriotic when challenged; when the fight is over they resume non-adherence. It may well be that

---

* On a recent visit to Belgium I idly turned on the radio one Sunday afternoon and heard two men having a conversation. "He's gotten a modicum of recognition in America," one of them said, "so he comes back to Belgium and thinks he's a big fish, but over here nobody shows him any respect, least of all his old friends." "He can't even speak French anymore," the other joined in. "He doesn't remember idioms, and translates American expressions instead. People laugh at him behind his back." *What?* I thought. At first I had no idea whom they might be talking about. *On n'est jamais prophète dans son pays.*

those *histoires belges,* and the contempt or indifference displayed by the rest of the world, spur national feeling more than any mediocre exhortations to pride ever could. It is not possible to imagine Belgians succumbing to the sort of pep-rally self-congratulation that appears to sway Americans, any more than they would be likely to indulge in the blood-and-soil occultism of the Germans or the pissing contests concealed by the rhetorical velvet of the French. Then again, Belgium is a monarchy, and it is rather difficult to take a nation seriously that in this day and age resorts to such a contrivance, however federal and constitutional it might be. The kingdoms and principalities and grand duchies that persist in the present era—Britain not excepted—are inevitably tarred with a comical irrelevance in the eyes of the world. Like an orange wig on a judge, the effect falsifies the gravity of the proceedings. But the monarchy has its uses: many Belgians of varied persuasions credit the late Baudouin with having kept the country from fragmenting at critically difficult junctures in the past few decades. The glue seems to have been some combination of personal charisma and weight of office; perhaps its success was itself symptomatic of the nation's core artifice.

It seems to be a rule that levels of popularity alternate among Belgian monarchs. Leopold I (d. 1865) was by all accounts not a terribly warm or inspiring personality, but he was the first, hence automatically popular. His son, Leopold II (d. 1909), was widely disliked, at home as well as abroad. It did not sit well with anyone that he appropriated the Congo as his own personal fiefdom—he claimed it in 1884, and Belgium did not annex the territory until 1908, having been virtually forced to do so by the pressure of world opinion regarding Leopold's administrative record of seizure, exploitation, and atrocity (not that the annexation changed conditions very much). Even people who did not care one way or the other that the native population was being tortured and worked to death in the mines and on the rubber plantations disliked his high-handed style, which extended to domestic issues. His queen, Marie-Henriette, was no exception to this sentiment; she walked out of the palace one sunny day and established her own residence at Spa, never again sharing a household with her husband.

Their nephew, Albert I, on the other hand, attained the very acme of popularity. Indeed, he was genuinely brave, and during World War I resisted the Germans for as long as he was able, staying with his troops rather than join the government in exile, and thereafter kept the country from falling apart altogether. Everything about him was dashing, as if he were a king in a novel. When he was not on horseback he was out riding his motorcycle incognito; his death in 1934, in a rock-climbing accident, further burnished his reputation. But his son, Leopold III, sank to the very nadir of esteem. His slide began only a year into his reign, when his enormously popular queen, the Swedish-born Astrid, was killed in a car crash while Leopold was at the wheel. He was thought to have profaned her memory when in 1941 he married a commoner, Liliane Baels; the fact that she was Flemish did not improve his standing among the traditionally republican Walloons, either, and the timing of the nuptials, in the middle of the war, did not please anyone. Although he refused to desert his country and decamp to London in 1940 along with the better part of the government, Leopold surrendered quickly. He did not offer much in the way of leadership or resistance to the invader, and his attempts to negotiate on behalf of Belgian prisoners and deportees were viewed as feeble. He was widely believed to have been a covert

German sympathizer. When the Allies invaded the continent in 1944, Leopold and family were ferried to Germany and then Austria; although involuntary, this flight was seen by his subjects as the final indignity, if not plain treason. When he was freed from confinement in May 1945 he could not return to Belgium, where for all anyone knew he might have been lynched. He moved to Switzerland instead, and his brother Charles was appointed regent. In 1950 a referendum indicated that popular feeling had not substantially improved in his favor; that summer, in fact, three people died in a demonstration against him in the industrial town of Grâce-Berleur. The following year he abdicated and his son Baudouin, not quite twenty-one, acceded to the throne.

Baudouin was tall, thin, and bespectacled, and until he was over forty looked rather like the bass player in some diffident English rock group of the era before the Beatles. He was wary of his role, although he applied himself diligently. He was a teetotaler, and extremely religious; he had wanted to become a Trappist monk. He remained so long a bachelor that the country became nervous, and rumor had it the Church itself discreetly played matchmaker. In 1960 he wed the pretty, pious, flip-hairdo-wearing Fabiola Mora y Aragon; the marriage seems to have been genuinely happy. When it proved impossible for her to bear children, the nation suffered along with the couple. Pageant and proxy substituted for actual reproduction. By tradition, the king is godfather of all seventh sons in the land (there was one such in my primary school class, a certain José), and the queen godmother to all seventh daughters; when a reunion of all the royal couple's godchildren was held in the early nineties, the total number was over six hundred. Baudouin presided over the independence of the Congo amid bloody circumstances; the decline of the coal, steel, and textile industries; the sharp increase in tension between the Flemish and Walloon halves of Belgium over the course of the 1960s and '70s; and the reorganization of the government along federal lines. It was during his reign that Brussels was trimmed of its architectural coherence and laced with elevated roadways, became the seat of NATO and the European Community, became an abstract and flavorless entity. When in 1990 the Belgian Parliament passed a measure legalizing abortion on demand, he resolved his moral-ideological quandary by abdicating for a day, so that he would not have to sign the bill. He made sincere efforts to encounter his subjects and minister to them, showing up at homeless shelters and meeting with distraught indentured Filipina prostitutes.

His image was displayed at least as widely as the flag: I saw him in every classroom, post office, hospital, Boy Scout clubhouse, and bureaucrat's warren I entered as a child. After the Kennedy assassination, when politico-religious iconography saturated the United States, it was the picture in *Life* that showed him alongside Haile Selassie, heading the procession of foreign dignitaries at the funeral, that was prominently displayed in our house. Thirty years later, in May 1993, I found myself in Amsterdam. Bound on an errand before catching my train back to Liège, I saw a crowd gathered in front of the royal palace in Dam Square. An obscure impulse caused me to stop and wait with them; I expected to see some banal performance by the guards. But then the band struck up the Brabançonne, the Belgian national anthem, and a minute later Beatrix and Bernhard emerged accompanied by Baudouin and Fabiola. They reviewed the troops the way dignitaries are always doing on the TV news in countries other than the United States, where visits by foreign heads of state are seldom considered newsworthy. Baudouin now looked like a well-heeled ascetic, perhaps an abbot in mufti. Fabiola, who may not know that her name has become an approbative exclamation among other sorts of queens, looked like an aging bisque doll. They possessed that glow that celebrities seen in the flesh often have, whether it is due to better health, greater self-confidence, manifold opportunities for tanning, or just the fact that they look so much like themselves. I tried to locate an appropriate emotion within myself: I was gazing upon my nominal ruler. Part of me, admittedly, returned to the age of six, while another part chafed at the notion that I could ever have tolerated the indignity of being a *subject,* and yet another luxuriated in a lukewarm tub of irony. Then I remembered a photograph I had seen, taken in the early 1960s, that showed Baudouin, in his commander-in-chief uniform, flanked by Frank Sinatra and Sophia Loren. As usual he looked shy, modest, reflective, intelligent, unpretentious—with icons to either side he was the *commoner;* he was, in fact, Belgium amid the great powers. I felt a small surge of identification.

Less than three months later, on July 31, Baudouin lay dead, of a massive heart attack, at the royal vacation villa in Motril, Spain, HIS CORPSE STRETCHED OUT BESIDE A CHAIR, as *La Dernière Heure* dramatically bellowed. Within hours, the mechanism of national mourning was under way, and soon the country had worked itself into a frenzy. People jammed the Brussels-bound trains, wept in the streets, stood on line for hours to view the cadaver, stood on line for hours just to sign the memorial book at their local town halls, wrote testimonials to which newspapers devoted many pages. Every place of business displayed a black-draped portrait at its entrance. Florists sold out the contents of their shops. Hysteria loomed, burst. One Cecilia M., of Bruges, drowned herself in the canal; her room was found choked with photographs of the late monarch and newspaper clippings regarding his passing. A friend of mine remarked that if you had publicly declared yourself a republican that week, you would have been taking your life in your hands.

Baudouin's brother, Albert, who had spent the previous sixty years primarily taking his ease, was hurriedly crowned successor. He stepped into the role looking like a successful self-made building contractor. Judgments on his rule thus far have been muted; they will probably never be more than that at least in the public sphere, given the country's stringent laws regarding respect of the monarchy. The wish to believe in a king is like the wish to believe in heaven. The frightened population yearns for the embrace of extrahuman arms. The king is a big father, a walking myth, an incarnate fortress. The humble and unworldly Baudouin was superbly cast. That the constitution prevented him from doing much of anything only added to his luster. He appeared to the lowly but was always just out of reach of the rest. In a troubled and impotent country he stood as the fireaxe, waiting to intervene when the final battle came. After that all would be well. His reign would usher in the reign of heaven. His namesake Baudouin IX, count of Flanders, was crowned emperor of Constantinople when that city was seized by Crusaders in 1204 and a year later was captured and executed by the Bulgarians. It was thereafter said that Baudouin was *not dead*, but *sleeping*. Even after a hermit who passed himself off as the late ruler had appeared in Flanders, even after the hermit was crowned to popular acclaim, with crowds fighting for a hair of his head or a drink of his bathwater, even after the hermit was exposed as a fraud and killed, even after Baudouin's daughter was accused of parricide for having exposed the hermit, even many decades after that, it was still said that Baudouin *was sleeping,* and would awaken.

XI Mirage

When I came along in 1954 my father was employed by the Duesberg-Bosson foundry in Verviers, one of 450 foundries operated by the company. The Verviers branch manufactured textile-industry machinery, looms and carding machines and the like. My father was production manager, in effect functioning as an engineer without benefit of degree. He pulled down ten thousand francs a month, about two hundred dollars, which at the time was a solid income; young engineers who possessed sheepskins averaged only three thousand francs per month. Meanwhile, the industrial crisis was beginning to take shape. The textile industry and all other heavy industries in southern Belgium, along with their counterparts in other western European countries, were in grave danger, although most people couldn't imagine how this could possibly be and so shrugged off the threat. Within five years Duesberg-Bosson was to close three hundred of its plants. Men like my father, who had come up through the ranks solely on native smarts and practical experience, were especially vulnerable. Indeed, the Verviers foundry closed on an interim basis in 1955, and my father was out of a job.

So my parents did what they could. They had friends who ran a Bata shoe store franchise in a suburb of Brussels. The friends put in word for them, and soon my parents left Verviers and relocated to Jemeppe, on the Meuse west of Liège, where there was an available Bata branch. The business was not en-

tirely a new experience for my father, who had learned cob-
bling during the war. Bata, a company that had originated in
Czechoslovakia during the 1920s, was Europe's leading mid-
level footwear manufacturer, and so the brand appeal was
built-in. The store would provide a solid, guaranteed income
without frills, and could be run in partnership by both my parents if need be. They could even put my crib in the rear of the
sales floor. They were not, however, prepared for Jemeppe.
Along with its slightly larger twin, Seraing, across the river,
Jemeppe was a steel town. Enormous factories such as Cockerill and Ougrée and Vieille-Montagne kept blast furnaces going
around the clock, blackening the air and producing a perpetual
rain of soot. When my mother took me for a walk in the fancy
navy-blue English baby carriage she would cover it with net-
ting to protect me, but upon arriving home would nevertheless
have to change my blanket, which was covered with black
speckles. Jemeppe was a grim place, where people led stunted
existences, work and sleep, drink or prayer, no more.

My parents sank into depression. They were still young and
had been through worse things, but those had nevertheless
allowed for hope, while this situation seemed to present them
with a blank wall. Meanwhile, I was coming awake. I rattled
the bars of my playpen in the back of the store and yelled
"Pantoufles!" (slippers) at the customers, and maybe I functioned as unintended advertising. Here's a photo postcard of
the store, which looks a bit Bauhaus: plain steel shelves of shoe-
boxes, a row of simple modern chairs with curved wooden
backs and seats and tubular legs and arms, a row of small signs
reading "California"—that European advertising strategy of
dressing up unglamorous necessities in American-movie trappings—and at the rear a large poster showing a padlocked

purse beneath the exhortation: "Refuse to pay more than Bata prices." I suppose I spent many days underneath that poster. We lived above the shop. The situation sounds cozier than it was. Every year for more than three decades my father drew a cartoon for his and my mother's wedding anniversary, a state-of-the-household summary featuring stick figures of the two of them and then the three of us, standing on a crescent moon. The first four years the moon bears the name of a brand of honey (a different one each time), but number five carries a company slogan: *"Tout est bas—chez Bata"* (everything is low—meaning prices—at Bata), followed in parentheses by "even morale."

I seem to have memories from that time, or maybe I've simply annexed stories told to me later and retrofitted them. I can picture, dimly, being wheeled down the street to a shrine to the Virgin in an alcove between buildings. As the badly scratched mnemonic filmstrip continues, however, I see the carriage coming to a halt at an intersection as a parade goes by, featuring a brass band whose musicians wear busbies and red jackets. I marveled at this memory until one day I realized that I had simply devised the whole band from the image of a red-jacketed, busby-wearing figure pounding a big bass drum that I had seen on the wrapper of a bar of Victoria chocolate. Years later, in Montreal to visit Expo 67, I bought an anthology of French poetry and, lying on the motel bed in Longueil across the St. Lawrence, first excitedly read Apollinaire's "Zone" and claimed it as my own, the whole poem in my possessive reading radiating out from the lines: *"Voilà la jeune rue et tu n'es encore qu'un petit enfant/ Ta mère ne t'habille que de bleu et de blanc."**

---

* "Here is the young street and you are only a little child/ Your mother only dresses you in blue and white."

My mother did indeed dress me only in blue and white, scrimping on her own clothing allowance to buy me clothes fit for a small heir, so that her friends called me "le petit prince"; the "young street" had to be that very one off Grand'Rue in Jemeppe-sur-Meuse. If I first imagined that Apollinaire had written the poem for me alone (it dazzled me by evoking among other things a collision of religious and technological imagery that felt as if I had imagined it myself), I later wondered whether I hadn't somehow constructed an artificially dated memory on the basis of the poem. I could without difficulty see myself in Marseilles among the watermelons, in Coblenz at the Hotel of the Giant, in Rome under a Japanese medlar tree, my face inserted into the arcade hole represented by the word "you" in Apollinaire's snapshot lines.

I thought I remembered sitting in a high chair at the kitchen table. The picture was vivid; I saw the calendar on the wall, the stove, the fringed tablecloth. What I couldn't quite figure was the pervasive grayness of the scene. Eventually I realized that I had borrowed the memory from an underlit photograph, with calendar and stove prominent; although in the picture I am lying on the table on a plaid blanket, it does have a fringe. On the other hand I have a fairly traumatic memory from babyhood, of burning myself on an electric iron that had been unplugged and left to cool behind a small yellow checked curtain covering a shelf. When I asked my mother about it a decade or so later, she denied it had ever happened. It was only two decades after that that she admitted the event had caused her such grief and shame she had repressed its memory. Far more difficult to place are memories of internal experiences. I seem to remember fragmentary word associations, presumably from the earliest days of language: there was a word that was a door

loosely swinging both ways, with cartoonish whoosh lines indicating its path, and another word that was a black-and-white
rocking horse set against a red wall. I don't know what the
words themselves were, only that the mnemonic images were
not at all literal; I also know that these were but two of a long
series of such visual associations. When I read A. R. Luria's
The Mind of a Mnemonist (1968), the Yiddish-speaking subject's account of his childhood word associations prompted my
instantaneous recognition:

> For some reason the word *mutter* produces an image of
> a dark brown sack with folds, hanging in a vertical
> position. . . . *Milch*, though, is a thin thread with a little
> bag attached. *Leffel* is braided like a *hallah*, while *hallah*
> itself is such a hard word, you have to snap it off.

My memory, obviously, is nothing like the total recall enjoyed and suffered by the titular S., a complex phenomenon
probably neurological in origin. Mine is scattered, its specifics
possibly random and possibly not, its structure undoubtedly
determined by events. I remember a visit to a little zoo in Spa
when I was maybe three, because I was unnerved by the tortured frustration of the tiger, who paced endlessly back and
forth in his ridiculously small cage, maybe also because of the
coincidence of the bars and the stripes. I remember an ice-
cream vendor pushing an ornately painted cart with a canopy
and towering domed brass lids over the compartments that held
the invariable vanilla, chocolate, and pistachio, because of my
parents' shock when it turned out I didn't like the stuff. I remember the one-ring Italian circus that pitched its tent in a va-

cant lot a block away from our house in Pepinster in 1957, but who wouldn't remember a circus just outside the door? I remember the day in 1958 when my friend Paul Detiffe, who lived across the street in Pepinster, was hit by a motorcycle, because he had to have stitches in his tongue, and the pain of that idea ran through me. It is possibly the pain's specific physical location that accounts for an odd component of this memory: my mother's voice slowing down like a phonograph losing power as she tells me the news.

But Paul himself now doesn't remember the event, and only knows that it happened because his parents have told him so. It may well be that Paul's failure to remember the accident is a direct result of the trauma he suffered. Still, when I compare notes with him and his older brother, André, whose ages lie a few months to either side of mine, and whom I have known since I was two, I remember far more about our collective early childhood than they do. Neither can remember a time when their parents had no car, or when their house lacked central heating or a refrigerator or a television; those innovations occurred during Belgium's "economic miracle" years, the early 1960s, when the postwar period finally ended. By that time we had already gone to America; the change was in full swing in 1962 and 1963, the years when my mother and I spent several months at a time back in Pepinster. In 1963 the Detiffes had a TV set and a telephone, but no car, and the house was still heated by a mazout stove in the parlor. The reason I can remember such things, and that I can remember, say, Paul and me having our tonsils jointly removed by the doctor in the parlor of my parents' house in 1958, and the white Porsche the doctor drove up in, and the deck chairs—the striped-fabric *transatlantiques*—in which we reclined to eat our post-operation ice cream (I'd come to tolerate it by then), and the kind of day it was (cool and sunny), is because I had to. Less than a year later the ground cracked under my feet, and I clung to my memories for dear life. Later, the memories became a way of establishing order in the chaos of my world.

The Jemeppe interlude was fortunately brief. After a bit less than a year, my parents' great wish was fulfilled: the Duesberg-Bosson foundry reopened and my father was offered his old job back. Flush with optimism, my parents put a down payment on a corner house in a new development being built in Pepinster, a small town southwest of Verviers that had lately become ambitious. While the house was under construction we lived in Ensival, a colorless factory suburb just west of Verviers. We lived somewhere down the line from the Île Adam (not an island, and no relation to the author of *L'Ève future*, but an upmarket styling of the Walloon name, Èlahan, which derives from the word for interlacing, probably a topographical reference); in any case the site of the house now lies under the E42 superhighway. Past Verviers, Rue d'Ensival stretches west along the Vesdre across unbroken miles of gray three-story houses and brown three-story houses, with garages and small factories interspersed, past Lambermont and Wegnez, past such neighborhoods as the aptly named Purgatoire, with sidewalks sparsely populated by beleaguered mothers dragging recalcitrant kids and shell-shocked pensioners dragging grocery bags, nowadays also with women in chadhors and men in djellabas. The road continues on to Liège, but at Pepinster it meets Rue Neuve, which follows the Hoëgne River, at a T, and down that way the landscape opens up.

Pepinster, named after Pepin le Bref, father of Charlemagne, doesn't stray too far from its main street, even now, when, for example, it inexplicably fields one of the country's top professional basketball teams. Proceeding down Rue Neuve you cross the Vesdre on Pont Nicolaï, duck under the railroad overpass, see St. Antoine to your right and the principal café directly across to your left (in my childhood it smelled as if it were regularly washed with beer, but now it has acquired large tinted windows and subdued lights and brass fittings), note the *Hôtel de Ville* with its war monument in front, where the tram stop became a bus stop when the trolleys were taken out of commission in 1969. The rest of the vista consists of pale gray three-story houses containing shops of minor significance, crisp and white, many of them barely altered from my childhood. The residential area extends no more than three blocks beyond in either direction. Turning right on Rue des Jardins you pass the middle school with its ten-foot karyatids and directly across the street the large newer high school. A block farther is Rue Alfred Brabant. The development looks exactly as it did when we moved in, except that there are now cars parked along the curb and in the garages that lie below and in the rears of the houses, accessed by a driveway that plunges just past each corner house and then runs down the center of each block. The houses are attached, with brick ground floors and white stucco second stories and roofs whose end points are sliced off at an angle and capped with a small triangular patch, giving them a certain Dutch-barn effect. Our old house, number 86, being on a corner lot, is attached only at the rear, to the house of Mr. and Mme. Laplanche, who are probably dead by now (despite the fact that my parents knew them for at least seven years, in true Belgian fashion they never learned their first names). The top part is a blank expanse of white broken only by the small attic window under the roof angle and a tiny bathroom window on the second floor that is set off-center, giving the whole a restrained modernistic look. The neighborhood is almost aggressively uncluttered, but it is saved from sterility by the steep wooded hill that looms behind it across the Hoëgne.

My parents had achieved their dream. They had fought their way into the middle class, with suburban homeownership and even for a while a car, a Morris Minor named Pâquerette, or Daisy. They were both approaching their mid-thirties by that time, having lost the better part of a decade to the war and its fallout, but if much hard work lay ahead, at least anxiety had been leavened. My father, though, had entertained large ambitions not very long before. He had been so forward-looking that he had never even picked up the medal and ribbon to which he was entitled as a *réfractaire,* one who had resisted forced deportation by the Germans. The Socialist Party had been interested in grooming him to be one of their bright young men. For several years beginning in 1946, he had been a contract player with the Théâtre Walloon Verviétois, known as "Amon Nos Autes" (literally "among us," with the flavor of "our gang"), the most significant Walloon theater company in Verviers, and in addition he had written a short play that the company produced. He had also written the lyrics to a football-team anthem that was recorded, as well as a short story, "Le Cadeau du Père Noël" (The Gift from Santa Claus), that was published in a local arts-and-entertainment newspaper, *Heures d'Oubli* (Leisure Time). Its hero, Raoul Dambert, is ambling down the street one Christmas Eve, lost in his thoughts, when the wind is suddenly knocked out of him. He has collided with a beautiful young woman with long blond hair. She must be his Christmas present, he tells her. She replies smartly; he parries, then gallantly offers to see her home. One thing leads to another, and in due course they are on their way to the altar. "Today," the story concludes, "Raoul Dambert no longer believes in Santa Claus." The byline reads: Luc Sante.

Once he met my mother, however, he put away such ambitions, since their rewards were not likely to be sufficient to support a family. He did occasionally think with a twinge of envy of an acquaintance from the foundry whose facility at writing had allowed him to quit his job and live on the proceeds of the pulp mystery novels he produced at the rate of one per month. To be a paperback writer was the great aspiration in a country not known for its film industry. Examples included not just the great Simenon but also such largely untranslated notables as Stanislas-André Steeman, Jean Ray, and the man who called himself Thomas Owen, all of them chiefly distinguished by their inexhaustible serial manufacture. Most of these writers were from working-class or lower-middle-class backgrounds, and they were as driven as if they were still on the assembly line. My father wasn't inclined toward mysteries, however. His bent was toward thick historical sagas by the likes of Samuel Shellabarger, the mandarin style of Jean de la Varende, the dry English absurdism of Jerome K. Jerome, the mountaineering chronicles of Frison-Roche, the rustic comedies of Arthur Masson, which wove in and out of Walloon, as well as innumerable accounts of the war. Many of these books were published by Marabout, of Verviers, a pioneer in the field of pocket-size paperbacks, a publishing phenomenon on the Continent at about the same time as in America. Their colorful and sometimes lurid covers were always around, catching my eye. More in keeping with the style of the house were the slipcased hardbacks put out each month by Le Club des Amis du Livre, primarily intended to look smart on the shelf, but which at our place actually got read.

But they did look smart on the shelves in the parlor, which doubled as formal dining room and took up nearly half the ground floor. It featured a black-enamel mazout stove backed into the hearth, and a massive table and carpet-upholstered chairs and a large Belgian-Oriental rug and accumulations of bibelots, not to mention the handsome moderne leather club chair my father designed and had built by his friend Jean Simar. In my mother's favorite family portrait she is sitting in that chair, and I am perched on its arm, and my father sits in one of the carpet-upholstered dining chairs next to a standing lamp with a frou-frou chintz shade. We are all smiling, quite unaffectedly, genuinely blissful, the ideal young family, suitable for framing. Our existence was unquestionably comfortable, curved if not padded, with steps leading upward toward a future that could not help being even better.

Everything was in easy reach. Grandparents were just minutes away, the rest of the family not much farther. Belgium's compactness made vacations and day trips convenient. A two-hour train ride would take us to Le Coq (De Haan) or La Panne (De Panne), resorts on the North Sea coast, while the mountains were even closer, less than an hour to Rochefort or La Roche, where we'd rent a room in a guest house and spend our days in the meadows and the evergreen woods, with pleated khakis and walking sticks, gulping the air that was measurably purer than the stuff that coursed twenty miles away. The falls at Coo, with their exciting cable-car ride, and the many pleasures of Spa—pony rides, mineral springs, ten thousand cafés with garlanded outdoor terraces—were virtually next door. Shopping was easily accomplished: the bakery (pies, loaves, the torpedo-shaped rolls called *pistolets,* commemorative specialties such as the special waffles made only on the feast of St. Antoine) and the butcher's (meat chopped into *hachis* right in front of you with two tiny cleavers, the ambrosial homemade *pâté de foie*) and the *friture* (hot twice-fried potatoes in a newspaper cone with mayonnaise on the side) were two blocks away, while the *épicerie* (huge wheels of cheese, the pervasive aroma of Chat Noir coffee) was just a bit farther. Vegetables came right to the door several times a week by truck, and so did fish on Fridays and ice cream in the summer, and beer and *eau gazeuse* and *citronade,* and for that matter the knife-grinder on Saturdays.

My two best friends lived across the street, and other friends, beginning with the fourth member of our quartet, the round blond Philippe Wergifosse, in houses all around. I developed my first crush on a girl who lived half a block over in the slightly older development west of Rue des Jardins (I seem to think she was the beautician's daughter, although I may only be incubating a country-and-western song in my brain's recesses). It was around the same time, I think, that I received a crucial lesson next door at the crowded house of the Voos family, whose nine children ranged from a sullen teenage boy whose bedroom walls were plastered with pictures of Elvis down to a newborn girl. They had the first television set in the neighborhood, which may be why I dropped by, one day, and happened to walk into the kitchen when the baby was being changed; abruptly I learned the difference between boys and girls. My friends and I played soccer in the safely empty streets; in winter we'd ride our sleds (made from three pieces of wood by somebody's father) down the gentle driveway inclines. Indoors we'd play with toy soldiers and Steiff animals and Meccano sets and Dinky cars, possibly all at the same time. The Detiffes were for some reason fond of playing church; André, who never failed to exploit his status as the eldest, always got to be the priest.

For a bunch of tots, we led busy lives. We all started school shortly after our third birthdays, and it was no mere kinder-garten—we began learning basic reading, writing, and arith-metic right away. Some months previously I had amazed my family by sitting down with a book (I remember it as being *Le Secret du castor*—The Beaver's Secret—a translation of a Little Golden Book by P. and R. Scarry, although my mother disputes this) and reciting its text while turning the pages. My grand-mother thought that I had somehow taught myself to read, but actually I had heard it so many times that I knew it by heart. I loved books immediately, almost as much as I loved to draw—some relative was moved to predict, with the usual accuracy of such divinations, that I would become an architect. Numbers posed more of a difficulty, as did music, but that was only be-cause when the teacher handed out instruments for us to make noise with I received the lowly triangle. In school there was also a great deal of drawing and cutting and pasting, even some heavily supervised baking. What remains most vivid from my first two years of education, however, was the day the teacher read us a story that caused me to have nightmares for years af-terward. It concerned a brave and selfless knight who ventures into the underworld, to the chamber where human life spans are measured by burning candles, to exchange his tall taper for the guttering stub of a dying baby. The story echoed and echoed, vertiginously. I suppose that was the day when I learned about mortality.*

In general, however, the matter of the schoolroom made much less of an impression on me than the reading I did on my own. In those books I still possess, the illustrations preserve

---

* Decades later I saw Fritz Lang's silent film *Der Müde Tod* (Weary Death). My hair stood on end; it was the same story, adapted from the Brothers Grimm.

much of their original force. It was the animals' tidy post office that I especially cherished in *Le Secret du castor*, the bedroom lined with sacks of hazelnuts in some squirrel's tale, the neatly stocked larder in a version of the story of the ant and the grasshopper. The taste of the piles of crêpes cooked up by Petzi the bear remains vivid, as do the various flavors I imagined for the black stuff the characters drink in the Tintin adventure *L'Île noire* (since the story is set in Scotland it is undoubtedly stout, but I identified it as everything from Coca-Cola to game marinade). I had absorbed the Belgian passion for contained order, and so I was drawn to neat toy-towns with everything in place, was always organizing my stuffed animals and assigning them jobs, ranks, and family ties. Toy shops were miniature worlds, their windows glowing through December fog to reveal crusaders' castles with hundreds of tiny knights marching around model-railroad shrubbery. Pleasure was expressed in series, which promised scale-reduced bounty. You could collect all three hundred knights, theoretically, and at the newsagents' shop stare in wonder at the massed ranks of all the bound Tintin adventures, as well as those of Spirou and Fantasio, Johan and Pirlouit and their allies the Schtroumpfs, Lucky Luke with whom I naturally identified (although it was many more years before I understood that series' clever parody of Western genre conventions), and on and on, shelf upon shelf of sixty-page books bound in boards. For similar reasons I always begged my mother to buy Jacques chocolate. Although inferior in flavor and quality to Côte d'Or it possessed the indisputable advantage of equipping each bar with a small, thin card which had a picture on one side and an explanatory text on the other. The cards also ran in series—famous cyclists, our ancestors the Belgae, the history of the automobile, the royal family's visit to the Congo—which could be mounted in albums, and the albums in turn could be acquired by mailing in so many flattened wrappers. Packaging of all sorts, from detergent box tops to the printed white tissues that enveloped Valencia and Jaffa oranges, contained *bons* that could be saved and redeemed for prizes. The acquisition, organization, and appreciation of all these things were activities that promised to stretch reassuringly into the far future, in never-ending abundance.

But then, at some point in the spring of 1958, my father happened to notice that the management of Duesberg-Bosson was conducting a stock inventory. This, he knew well by now, was a harbinger of doom. The jig was up. Quite fortuitously, Jeanne Dosquet chose that time to come to Belgium on a visit. She was married to Léopold (Pol) Dosquet, my father's oldest friend, and they had emigrated to the United States in 1955, the last year in which immigrants passed through Ellis Island on their way to New York City (Pol was kept there in quarantine for three days, something to do with his lungs). Pol was the youngest of the Dosquets. The eldest, Anna, was the brainy, bookish one; she never married. The middle child, Lucy, tall and coltish, was the gregarious one. In 1945 she met an American G.I. from New Jersey. Like so many thin, weary, bright-eyed young European women and triumphant, suddenly cosmopolitan young American soldiers, the two promptly fell in love, learned the rudiments of one another's languages, got married, and took off for America (one of the Marabout paperbacks in my father's collection was a memoir by a Frenchwoman entitled *G.I., marions-nous*). They settled on the shores of Lake Hopatcong and both obtained secure government-issue jobs at the nearby Picatinny Arsenal. Lucy's letters home were sufficient inducement for Pol and Jeanne, somewhat at loose ends, to pack up and follow suit. They spent a few years attempting to take root, living in urban Essex County while Pol was employed at factories in and around Newark and Jeanne worked in a beauty parlor. One day a client of Jeanne's mentioned that the large chemical firm Ciba, her husband's employer, was in need of personnel at its branch in the suburban splendor of Summit. The deal was done, and there they moved, permanently.

I dimly knew of the Dosquets, less perhaps because I heard my parents talking about them than because of the colorful foreign greeting cards with which they were associated; for my third birthday they sent a picture of an impossibly round and fuzzy fawn, with marshmallow antlers and eyes the size of gingerbread cookies, bearing the legend: "To a Real Deer" (I don't know at what point I came to understand the pun). They also sent snapshots that were perfectly square and in color, quite unlike our rectangular sepia items. When Jeanne arrived we all went off by train to La Panne, on the coast at Belgium's northwest extreme, and booked rooms at a Socialist guest house called the Hôtel Germinal. Jeanne had brought me a small American flag, and I planted it in my sand castles. It rode, too, on the various conveyances I pedaled around, which were a fixture of Belgian beach resorts: tricycles done up as horse carts, bicycles as rockets, four-person velocipedes as fire trucks and jeeps. My parents and Jeanne were deep in tactical negotiations and soul-searching, but I was happily oblivious. I admired as ever the endless reach of the strand between hotels and gently lapping waves, the stiff breezes, the circling gulls, the bounty of the self-service tearooms and the seafood restaurants, the impression that the whole town was a carnival in continuous motion, and the image that I clung to for some reason above all: a shack in the shape of a giant beehive, a promotional device for a brand of honey. It was always just down the beach and we were always approaching it but never seemed to get there, much as I desperately wanted to visit it. It hung as a sort of mirage behind a screen of fine white airborne sand.

The gravity of everything was quite beyond my ken. How did my parents speak to me of their plans? Did they resort to parables, or tell me that we'd soon be taking a long fun-filled trip? All I can remember is a buzz of excitement, that of going all the way to Antwerp, for example, where my parents obtained our green cards from the American consulate, but where the errand for me consisted of going to the zoo improbably nestled against the cavernous hall of the train station, where there were birds that seemed to float on spindly legs and that weirdly bore the same name as the people (flamingos in French are *flamants roses,* which is homonymic with "pink Flemings"). But Christmas that year was somehow weighted with significance, although I don't really know if that was true at the time or an overlay later supplied by retrospect. I just remember December as a blur of snowflakes and activity, with many visitors and many visits. I had in some way been given the message that we would be leaving the country, however, because as I sat at my desk in a large old classroom on the second floor of the *école des soeurs* by Pont Nicolaï, punching out a picture of the king from a newspaper with an awl and then gluing it on coarse paper above a flag made of strips of black, yellow, and red cellophane, I was overwhelmed with a sense of leave-taking.

The foundry had closed in June, for good this time. My father got six months' severance pay, and in January he collected a month's unemployment, for the only time in his life. He remains proud of this feat. (The worst fight I ever had with my father, despite my expulsion from high school and inglorious college record and at least one brush with the law, among many assorted torts of late adolescence, came when I revealed to him my plan to quit a dull job and collect unemployment, a plan that anyway failed; he accused me of proposing to take bread from the mouths of workers.) He spent his time doing paperwork and adding columns of figures in his tiny, modernistically minimal hand. In 1958 my parents also traveled to Brussels to take in the World's Fair (I was deemed too young to go along). There they visited the American pavilion and marveled at the 360-degree movie that displayed the country in all its glory and put you in the middle: riding a fire truck down Main Street, hurtling through Monument Valley, plunging through Iowa cornfields. They remained apprehensive, but they were now filled with a certain muted sense of adventure.

My father built nine large crates from wood that was scrap but solid, and into them went the twelve-piece cream-colored Occupied-Germany dinner set, the twelve-piece silver service, the colorfully patterned woolen blankets, the Val-St. Lambert crystal ashtray with matching teardrop-shaped butt-grinder, the cut-glass cigarette box, the dolls in national costume that my mother had collected on their honeymoon in Switzerland and northern Italy, the pair of hand-painted eighteenth-century Chinese-export plates with their wire wall hangers, the crucifix with its silver cross tips mounted on scarlet satin in an oval frame, the several pewter dishes embossed with obscure crests, the brown-and-yellow Luxembourgeois coffee service, the good glasses including the crystal wine goblets, the artificially aged parchment scroll bearing a translation of Rudyard

Kipling's "If" ("... you shall be a man, my son"), the prints of
Van Dyck's self-portrait and of his painting of St. Martin divid-
ing his cloak, the gilt-framed wedding portrait and the carved-
framed portrait of my father's father and innumerable portraits
of me at various key ages, the lace pillowcases and tablecloths
and table runners and antimacassars, the bespoke suits and formal dresses, the hand-knit sweaters and socks, several dozen
stuffed animals and a couple of dozen Dinky cars and regi-
ments of toy soldiers, and nearly a hundred books painfully selected from the shelves.

The crates were shipped off by freighter. We, however,
were going to travel in style, expensively, by air. After paying
freight charges and the cost of two and a half seats aboard a
Sabena prop jet going from Brussels to Idlewild, my parents
were left with their nest egg for the new world: six hundred
dollars. On February 7, 1959, four days before my parents'
ninth wedding anniversary, we entrained from Pepinster, accompanied by many suitcases as well as by my maternal grandparents and my mother's brother, René, bound for the airport
on the outskirts of the formerly quaint Brabant village of Zaventem. A storm was blowing in, however. Tearful closure
was unsatisfyingly left to drag on; the flight was postponed
overnight. On the other hand, those being the luxury days of
air travel, the airline took care even of second-class passengers
in such circumstances. They put us up at the grand old art-
nouveau Hôtel Métropole, in the heart of Brussels. I seem to
watch a fragmentary little movie, on aged color stock gone
to staticky brown: a rain-slick tarmac runway, the dramatic
nighttime streets of Brussels filled with rushing headlights and
crowned with red neon words above the black silhouettes of its
hulking buildings, the deep awnings of the Métropole, the

suavely darkened dining room, a round table lit at its center by a small shaded lamp, the six of us around it, René raising his glass in a toast. This footage is, I suppose, partly imaginary, partly remembered. In any event, no one took any pictures that day.

XII Atlantic

In Kafka's *Amerika* the Statue of Liberty stands guard over the harbor holding aloft a gigantic sword. In my family's version, probably not original to us, the item she bears is an ice-cream cone. *La marchande de crème glace*, she was always called, before and after immigration. The overtone was ironic in both cases, but the nature of the irony changed. On February 8, 1959, my parents and I were on our way to set our material selves down in a preposterous El Dorado, a candy mountain that existed only in rumor and representation and could not by any standard of logic or reason actually exist. The verified presence of three actual Belgians in America, two of whom had proposed to act as our sponsors, did not substantially alter our impression that we were plunging into a void in quest of a chimera; it merely served a talismanic function. The very physical approach my parents took to this absurd leap—those nine packing cases—can primarily be attributed to my father's propensity for meticulous long-range planning. If my father had gone down the rabbit hole he would have had the foresight to equip himself with a compass and a box lunch. He had planned for America imagining such contingencies as semiformal dinners and evening promenades.

But then the model he envisioned, the only available parallel, was the Belgian experience in the Congo. My uncle René came home from there and was on hand to advise, and every year my mother's cousin Pierre Stelmes, Tante Fonsine's son,

returned on leave with his wife and two daughters, the elder of
whom, Myriam, was born in Léopoldville exactly a month before my birth. The Congo was referred to by all as *"un stage,"*
an apprenticeship, a temporary stepping-stone for those whose
futures at home would otherwise have been uncertain. It was
also known that colonial society was both more grandiose and
more volatile than everyday life in Belgium. It was overheated
in ways other than the literal; René had lost his wife to the ongoing soap opera to which domestic relations were subject over
there. But, of course, Belgians however dissipated were the
masters of the land. Even if you were taking a job as assistant
file clerk in a lesser ministerial agency, you would be moving
into a villa in a palm-shaded suburb. You would be entertaining
on a regular basis; you would have servants. Nobody that we
knew ever questioned the premise. Stories of the mistreat-
ment—not to say enslavement and torture—of native Africans
did not circulate at home. Everyone simply accepted that the
Belgians were helping the Africans enter the twentieth century
(by 1959 it was common knowledge that the Congo would
eventually be granted its independence, perhaps in a decade or
two) and furthermore had brought them the treasure of Christian salvation, without which those unfortunate animists would
be consigned to Limbo for eternity.

So, for planning purposes, it was a matter of superimposing
the structure of colonial life—high salaries, material comfort,
cultural and spiritual dislocation—onto what was known about
America. The body of available folklore concerning the United
States did not really add up to a coherent picture. It was known
that American pharmacies, for example, provided nearly every
imaginable service with the possible exception of filling pre-
scriptions; they copied keys, repaired shoes, sold magazines,

and furthermore doubled as nonalcoholic cafés where one could consume such exotica as malted milk and pimento-cheese sandwiches, whatever those might be. Their nominal association with the pursuit of health probably accounted for their failure to serve alcoholic beverages, since it was known that Americans went about their business in a perpetual mild drunken haze—although Americans did not drink wine, they consumed cocktails with every meal perhaps excepting breakfast. The national drinks, in an odd paradox, appeared to be milk (which no Belgian adult would have thought of ingesting in any form but as a cloud in coffee) and something called the martini, about which all one knew was that it bore no resemblance to the apéritif of the same name, which was merely vermouth, most often red. Americans could afford to be drunk all the time because there was nothing for them to bump or bash into—roads were three or four times as wide as those in Europe, houses were set far apart, the scale of everything could be multiplied many times over. This in addition accounted for the size of American cars; not only *could* they be big, since there was so much room for them, and materials for constructing them were unbelievably cheap, but they almost *had* to be, since the daily distances they needed to traverse were beyond any European's reckoning.

The Brobdingnagian dimensions of the country would all by themselves have provoked wonder and wild speculation among Europeans. Obviously it was known that Russia and China and Australia were on the same scale, but those territories were largely untamed, wastelands barely mapped. America was more like Europe, albeit colossally inflated. But size correspondingly affected psychology. For instance, Americans ate vast quantities of beef, nearly raw (for this reason steak tartare

was called *filet américain*) and glistening with broad bands of
fat, exactly those portions that Belgian butchers took trouble to
trim away. This revealed the crudeness of Americans, and
showed the lamentable lack of craftsmanship that attended
most professions over there, but it also shed light on the primi-
tive logic that ruled the American mind. Not only could Americans eat all the beef they wished, since there it was on the hoof
in the prairie just outside the door, but they also needed to be
physically large, both to occupy as much of the landscape as
possible in order to adapt to its scale, and in order to compete
with each other, in the manner of pouter pigeons inflating their
necks and chests. Regarding this last detail Belgians knew
whereof they spoke; they had seen them in '44 and '45, all those
giant Iowa farmboys with muscles in their ears, and they had
seen them ten years later, roughly doubled in bulk, wearing
straw hats and Bermuda shorts, with cameras in their paws.
One guessed that another reason Americans required large
quantities of beef was because so much of the balance of their
diet consisted of bizarre waste products: maize, which *chez nous*
was exclusively fed to chickens, and pumpkins, which were
thrown to the hogs.

American culture could be said to be predicated on the pursuit of beef, quite literally, since what else were Westerns but
the heroic saga of the cultivation, transport, and marketing of
beef? Could one imagine a Belgian cinema and literature in
which the story always boiled down to *francs-tireurs* defending
the endive crops of the Campinne from foreign invaders?
Westerns could be good fun, but they were issued in such numbers, with so much repetition, that they blurred into one long
chase. The other half of American culture appeared to be the
saga of the cocktail: Humphré Bogart (the *t* is silent) feeding

martinis to Marie-Lynne Monroë in some pitch-dark *bar améri-cain*, suddenly interrupted by Richard Widmarque wielding a revolver, so that they never do make it to bed and we are denied the sight of her breasts in their full magnificence. This genre could be defined as one protracted tease. Americans were peculiarly licentious and sanctimonious at once. This was owing to their lack of roots. American civilization was a jerry-built edifice, as fascinating as it was wafer-thin. Again, this was quite literal: the cities had gone up virtually overnight. Concentrations of concrete monoliths appeared abruptly on pasturelands, and the poor Indians were forced to take down their teepees and shoulder their papooses so that highway cloverleafs could be poured. In that ceaselessly churning machine of a nation it was quite believable that a bootblack could in a trice become head of General Motors, or a minor provincial haberdasher wake up to find himself president of the country.

Such men had no families, no culture, no couth, but then neither did anyone else. America was a democracy of rough-necks who proceeded solely on native cunning and bare-knuckle force. Upon seeing a prize we had longed for, set out in front of us, you or I or any other European would negotiate for it, employing diplomatic skill and subtly deflected language; the American, however, would just grab it and walk. Americans did not read; they had produced no writers besides Jack London and some detective novelists—oh, and Faulkner. They had no painters, no composers, although the American Negro had invented jazz and spirituals, which were often sublime, so it was perhaps because of envy that there was so much prejudice against the Negro. Americans had nothing that could be called philosophy, either, and as for religion, they had divided themselves into an endless profusion of outlandish sects. Your well-dressed businessman was likely to spend Sunday morning handling poisonous snakes—or maybe they went on Saturday night in that godforsaken country. They called themselves Christians, but they attended temples, like any pagans, and wept and danced in them, and threw each other into water fully clothed, and rang doorbells and tried to convert you, tempting you away from the true Church and your family.

Somehow there had to be an angle even in this, because the rock upon which America was founded was the almighty dollar. You had to admire them for their skill at making money. They could buy and sell not only you and me, but any Belgian industrialist or hereditary landowner you cared to mention. Of course, they did have certain advantages, such as the arable soil and the petroleum that they had hoodwinked the simple Indians into trading for beads and trinkets. And they had no end of cheap labor; the wretched of the earth, massed on American shores earlier in the century, comprised a renewable workforce that permitted the likes of Henry Ford to build cars at a rate of one per minute. You got what you paid for, naturally: such automobiles might be large and inexpensive, but they were made hastily, without the rigor or attention to detail that distinguished the European product. They were tin cans, however flamboyant. But what was truly astonishing about America was its open door. You could go there with only the clothes on your back and, if you had the mettle, you could find yourself drinking cocktails on a veranda in Miami Beach within a fortnight, a blonde on your arm and your Cadillac idling at the curb. It was understood that you had to be ruthless—nothing was free in America, and the citizens were inclined to shoot each other in the back, literally as well as figuratively. America issued a perpetual schoolyard taunt: Are you man enough to take me on?

The difference was that there was a bona fide prize backing up the challenge.

It was a challenge few Belgians cared to meet. Hustling and back-stabbing were just not their style. They were too passive, it might be averred, although some would say it was rather that they were sensualists, uneager to give up good food and drink and the beautiful landscape and the convivial pleasures of their café or their family circle for the frenetic pace and brute satisfactions of America, however great the eventual reward. Now, my parents hardly fit the image of mercenary fortune-hunters. Their emigration must in that time and place have seemed like a large and desperate gamble. To this day I find myself trying to account for it. There are no augurs in their earlier lives, unless you want to count their parallel flights in May 1940, but those were different in essence, and different from one other. My parents always erred on the side of caution; like people building a house they were careful to brace each step before proceeding. My father will never leave home even for a brief errand without checking all the locks, making sure all the burners on the stove are turned off, patting his pockets to make sure he has his keys, money, identification. My parents assembled the foundation of a quiet middle-class life item after item, year after year, with no decision made hastily, no impulse unsupported—and then they suddenly threw themselves into the wild unknown. It can only have been that the alternatives were worse. There were no jobs in Belgium; the *crise,* for all one knew, might have lasted a decade or more. The Congo was out of the question for many reasons, from the climate to René's experience to a whiff of uncertainty perhaps already detectable. They didn't happen to have intimate acquaintances who had emigrated to gentler and more familiar lands. The best they could do was to equip themselves for the alien shore as fully as they could. Those nine crates were a turtle's house: wherever my parents were, they would erect a Belgium around themselves. Nevertheless, as I examine all the available evidence and weigh the alternatives and try to look at the veiled future through their eyes aged thirty-six and thirty-four years respectively, I am still brought up short. Their decision to emigrate still seems like an act of reckless daring.

For one thing, it is a fact that, however bad things were looking in Belgium, there was no throng making for the exits. My parents knew a few others who had left earlier in the 1950s, mostly headed for the French-speaking areas of Canada, but there had always been a few emigrants in every generation, and the phenomenon was statistically insignificant. Nearly forty years and many huge global changes later, it may sound odd that we already had our green cards in hand before even touching down on American soil. But in the context of the century, the late 1950s represented a lull in worldwide migration, between the movement of displaced persons in the wake of the war, which peaked in the early '50s, and the first stirrings of the global diaspora that began in the 1960s and continues to this day. The world was relatively stable then; people who migrated did so individually rather than in waves. Even the Hungarians who arrived in the United States after the events of 1956 barely registered as a phenomenon. Furthermore, the United States assigned to every country in the world an immigration quota, and Belgium had seldom approached its annual allotment of 1350 (not that it would have occurred to the Department of Immigration and Naturalization to transfer some of those unused Belgian slots to, say, Haitians). We were a shoo-in, although none of these factors could help a foundry colleague of my father's who had applied for a resident visa at the same time we did; his own father had at one time been a member of the Belgian Communist Party, and so he was refused admission.

Belgium, unlike England, Ireland, Scotland, Wales, France, Germany, Italy, Spain, Portugal, Greece, Denmark, Norway, Sweden, Finland, even the Netherlands, even Switzerland, had never sent large numbers of immigrants to find their destinies in the American wilderness. There were, it is true, early settlers from the future Belgium, mostly Huguenots who arrived on Dutch boats in the seventeenth century in the place whose seal was oddly enough inscribed "Nova Belgica." As previously noted, it is the opinion of many modern historians that the Walloons under Peter Minuit, who pulled off the first real-estate swindle in New York City's history by obtaining Manhattan from its original owners for a price traditionally rendered as twenty-four dollars, were mostly Picards from the Aisne, then part of the Spanish Netherlands but later part of France. Be that as it may, nationalities were much more fluid in the seventeenth century (as they continued to be until World War I; passports and visas are an invention of our era), and the Low Countries, although separately governed, were culturally mingled in many ways. It is just about impossible to differentiate Dutch and Flemish migrants to the new world, for instance, and while it is certain that Walloons from the lower five provinces were among the original settlers of New Amsterdam and the lower Hudson Valley, the specifics of numbers and names are murky.

It may be that Corlear's Hook, the jutting hip of Manhattan's Lower East Side, owes its name to someone originally called Corlier, and that the name of Brooklyn's brackish

Gowanus Canal is a heavily Dutchified rendition of that of the Brabant village Ohain, where there were people called Minuit in the sixteenth century, and that the Delano family, Franklin Roosevelt's mother's side, began its lineage in Tournai as De Lanoy. It has even been alleged that the Roosevelts themselves were originally Walloons called Martin, whose later appellation was derived from their farm, Rose Field, on the East River shore (one of its boundary roads continued to be called Roosevelt Street until it was erased by the building of the Alfred E. Smith Houses in the 1950s). This speculation is the work of Robert Goffin, a native of Ohain and a prolific writer who among other things served as Louis Armstrong's earliest (if unreliable) biographer. His book *De Pierre Minuit aux Roosevelt: L'Épopée Belge aux États-Unis* (1943) is a rather single-minded and sometimes tendentious work that attempts to claim a Walloon heritage in America to rival that of the Mayflower colonists. Its very premise may seem idle today, but it is not without a certain poignancy, given that Goffin wrote the book in exile in New York City in the early years of the Nazi occupation of Belgium. His work also capped a small pile of similar works, such as William E. Griffis's *The Story of the Walloons* (1923) and Henry G. Bayer's *The Belgians: First Settlers in New York* (1925), that were spurred both by the 1924 tricentenary of the Walloon landing in Manhattan and by the great rush of American feeling for Brave Little Belgium in the First World War.

Sentimentality and wishful thinking aside, there are indeed Belgian traces left from those early settlements. Hoboken is a suburb of Antwerp; Kortright, New York, was christened after Kortrijk, in West Flanders; the Wallkill River's name means "Walloon stream," and Wallabout and Walloonsac have similar etymologies. The black-robe Louis Hennepin, the first European to see Niagara Falls and to set foot on the future site of Minneapolis, hailed from Ath, and his colleague Luc Buisset from Charleroi. After Belgium's annexation by the Dutch and then its independence in 1830, sporadic clusters of immigrants arrived in America: 104,000 between 1820 and 1910; 62,000 from 1910 to 1950; roughly 10,000 from 1950 to the mid-'70s. The grand total is smaller than the number of French people living in the United States in 1860, and a mere tenth the number of Irish immigrants in place that same year. The anecdotes are sketchy. An outpost called Nouvelle-Liége sprang up in Missouri, but its trace was already lost by 1833. Wavelets from the province of Luxembourg arrived throughout the 1830s, '40s, and '50s, in Ohio, New York, Iowa, Illinois, Minnesota, and in Boyle County, Kentucky. In the 1840s settlers from the region around Arlon and Florenville established a town called Leopold just north of the Ohio River in Indiana; in 1880 it held 200 Walloon families. Twin colonies appeared in 1848 in Elk County, Pennsylvania: New Brabant, its capital New Brussels, and New Flanders, its capital Leopoldsburg—they do not seem to have lasted long. The industry around Pittsburgh attracted immigrants who founded towns called Charleroi, Floreffe, and Philippeville. Flemings apparently preferred the industry of Detroit, where in the early 1960s the *Gazette van Detroit* was still published and a Flemish radio show was still broadcast on Sunday mornings. Smaller Belgian communities also arose in Providence and in Paterson, New Jersey.

The largest concentration of Walloon immigrants arrived beginning in 1853 from the region around Grez-Doiceau in Brabant and settled in Door, Brown, and Kewaunee Counties, Wisconsin, where they founded such villages as Belgium, Luxemburg, Brussels, Namur, Walhain, Rosiere, San Sauveur, Tonet, and Misere. Their leader was a man named François Pétiniot, who in a café in Antwerp had found a pamphlet, printed in Dutch, proclaiming that land in America could be bought for $1.25 an acre. His family and nine others promptly boarded the S.S. *Quennebec* and sailed from Antwerp to New York. They met some Hollanders aboard who were headed for Wisconsin and decided to join them, traveling by train via Milwaukee to Sheboygan. There they encountered a French Canadian who advised them to go on to Green Bay, where there were French speakers, but they continued past it up the peninsula, an appropriately icicle-shaped spike poking into Lake Michigan, because they heard of a Belgian priest, Édouard Daems, who was preaching in a place called Bay Settlement. Their first encampment was at Robinsonville, later called Aux Premiers Belges, eventually Champion. Waves followed in 1856 and 1857, although one ship was wrecked at sea with all hands lost, and epidemics of cholera and dysentery decimated the settled population.

Even though their towns are just a few miles north of places called Poland, Pilsen, and Denmark, the Walloons of the peninsula remain to this day an ethnically distinct community. Their first chronicler, Hjalmar Rued Holand, wrote in 1933 that they "are a people of rather short but very stocky frame with black hair and brown eyes. About 20% have blue eyes. . . . Their most noticeable characteristic is their friendly, convivial disposition." He describes them as garrulous beer drinkers, who "anathematized" Prohibition. Indeed, in the nineteenth century at least, the kermesse (locally spelled *kermiss*) went on three days a week for six weeks. "The Belgians read very little," Holand continues, "finding their intellectual stimulation in social gatherings." Today their descendants bear surnames like Quartemont, Dhuey, Jeanquart, Wautlet, Lampereur, attached to such first names as Elmer, Mildred, Lyle, Gladys, Homer. They eat Belgian Pie and something called Chicken Boyoo (which probably derives from *waterzooie*), and foregather in Namur at the Belgian-American Club, and sponsor annual tours of Belgium, and receive numerous visitors from Grez-Doiceau. The old-timers still speak some Walloon and sing Walloon songs (the first letter I got from club president Harry Chaudoir, Sr., was sealed with a yellow-and-red sticker reading *"Walons: Tortos por onk, onk po tortos,"* all for one and one for all, in the dialect of the other Namur), but, significantly, do not tend to know French.

Among individual Belgians who crossed the ocean in search of a better life, the most redoubtable, or at least the one whose activities are best documented, was Jean-Nicolas Perlot, from Herbeumont in the province of Luxembourg, who in 1850 made his way to California to join the Gold Rush. He failed to strike it rich, but after many adventures set himself up in Portand, Oregon, as a successful truck farmer. In 1867 he returned to Herbeumont, dollars in pocket, to fetch himself a wife. Duly spliced, he went back to Portland with fifteen Ardennais in tow. Once he had succeeded in finding jobs for all of them, he considered his changing situation. His farm lay within the city limits, and the city's rapid growth was encroaching on the conditions required for agriculture. On the verge of fifty, he felt too old to cut himself a new path in the American wilderness. On the other hand, his domain was now worth a fortune. He sold out, and he and his bride returned to Belgium to live in high style. He thus exemplifies the Belgian dream: to come home to the village after a ritual ordeal in terra incognita, equipped with a bankroll and a fund of stories.* His memoir, published just before his death in 1897, was an immediate best-seller and remains in print to this day. With its rollicking style and colorful tales of bold exploits in the deserts and mountains it became Belgium's answer to Fenimore Cooper and Jack London (and, the jacket copy alleges, Mayne Reid), a Western that Walloons could call their own.

Among the unsung remainder were farmers who fled in times of blight (the period of the Gold Rush was coincidentally one of these), former soldiers eager for the recruitment bounty posted by the Union during the Civil War, miners and factory laborers who imagined that at least they could collect better pay for such jobs on the other side of the water. I imagine a Belgian family arriving by wagon, sometime toward evening, in a semi-populated clearing called Bug Jump or Fly Dope, where ship-board rumor had it the potatoes grew to the size of cabbages and the cabbages to the size of boulders, and pitching a lean-to on the bramble-choked forty acres they had bought in the lobby of a New York hotel from an affable but unduly back-slapping land agent who spoke an odd sort of French, and unhitching the spavined horse they had acquired at the depot in the nearest railroad town three hundred miles away, and setting down what remained of their possessions after the unaccountable loss of two barrels in the ship's hold and a trunk vanished at the rail-head in Jersey City along with the friendly countryman who had volunteered to watch it while they bought their tickets. They have traversed six or seven Belgiums just to get from the

---

* Compare the story of Henri-Joseph Delilez, born in Pepinster in 1745, who hit the road at the tender age of eleven. He made his way to Germany, to Rome, to Vienna, worked (at the textile trade, naturally) in Italy and Carinthia and Moravia. He came home at thirty-two, wrote his memoirs, and settled into a quiet life as a schoolteacher.

port to their new home, and watched as the terrain passed from Campinne to Condroz to Ardenne over and over again, and seen houses standing all by themselves with no villages anywhere nearby, the houses and even the churches—even the train stations and the courthouses—built entirely of wood, which seems to them as rash as if they were made of paper. The days are either extraordinarily hot or extraordinarily cold. The trees are strange, the animals unfamiliar, the birds beyond all reckoning. They wonder if they haven't made a colossal error in coming here, taken the suspiciously unrutted road at the fork, the one that leads to the chasm. As the father tries to build a fire with the soaked available wood, the mother takes the little one by the hand and walks around the accessible part of the property in the deepening dusk. Suddenly her eyes light up. *"Regarde, fifi, un lapin!"* The child claps his hands in glee, scaring the rabbit. He bursts into tears as the white tail disappears into the dark undergrowth. He knows it is running straight into the jaws of a wolf.

All we did, though, was sit for eleven hours, or maybe it was fourteen, aboard a narrow Sabena prop jet, in the sun above the clouds. Just before takeoff the *air-hôtesse* had walked down the aisle with a tray of tiny boxes containing two Chiclets apiece, to relieve pressure on the ears during the ascent; just before landing she would repeat the procedure. At some point I had acquired a zippered flight bag with a shoulder strap and the airline's logo on the side; within were my most important stuffed animals. Despite the clement weather the flight was bumpy, and my father, always upset by motion unless he himself was at the controls, was terribly airsick. My mother clutched my hand and I prayed along with her during both takeoff and landing. My parents had never flown before, either. My father, trying as ever to let his wit buoy him, said something about how I was getting my whooping-cough cure—flying in an airplane allegedly relieved the symptoms—three years late. Sitting directly behind us was a man in a white robe and burnoose, returning from Mecca with a tall metal cylinder that occupied the seat next to him. Apparently it contained holy water, but people joked nervously about it, even in 1959.

Despite its length and its choppiness, the flight was suffused with the glamour of travel, the impression of being accorded an élite privilege. Even the canned air smelled of this rarefied condition, and the potted plants in the departure lounge were imbued with it, and the starched blue uniforms of the flight attendants—their small caps in particular—were its official garb. Dawn became glamorous forever, because it was workaday dawn I first flew over, casting a lordly eye down on the trucks blithely going about their miniature business, and on the tracts of houses waking up each foolishly persuaded of its singularity, and on a whole world of clocks that naively assumed they told the correct time without suspecting that time ran quite differently up where I was. It was the best of all possible circumstances to be in: to gaze upon and savor a perfectly ordered planet, and to be oneself exempt from that order. I could pretend as much with the toylands I ruled, but here above the ground no pretense was required. I almost felt I could waggle my index and cause cars to turn and trains to stop.

That is what the tiny megalomaniac was thinking; for him the trip was a lark, on a grand scale, with no consequences. Denise and Lucien, it can be surmised, felt otherwise. They were adults, which meant that for them any excitement came wrapped in a cold damp towel of anxiety. A few years later, when my head was still oversized, I retrospectively endowed the voyage with a ruling myth: The Flight into Egypt. My parents, an apt Mary and Joseph, were smuggling the small blue-and-white-garbed prophet away from the depredations of Herod. Adapting an illustration from some catechism, I imagined us camping in the sand by the side of a fallen pharaonic head, our donkey (he and his descendants thereafter bearing the cross on the spot where the saddle is placed) parked by a low wall. This fantasy was supported by the fact that our mission was always intended to be temporary. I knew that we would be listening for the call telling us that Herod was dead, or the factories had reopened, and that we could return unto Galilee. The notion that my parents were suffering on my behalf was not purely my invention, either.

We landed, passed through customs and immigration, were met and driven to the New Jersey hills; I remember none of it. I suppose we must have passed through Manhattan, since in those days before the Verrazano Bridge there was no other feasible way of crossing the Hudson, but I have no dazzling memories of my first view of skyscrapers. Instead I was preoccupied with seeing American television, especially since Jeanne Dosquet had told me about the *Mickey Mouse Club,* undoubtedly after spotting a copy of *Mickey,* the weekly collection of Carl Barks strips in translation, among my personal effects. I know that when we got to the Dosquet apartment, four rooms in a rambling Victorian pile in a part of town that had seen much better days, all I wanted to do was to see the show right away. My experience with television was minimal; I thought that whatever show you wanted to watch would start when you turned on the set. When I eventually did see the show I was bitterly disappointed anyway. Animation was restricted to the opening credits, and those prancing teenagers with their ear wigs, so stupid they had to wear their names in big letters on their shirts, did not approximate any idea I had of fun. Television failed to captivate me, and in those early days seemed like an adult experience and so barely comprehensible, but it had its moments. Although I had no interest in soap operas, I loved their credit sequences, which were terrifying: the circling globe and rumbling baritone of *As the World Turns*, the thunderstorm and screaming organ crescendo of the *Loretta Young Show*. I was hypnotized, mysteriously, by a program called *Continental Miniatures*, quarter-hour snippets of opera in creakingly low-rent productions, in the middle of the afternoon, with commercials in Italian for Progresso products. This could not have appeared any stranger to me than the rest of the stuff that was on, or for that matter what lay outside the door.

But since I did not exactly have a fund of experiences to measure the new ones against, everything to me was pretty much cake. My parents, on the other hand, had suddenly been handed an entirely new life, without benefit of operating instructions. An important aspect of the initial premise had been that my father could easily get a job at the Summit plant of the Swiss pharmaceutical giant Ciba (later Ciba-Geigy), which employed the Dosquets. (Pol was in charge of the laboratory research animals. For Easter that year I was presented with a flock of tiny yellow chicks; the following day they were whisked off.) As it turned out, Ciba had no openings, and the only job my father could get at first was as a grounds maintenance assistant, mowing lawns and trimming hedges, at the chemical research firm Celanese, which paid $1.37 per hour— $54.80 a week, or roughly fifty bucks after taxes. Somehow my parents managed to stretch this sum to cover rent and groceries, and even send money home to my grandparents, for mortgage payments and then some. The Celanese plant was a good three miles from the apartment, now our apartment, since the Dosquets had bought a house. My father walked. My parents established their household, buying odds and ends of furniture at the local Salvation Army outlet. The nine packing cases finally arrived; they had been roughly handled, and many of their contents, including nearly all the crystal stemware, had been smashed.

My father got the job at Celanese by telling the personnel department at the Summit plant that he had been sent there by the Celanese office in Newark. It was a small fib, but it worked, and anyway he actually had presented himself at the Newark office and been told about the Summit job. After he started working he continued his frequent trips to personnel offices and employment agencies in Newark, sometimes accompanied by my mother and me. My mother, who wore white gloves on these excursions, on Erie Lackawanna trains whose coaches, with their rattan seats and smeared windows, dated back to before World War I (they were still running those trains a decade later, when I commuted on them to high school in New York City), remembers how her face was always streaked with tears mingled with dirt. My father could, with some effort, make himself understood in English, but he was nowhere near fluent. He was a quick study, and he recalled enough of his lessons from more than twenty years earlier, however flawed they had been—he was always throwing in inappropriate Teutonic aspirates. But people very often heard an accent and fixated upon it without listening to the sense of what he was saying. And anyway the response was the same everywhere: having worked in management he was overqualified for mere labor, but his lack of formal education made him underqualified for management.

Those journeys to the Gothic, smogbound city of Newark produced a lasting twilight horror that I can feel to this day amid the bright chrome and plastic fittings of New Jersey Transit trains when they make their stop at Broad Street on their way to Summit. I hear the conductor's cry of *"Nyuuurk!"* as the carriage crosses the Passaic River toward the array of hulking, midsized gray office buildings curving off to the left along its bank, and my first solid impression of America returns: venetian blinds, cheap suits, pen-and-pencil sets, ersatz-pine paneling, thick plastic eyeglass frames, lacquered beehive hairdos, refinery-equipment calendars, dented green filing cabinets, dented brown wastepaper baskets, names painted in gold on frosted-glass doors, cracked linoleum floors, sweating elevator operators in undersized uniforms, luncheonettes, cigar stores, loading docks, pawn shops, bars with names like Alibi and Escapade and tiny rectangular windows, delivery entrances lit by bare bulbs, glittering pavements made of concrete mixed with ground glass, men selling neckties and windup toys out of briefcases mounted on legs, men selling tabloids from stacks weighed down with bricks, blind men selling pencils, men with jackhammers tearing up asphalt, the sound of jackhammers and sirens and car horns and car radios, the smell of hot asphalt and exhaust and grease and the smoke from smelters and refineries and the rotten-egg smell of sulphur.

*Pôves pitits mimbes du Diu,** I find myself thinking, as if I were the father of my parents, watching them trudge around that wasteland, tear-streaked and footsore and increasingly without hope. The search was never-ending, America an endless web of streets all of which came to dead ends. Everyone

---

* Poor little limbs of God; Walloon idiom.

gave my father cheap advice: In order to get a job you already
need to have a job; In America it's not what you know but who
you know; You can't afford to be modest; Honesty isn't worth
balls. It was the era of the Organization Man, of upward mobility, of three-martini lunches and sordid motel philandering and
car crashes and fatal heart attacks at forty. New Jersey, between
the hills of Summit and the Hudson River, was an industrial
dead zone wherein lay our destiny. My parents' new friend
Marie-Louise Lenihan put herself out to drive us all over in
search of job prospects and European groceries, all through
those end-of-the-world salt-marsh factory sites and entire
towns built from junk fifty years earlier for immigrants to live
in. All I have to do even now is hear names like Linden,
Carteret, Perth Amboy, and my stomach starts to heave as if I
were sticking in July sun to the Naugahyde backseat of a '52
Chevrolet with played-out shocks. My parents had packed their
crystal and silver, tweed suits and English shoes, only to end
up, most probably, in a rear apartment over a liquor store in
some burg like Elizabeth or Rahway or Roselle Park, nothing
but sad coughing cars with mismatched doors and buzzing
power plants and two-story asphalt-sided hovels, under a permanently pea-green sky. It was Jemeppe-sur-Meuse all over
again, but in a foreign tongue and with no family and no countryside anywhere around.

And then, one day, somewhere down toward the end of his
rope, my father happened by a small factory in Summit, over
near the railroad tracks, walked in and was hired on the spot.
The Ethylene Corporation—"fluorocarbons" it said at the
bottom of their stationery—made sheeting and tubing of
industrial-grade Teflon. He would be operating extruding
machines, on a rotating shift, at a starting rate of $1.75 an

hour, with a 10 percent night-work bonus; his second week there he was raised to $1.98 an hour. Ethylene was an old-fashioned, paternalistic sort of company, privately owned, with no union and no pension plan, although the boss wouldn't lay anyone off during lean periods, but kept the workforce busy doing things like painting the walls. The force was a bomber-crew mix: war veterans of Irish and Italian and German extraction, family men and drunks, and immigrants from Puerto Rico, England, Alabama, Russia, strivers and losers. The rotating shift was a trial—a week of day work followed by a week of evening work followed by a week of night work, and then back again. It was hard labor in a brutally noisy shed that was exceedingly hot all year round, and the ambient powdered polymer could not have been good for anyone's health; workers stupid enough to smoke on the shop floor were apt to get bits of it on their cigarettes, and then they would turn green and have to be excused for the day.

But it was a solid, decent job with a future, in a pleasant town with trees and good schools and well-kept shops. We had lucked out. We moved into a better apartment, having been all but ejected from the first because the landlord wished to save on heating costs and so didn't want women and children hanging around the place during the day. And then suddenly, in the autumn, the call came. My father's boss from the foundry in Belgium had opened a plant for the manufacture of scales, and he was offering my father a job at a good salary. So the grand emigration experiment came to a close, after eight months. We had gotten a taste of the U.S. of A. With Marie-Louise, born of the Antwerp bourgeoisie but married to an American merchant seaman, we had sped down the futuristic Garden State Parkway, attended a rodeo with bona fide cowboys, taken the sun on

New Jersey's beaches and tasted their pounding surf (my mother wrote to her mother that "the journey of 1½ hours was long for *pauvre petit Luc,* who was sick four times on the way down," but "I assure you we had a good time, we almost thought we were in Le Coq"). We had visited the great city of New York, taking in its touristic staples (*"petit* Luc climbed like an angel all the way to the top of the statue"). We had seen how the other half lived when we were invited by a Belgian couple who worked as caretakers of an estate in Tuxedo Park, New York, to a party when their employers were away—I fell asleep on a pile of furs. We had shopped in supermarkets so vast nobody in Belgium would believe it. We had laughed at the way Americans talked through their noses, had sneered at what they considered food, had marveled at how American women casually wore slacks, even shorts, even in town. There would be plenty to remember in the years ahead.

The nine crates were repacked and sent on their way, and my parents booked passage for us via the cheapest mode of transport, on a Belgian freighter, the S.S. *Tervaete,* bound for Rotterdam from Pier 14 in the Port of New York (its site now lies somewhere under Battery Park City). The day of our departure we took a farewell tour of Manhattan by bus. It was Halloween, although we didn't know what that was. Children ran through the streets wearing masks. There were clusters of them along Sixth Avenue, a whole tribe in the little triangular park at Thirty-fourth Street, in front of Gimbel's, tiny hoodlums in zippered windbreakers wearing the faces of Frankenstein and Bozo the Clown. I was dazzled and frightened by New York. The scale of the place made me queasy. In front of Grand Central Station I nearly lost my balance looking up. Along Forty-second Street were movie theaters decked out in massive cutout color blowups of monsters and strippers and giant words dripping ice or blood. My mother made me keep my head turned away, although I surreptitiously peered sideways, and caught one image that lingered inexplicably: a cowboy smoking a cigarette right through the bandanna that covered the lower half of his face.

The boat followed the New Jersey coast and rounded Cape May, then ascended the Delaware River to Camden, where it took on cargo. We visited Philadelphia, where to our slack-jawed astonishment crews were hanging Christmas decorations from the lampposts—on All Saints' Day! There were only two other passengers on the boat besides us. We ate our meals with the captain, although my poor father hardly touched a morsel during the whole twelve days. It was even hard to sleep, because the suitcases slid out from under the beds and banged across the cabin all night long. I myself was supremely unconcerned. I was the pet of the crew, who showed me every gear, every screw, every pump, and took me to the bridge to watch a whale spout, and let me help myself to ice-cold Cokes from the walk-in refrigerator belowdecks. I was experiencing a boy's own adventure, bound in boards and illustrated in color. None of my friends would ever be able to top it.

XIII Gloss

But somehow we were right back in New Jersey three months later. I don't remember what happened. My memory shows us disembarking at the port of Rotterdam, where customs agents seized some oranges the crew had given me as a parting gift, and made my father fill out all kinds of paperwork. Then we boarded a train, my mother holding me up on her lap as we passed through multicolored fields of tulips (although there could not have been any tulips in *November*). There follows a lapse, after which I see us aboard the S.S. *United States*, bound west from Le Havre, sitting down to a meal with our assigned tablemate, a crusty midwestern retiree who looked like one of Grant Wood's Daughters of the American Revolution and whom my mother described as *"verte comme la justice"* (green as justice; I'm not certain the phrase is even idiomatic, but it's what I remember). The boat was big. The tourist-class dining room was vast, and if I remember correctly had more tables on an open mezzanine level above. The rest is fog.

My parents are able to account for the lapse. According to them, my maternal grandparents were not thrilled to see us, or rather were not amused by our taking over most of the house that was still nominally ours, or rather were not enchanted by the prospect of my father's encroaching upon their turf. My grandmother blamed my father for everything that went wrong, which included every time I couldn't fall asleep and every single time I cried, which was apparently often, and she made a point of scheduling the evening meal for half an hour before he was due home from work. The situation was tense. I imagine I blocked out all memory of this period because I loved my grandmother, who doted on me, and I loved my father, and the conflict between them was more than I could process. My father's new job was a good one, though, and had it not been for my grandparents' antagonism, we would have remained in Belgium for keeps.

Instead my father borrowed twenty thousand francs (a big four hundred dollars in those days) from Armande, and we left again, just under a year after our first exodus, traveling by train from Pepinster to Le Havre, changing at Liège and again at Paris. The ship's photographer caught us as we walked toward the ramp. My father wears his black Jean Bart fedora, the kind you could fold up, stick in your pocket, and restore to its shape with a flick of the wrist (anathema on whomever stole it from me during college), and has our tickets in hand. My mother wears an interesting 1960 cross between a cloche and a pillbox and carries the leather Gladstone bag containing our small necessaries. Her other hand clutches mine tight. I am wearing a pale yellow knit cowl and a short coat I seem to think was of brown loden and a pair of ankle-high lace-up boots—the kinds of clothes only European kids wore in that time before transatlantic homogenization—and carefully support the belly of a vulgar stuffed animal, a blob with long trailing ears, you couldn't even tell whether it was supposed to be a dog or a donkey or a rabbit. Some relative (and it wasn't my grandmother; she had *taste*) had given it to me just before we left. I despised it, but I was dutiful. My eyes are duly cast down *(sage comme une image);* my mother seems motored by grim determination; my father looks tired but game.

We stayed with Marie-Louise for a while. Her husband, Bob, a very kind man who looked the part of an old salt and whom I soon conflated with the host of Cappy Dick's Fun Page in the Sunday color supplement of the *Newark Evening News,* had recently died in the Union County V.A. Hospital. We all mourned him deeply. He had been an indispensible guide, had taken us on jaunts to the then-rural middle of Staten Island, where he knew Italian farmers who grew leeks, which were unobtainable in supermarkets, and he had once taken my father on a memorable bar-crawl, to sailors' joints that still had free-lunch counters. Marie-Louise distracted herself from her widowhood by working long hours as a nurse's aide in addition to caring for her aged mother and devoting herself to her animals, who were everywhere: the collie Jimmy and his old mother, Souske, the small black-and-brown mutt Pijke (whose name significantly rhymed with that of my heroine Laika, the first dog in space), the white mare Stardust and the little roan pony, and any number of cats, as well as a loquacious parakeet. The beasts were friendly and unfettered, with distinct personalities and roles: Stardust was clearly the queen, and commanded deference, while Jimmy was as much a gentle figure of authority as any of the human adults. Marie-Louise lived in Westfield, which was quite suburban, but her spread was big enough to accommodate a barn for the horses, who peaceably grazed on the lawn.

My father got his job back at Ethylene, and soon we had moved into an apartment in Westfield, in a big house with a front porch. The town, like Summit, had been a prosperous suburb for a century; it had splendid, well-tended parks and a genteel business district. We were easing ourselves into America. This time around it was less shocking, less desperate, we could take our time getting acclimated. The spirit of adventure that had been obscured by anxiety and disappointment now returned. We were eager, amused, ironic—we were on more than a holiday, but were nevertheless tourists. We could preserve our detachment because despite the trouble back in Pepinster, we were still in the United States only temporarily, notching *un stage* on our belts. When the entity that held the mortgage on our house in Belgium began sniffing around, investigating whether my parents might have surreptitiously rented out the property, in contravention of contract, and suggesting that it might demand immediate full payment of the balance owed, my father fired back a reply:

> To effect a complete understanding of the situation, it is necessary that I establish the full historical account of the relevant facts, in order that you may judge for yourselves the grounds on which my position rests. Having lost my position in 1958, as a result of the shutting down of the enterprise that employed me, and, owing to the recession, being unable to find another job, I found myself obliged to accept an offer of employment abroad (in the U.S.A., to be exact). This decision has presented me with diverse problems. My sojourn in the U.S.A. (of a professional nature, let me emphasize) being but temporary, I naturally wish to preserve my house for that time when my current obligations will have been fulfilled. Moreover, since the distances involved do not permit continual transit, I could not without prejudice to the proper upkeep of the house and its dependencies keep the house closed in the intervals between my visits, and so I begged Monsieur and Madame E. NANDRIN, my parents-in-law, to supervise its upkeep,

and in order to facilitate this authorized them to reside in my house during my absence, without fee or charge of any kind. . . .

Given the professional and temporary nature of this sojourn in the U.S.A., there could be no question of contravention, considering that our legal address remains 86, rue Alfred Brabant, Pepinster, and that furniture, clothing, and sundry possessions belonging to us remain permanently in the house, and that since our departure we have returned to dwell in the house in 1959, in 1960, and expect to do so again in 1962, all the while anticipating our definitive return. . . .

To forestall any further questions, permit me to add that it should be evident that if our intention were not to return to Belgium, it would be much more advantageous for us to direct those sums that are currently devoted to payments on and upkeep of the house toward investment opportunities in the U.S.A. instead. Furthermore, it is barely understandable that I should have to defend myself, since the charge is that rather than collecting unemployment insurance and requesting incessant extensions of my payment schedule, I have instead sought work under any circumstance and chosen to meet my obligations.

"To effect a complete understanding of the situation, it is necessary that I establish the full historical account of the relevant facts, in order that you may judge for yourselves the grounds on which my position rests . . ." The phrase echoes. It might be the opening line of something, some panorama of self-justification (this one, perhaps). My father may present the situation in a somewhat grander light than it warrants (that offer of employment, those investment opportunities), but he does not actually lie. He is addressing a body of unknown worthies attached to the government, the Intercommunale de Crédit au Logement de l'arrondissement de Verviers, presumably seated at a long table in a paneled room under portraits of sundry Leopolds. He is fluent in their mandarin tongue. He is a man of the world, drawn by adverse circumstances into a situation which, while somewhat embarrassing, you can certainly understand, not that it would be likely to happen to any of you gentlemen, granted, but . . . In the last sentence he rises from his chair, impassioned, his face taking on color.

Actually, he composes it on a borrowed typewriter, with an annoying QWERTY keyboard and lack of accent marks, at the kitchen table, on his day off, perhaps with a stemmed goblet of orange Kool-Aid by his elbow, as in one of the photographs taken to impress relatives with the splendor of our material appointments. My father is a mere prop for showing off the refrigerator, and my mother displays the range as well as the expandable Formica-topped kitchen table with its tapered steel legs. I, meanwhile, am set wriggling in the tub in the gleaming bathroom. The Westfield house has those featureless white walls of new apartment conversions everywhere. All I remember now is the window that gave out onto a bit of roof, where metal boxes of frozen strawberries were set out to thaw.

We got ourselves a car, a stately blue '53 Buick with a radiator grille that looked like two rows of whale teeth. We frequented an enormous supermarket that called itself Bardy Farms and displayed a large molded cow's head in poignant commemoration of what its recent construction had displaced. There we inspected, debated, and experimentally purchased

American foodstuffs—Velveeta cheese, for example, which came in yellow coffin-shaped boxes and tasted more like the product of a laboratory than of a cow. We tried to find our own food, rarely with success, and flirted with substitutes. Cottage cheese, ricotta, and even sour cream were auditioned as stand-ins for the farmer cheese called *makée*, none very successfully, although in German pork stores in Union and Irvington we did locate *sirop*, a dense concentrate of apples and pears that is the color and texture of heavy-gauge motor oil and is spread on bread (*sirop* and *makée* together compose *caca de poule*). In place of *eau gazeuse*, we had to make do with sodium-laden club soda, being far from the seltzer belt, and *bière de table* could be faintly impersonated by Piel's. After gagging on Wonder we found that a reasonable facsimile of bread could be obtained from Italian bakeries, although their pastry was strictly, in my mother's phrase, *grosse cavalerie*. The produce department was the greatest disappointment. Not only had no one ever heard of chervil, but the tomatoes and the apples were oversized and tasteless, the potatoes were mealy, the apricots were dull and hard. And, mystifyingly, Americans seemed to go for pale, drab iceberg lettuce, distinguished by its total absence of any flavor. (Little did my parents suspect that iceberg lettuce would later find its way into Belgian markets and sit alongside tomatillos and jicamas in the bins devoted to exotic vegetables.)

We visited parks, where we undertook picnics in our European style, with rolls and cheese, as barbecues sizzled around us and the odor of grilled flesh mingled with the sound of Curt Gowdy's amiable undertone in running commentary on the Yankees wafting out of radios of cars parked up on the grass. We visited Wild West City and Fairy Tale Castle and Santa Claus Land and Washington's Morristown headquarters and

the adjacent Fort Nonsense and various petting zoos. I particularly liked a forlorn place near Gillette that had once supplied
animals for Hollywood movies but had gone into decline; besides a handful of aged goats and retired horses it featured the
grave of the MGM lion (I cried a little), as well as a significant
portion of the HMS *Bounty*, from the 1935 production. I also
liked the old Bertrand Island amusement park on Lake Hopatcong, a relic preserved from the ice-cream-suit era, down to its
wooden roller coaster and its penny arcade, with Mutoscope
machines that dispensed pictures of forgotten cowboy stars. On
the other hand, I had to suffer through ritual visits to model
homes. Those empty houses, with their generic furnishings,
had a smell of formaldehyde about them. I think my parents
searched them for clues to the home lives of the Americans, but
they seemed more like decoys, traps set out for unsuspecting
humans by some cunning anthropophagic species.

America in those days was trying to achieve a gleaming,
diamond-hard, aerodynamic surface. You weren't supposed to
notice the past that stood all around you in any three-story
brick downtown, but concentrate instead on the stylized neon
and the harsh lights reflected off the hoods of long, low, wide
automobiles. The air was filled with authoritative baritone an-
nouncers and string orchestras playing glissando swooshes and,
when you drove down residential streets in the evening, the ric-
ochets of Winchester rifle bullets echoing from Philco to
Zenith. Diesel fuel and suntan lotion and hairspray and asphalt
softening in the sun made up an acrid, poison-sweet perfume
along the roads and in the parking lots. Women wore their hair
up and showed their teeth, and men wore short, tight gray suits
and grunted by way of conversation. They took off their
stingy-brim hats to mop their crew cuts; cops' short-sleeved

uniform shirts were drenched three inches around the armpits. We were on the road and it was mercilessly hot. I was carsick and thirsty and wanted fun, more of it all the time, and I got fooled again and again by those strings of multicolored pennants along the highways, always thinking a carnival lay ahead but it was always a used-car lot. Sometimes at night I'd catch a glimpse of a drive-in movie along the side of the road, and my mother would tell me not to look, but if I wanted to defy her she couldn't stop me; once as we were pulling out of the parking lot of a discount store on Route 22 I watched Samson snap his chains and lumber over to a set of pillars and push out with both arms. And between the big, wide, loud, shiny things were zones of crabgrass and plywood shacks and Quonset huts and piles of automobile cadavers and here and there an old farmhouse.

We were entranced and baffled by all of it. We were picking up the language piece by piece. We knew just enough to laugh at the hyperbole. Everything was "new"; every jar lid said, "New! Twist-Off Cap," in 1959, and most continued to say it three or four years later. Everything was the World's Biggest: linoleum showroom, discount tire warehouse, indoor lighting display, selection of shoes for the whole family. Shopkeepers along 22 in particular did not stint themselves. That was, after all, the site of the Flagship, a large, literally boat-shaped building that had perhaps begun life as a nightclub but by now sold cheap suits with incongruous flamboyance. Anybody could open up a four-thousand-square-foot single-story shed and proclaim The Lowest Appliance Prices in the Universe, hardly expecting someone to come along and challenge the assertion. Nothing could have been farther from the Belgian mentality of the time, which prized understatement of the British sort, such

as calling a thirty-bedroom mansion a "cottage"; if you owned
Macy's, you'd say you had "a little shop downtown."

British understatement was as much a part of our cultural
equipment as Harris tweed and chocolate-bar wrappers illustrated with pictures of the Coldstream Guards. I had pail-
and-shovel sets and watercolor tins that featured images of
rosy-cheeked little children in idealized seashore or countryside
or village surroundings. Their vision of apple-pie order and
their primary-color schemes were somehow immediately iden-
tifiable as British, maybe because Belgians had a darker out-
look, so that our kind of saccharine was more halfhearted, if
not flat-out vulgar. For that matter, my parents' principal guide
to the English language then, the 1945 edition of a conversation
manual entitled *L'Anglais sans peine* (English without toil),
published by the Assimil firm of Paris and Brussels, was entirely British in its vocabulary and references. This volume is
sufficiently embedded in francophone consciousness that you
can still raise a snicker by quoting its opening phrase, "My tailor is rich." (A panel by the Belgian cartoonist Benoît van Innes
shows a European conceptual artist preparing an installation at
the Whitney; peering at an open book, he is writing on the wall:
"My tailor is rich.") The book, distinguished by its dry humor
("Waiter, I have often eaten better fish than this, I must say."
"That may be, sir, but not here"), could not have been much
help, since its frame of reference was so thoroughly alien to the
America of the 1960s: "The Smiths had wired ahead the time of
their arrival, and were expected for lunch at Fairview." This
was also true of my parents' other principal textbook, a reader
called *Short Narratives*, published in Ghent: "The proprietor of
an eating-house ordered some bills to be printed for his window, with the words, 'Try our mutton pies!'"

Imagine, if you will, earnest French speakers rehearsing

their exercises, studiously following the Assimil pronunciation guide: "Iz shî bioùtifoul? Shî iz not bioùtifoul beutt shî iz in'ter-estign'e." It's a wonder my parents could make themselves understood at all. Their circle of acquaintances was almost en-tirely Belgian. Besides the Dosquets there were Marie-Louise and her mother and her sisters Bie, married to an Englishman, and Hilda, married to another Fleming. There weren't a lot of Belgians around, of course, and such French people as one en-countered tended, it was said, to be unapproachably snotty. My mother kept an ear cocked everywhere, in supermarkets, on trains, in the city, poised to pick up those drawled French vow-els, those aspirate *h*'s that were the Walloon signature. Now and then, at long intervals, she found a candidate, maybe a student or an au pair; some of those have remained their friends. In the early sixties, though, the pursuit of other Belgians was more than a casual interest. It was a lifeline. It was like finding other humans in the jungle. Just the opportunity to compare notes, to take *une tasse de café* and palaver about nothing much, to recre-ate a corner of your world on alien soil and pretend that life was normal, to watch television with others of your kind and pool your comprehension of the arcana on display—it was meat and drink. My mother seized upon any French word in ad-vertisements (more often than not misspelled or misused), any French-sounding name, any rumor of Belgianness. One half of the Vegas lounge duo Sandler and Young turned out to be Bel-gian, and my mother became an instant fan. The Singing Nun was Belgian—need I say more? By contrast, television news-casters were judged according to their perceived degree of friendliness toward the Belgians when reporting on the bloody events in the Congo—Robert Trout yes, Charles Collingwood no—and those who failed the test were consigned to perdition.

Marie-Louise and her sisters had a Belgian friend also called

Marie-Louise, who was referred to as Marie-Louise *du facteur* because she had once been married to a mailman. Later I was to get a brief glimpse of her face every time I encountered the phrase "ex post facto," but she had contributed to my burgeoning English vocabulary long before. One evening, while we were all watching television, Cesar Romero appeared on the screen; "Such a handsome man!" Marie-Louise exclaimed in English, forever wedding the word "handsome" to the faint but unmistakable impression of Cesar Romero in my mind's eye. I was accumulating a vocabulary from scraps, like a bowerbird. Packaging could be useful or not. I learned "coffee" from a can of Chock Full O'Nuts in our Westfield kitchen, impressed by its insistent doubling of *f*'s and *e*'s. I translated but could not figure out the meaning of the slogan on the Morton's Salt box—"When it rains, it pours"—and its possible significance was further complicated when *Million Dollar Movie* showed *The Rains of Ranchipour* (1955). I was mystified by a local storefront whose shingle read "Jalousies"—how could a shop sell jealousy? We must have spent a lot of time in furniture showrooms, because I compiled a list of near-synonyms I still find confusing: sofa, couch, lounge, divan, settee, chesterfield, davenport, the latter pictured as modernistically curved, owing to conflation with the trademark boomerang shape on the Newport cigarette pack.

The creative spellings indulged in by commerce in the early sixties stumped us: what was "kleen"? "Sta-prest"? "E-Ze-Wash"? "Kwality"? (We did figure out "Sansabelt.") We shopped for years at a place called Sav-On Drugs before realizing that its name had nothing to do with soap, although it took less time to decipher the penguin's invitation on its glass door: "Come in, it's KOOL inside." I never did succeed, though, in cracking the code teasingly advanced by the name Chef Boy-Ar-Dee, whose C-ration canned spaghetti was often a feature of meals in those early years, when everything in the supermarket was a mystery. Pasta packaging actually taught me a useful lesson about the limits of truth, one day when I spotted a box of Buitoni Wagon Wheels emblazoned with the breathless promise: "Inside! Free Lifelike Statuette of U.S. President!" My parents agreed that this would be something to see. We bought the box, took it home, and, still debating the possible meaning of "lifelike," dumped its contents into a bowl. At the top of the heap was an inch-high gray plastic figurine whose tiny pedestal read "Garfield."

I first encountered the American educational system in the spring of 1960, when I was sent to kindergarten for a week. The experience was shocking. I couldn't speak the language, which might have made a difference, but in every other regard felt as if I'd been relegated to an institution for babies, and slow ones at that. There was a scheduled period for drinking milk! And then nap time, when we were urged to prostrate ourselves on green plastic-covered mats on the floor. What could be the point? I was not about to shut my eyes in the company of strangers, anyway. Insulting tests were administered, which measured students' ability to tell time, comb their hair, tie their shoelaces—as if the simplest cretin hadn't mastered such skills years before. My parents were even more critical of these matters than I was. It could hardly be called education, this time-serving nonsense. It might well have been deliberately designed to slow children's progress! You didn't need to be fluent to know that such books as were available were pitched at three-year-old readers—*the cat sat on the mat*—the cat could probably read the book! (My parents were not infallible in their evaluation of reading materials; for years I had to go to friends' houses to read the Dr. Seuss books surreptitiously, because they too were deemed infantile.)

My kindergarten experience was mercifully brief. However, as the summer drew to a close and the prospect of first grade loomed ahead, I became increasingly nervous. Somehow it failed to occur to me that grammar school would necessarily be but an easy step up from what had preceded it. Just before school opened I had a nightmare in which hooded authorities forced me to read and interpret enormous volumes, which I pictured as ancient, crumbling, leatherbound, perhaps written in Old Norse or Aramaic. I'm not sure how I might have devised the image. The fattest book in our house was *Bombes sur Shanghai*, by Vicki Baum, author of *Grand Hotel*, and I actively looked forward to reading it thanks to its lurid jacket; the only leatherbound volume I was likely to be familiar with was the daily missal. Anyway, I needn't have worried. I was in for Dick and Jane and Sally and Spot, quite literally. Reading was not much of a problem, even at first. As it turned out I had amassed quite a number of words, although putting them together into sentences was another matter altogether. My first day of school remains vivid in its discomfort. To begin with, I didn't know how to ask to go to the toilet. In addition, my mother had dressed me in a yellow pullover with a white shirt-collar dickey. It was a warm day, and the nun in charge suggested I take off my sweater. Since I didn't understand, she came over and yanked it off me, revealing my sleeveless undershirt.

But time passed, and I started to immerse myself in English. For a while, though, I would pass through a fugue state lasting an hour or so, a sort of period of decompression between home and school and school and home, during which I could not use either language. My mother tackled the problem by tutoring me in French grammar and vocabulary as soon as I got home. I wasn't crazy about this enforced extension of the school day, and all I can seem to recall of it is my staring fixedly at the mottled black-and-white covers of the composition books we used for the exercises, deliberately making myself dizzy by crossing my eyes and watching the pattern swirl. It was probably valuable, though, especially in conjunction with the issues of *Spirou* I would then rush off to read, when I wasn't spending my time drawing my own wretched cartoons on the reams of inter-office-communication paper my father brought home from work. But the autumn was full of signs and wonders: I saw my first movie at the Rialto, got a glimpse of Richard Nixon on a campaign stop, withstood my and our first hurricane—on the sunny following day there were trees and parts of trees all over the lawns and the sides of the roads. I learned what Halloween was, and posed for the camera in a Robin Hood costume, although I'm not sure my parents went so far as to allow me to go trick-or-treating.

In the late fall we moved back to Summit, to our old apartment and eventually to the two-floor apartment upstairs. It was bigger and much more homelike; indeed for me it quickly overtook any previous notion I had of home. Summit was and remains a pleasant suburban town—technically a city, although few buildings stand as high as four stories. The place was founded in the days when planning really counted, so that it is abundantly stocked with parks, and it is sufficiently rooted and endowed to have warded off strip malls and such assorted high-turnover detritus. When we had been living there a few years I began reading the Hardy Boys books, and also became fascinated with boys' activity books of the interwar period, profusely illustrated and packed with crafts projects, ideas for clubs, and modest moneymaking ventures. The Hardy Boys lived in Bay City, a suburban utopia that seemed to contain one of everything in the known world: a forest, a movie theater, a haunted house, a hill, a railyard, a dark alley, a cave, an office building, a bridge, a newspaper bureau, a field, a nightclub, a barn. The activity books were also set in such a place, an un-named Anytown where, as the pictures showed, you could climb the tree behind the old fence on the hill and look out over the field and across the river, through the smoke rising from the funnel of the boat, at the radio tower and the skyscraper. I was frustrated by this ideal; Summit lacked the orchard, the inlet, the cave; the nightclub, the radio station, the skyscraper. I couldn't earn money delivering sandwiches to offices high above the street, nor could I devise a ten-minute weekly pro-gram of interest to other children.

But I was a malcontent; Summit came close enough to the model. A block from our house in one direction was the for-est—a ragged few acres of saplings, really, but big enough for me—past which lay the railyard. Two blocks away in the other direction was the business district, which contained the dime store, the haberdasher, the bookshop, the grocery, the bakery, the movie theater, the stamp-and-coin shop, the toy store, and so on. Across from the train station was a small string of busi-nesses that in a Hardy Boys way could pass for disreputable: the bar, the diner, the barbershop, the poolroom, the liquor store, the cigar store that sold men's magazines under the counter. With exquisitely commonplace irony, the charm school was sit-uated one flight up and just to the left of this toyland Bowery. The place of business nearest to our house was a penny-candy shop, run by an aged Italian couple, that was dark, slightly dusty, familial, welcoming, untouched by fashion or merchandising, and had a clientele made up exclusively of small children—a preposterous cliché. On my way to school I would walk by the candy store, cross over the railroad bridge, traverse the town green, pass between the YMCA and the post office, and then navigate a two-block section of slightly run-down houses: the slum, whose candy store sold the gory Mars Attacks and Civil War bubble-gum cards my old Italians wouldn't handle. In the spring the green's cherry trees blossomed; in summer the whole town was verdant; in the autumn everything was fragrant with the smell of burning leaves; in winter it all lay under a fleecy white blanket. It seems scarcely credible now. In photographs as well as memory, Summit of the early 1960s looks like an archetype in a *Life* feature, like the native habitat of Dick and Jane. To emigrate to the United States and wind up in such a place was like hitting some kind of jackpot.

Despite our initial fears we were spared tenements, factory towns, hardscrabble, not that this prevented my parents from constantly fearing the disaster that would strike suddenly and break us (it's a fear I've inherited), nor from being inordinately self-conscious about our material status. Summit was a rich town, and we were among its poorer inhabitants. We lived in an apartment; that set us apart right away in a town where, at that time at least, apartments were few. At first, too, my parents couldn't afford those desirable Ethan Allen colonial sets and so had to furnish the place with secondhand items. Here's a photograph of my mother, obviously taken for export purposes, that were it not square and glossy would appear to have been taken in the 1930s: She's feigning a phone call, like an administrator in a high-school yearbook (the telephone is clearly the point of the shot), sitting in a small overstuffed chair with a checked slipcover that makes it look like an oven mitt, her feet resting on the big, threadbare oriental rug with the pattern I spent much time trying to decode. The black Western Electric telephone sits on a radio cabinet smaller than the one we had in Belgium, only about the size of a TV set with a thirty-six-inch screen (measured diagonally), alongside greeting cards (the humorous one is from my father, the others belong to the genus *cute*) and a small bridge lamp with a frilled shade that looks like a can-can dancer's garter. The only Belgian element present, if Belgian it can be considered, is nearly hidden by the cards: the ebony bust of a woman with tubular headdress and artfully chipped ear that René brought back from the Congo.

My parents were shy about their castoffs, and were sensitive about people seeing the inside of our home. They were uneasy about their used car, about their difficulties with the language, about the fact that my father worked in a factory when the fathers of most of my playmates and schoolmates worked in offices. They did not socialize with the other parents, nor with very many Americans beyond a few strays and some immigrants from other lands. They were discreet, circumspect, diffident to a fault, helpful to neighbors—my father was always doing chores for the elderly. Had either of them ever committed a murder, the neighbors would have characterized them on the TV news as "nice, quiet people who kept to themselves." My father was a hard worker, prized by his bosses, who volunteered to countersign bank loans and now and then took him out to dinner at some French joint, where they would solicit his advice on the choice of wines and ask him to repeat the correct pronunciation of their entree selection. My mother eventually went to work, first in the cafeteria of the local high school and then in the executive dining room of the nearby Bell

Laboratories; she once waited on Leopold Stokowski, and once she caught an eminent scientist absent-mindedly putting both milk and lemon into his tea. She, too, was highly thought of.

My parents made certain that the telltale signs of the working class would not show on me. My clothes and my manners were never less than correct. At my first communion, when communicants were required to dress from head to foot in white, I was the only boy wearing black shoes, because all the available white shoes had red rubber soles, which my mother considered vulgar. Once, when my mother was still walking me home from school, she was unavoidably delayed, and she called the nuns and asked them to look after me for half an hour. I was invited into the convent and offered a glass of milk and a large slice of homemade chocolate cake. The cake, perhaps the finest specimen I have ever seen, beckoned to me, but I steadfastly refused it, because I was persuaded that good manners forbade my accepting it. I was prompt with my apologies and my gratitude, however. I always was. Otherwise, I did not readily speak to adults. It may be that I did not readily speak to anyone.

XIV Dummy

In order to speak of my childhood I have to translate. It is as if I were writing about someone else. The words don't fit, because they are in English, and languages are not equivalent one to another. If I say, "I am a boy; I am lying in my bed; I am sitting in my room; I am lonely and afraid," attributing these thoughts to my eight-year-old self, I am being literally correct but emotionally untrue. Even if I submit the thoughts to indirect citation and the past tense I am engaging in a sort of falsehood. I am playing ventriloquist, and that eight-year-old, now made of wood and with a hinged jaw, is sitting on my knee, mouthing the phrases I am fashioning for him. It's not that the boy couldn't understand those phrases. It is that in order to do so, he would have to translate, and that would mean engaging an electrical circuit in his brain, bypassing his heart.

If the boy thought the phrase "I am a boy," he would picture Dick or Zeke from the schoolbooks, or maybe his friends Mike or Joe. The word "boy" could not refer to him; he is *un garçon*. You may think this is trivial, that *"garçon"* simply means "boy," but that is missing the point. Similarly, *maman* and papa are people; "mother" and "father" are notions. *La nuit* is dark and filled with fear, while "the night" is a pretty picture of a starry field. The boy lives in *une maison*, with "a house" on either side. His *coeur* is where his feelings dwell, and his "heart" is a blood-pumping muscle. For that matter, his name is Luc, pronounced *lük;* everybody around, though, calls him "Luke," which is an alias, a mask.

He regards the English language with a curiosity bordering on the entomological. Watching the *Amerloques* moving around in their tongue is like seeing lines of ants parading through tunnels bearing sections of leaves. He finds it funny, often enough. In school, for instance, when nutrition is discussed, the elements of a meal are called "servings," a word that always conjures up images of footmen in clawhammer coats bearing covered dishes. Since he knows that his classmates, however prosperous their parents might be, aren't likely to have servants, he substitutes the familiar advertising icon of Mother entering the room with a trussed turkey on a platter, which is no less alien or ridiculous. He gathers that this scene has some material basis in the lives of Americans, although it appears to him contrived beyond belief. American life, like the English language, is endlessly fascinating and hopelessly phony.

His vantage point is convenient, like a hunter's blind. He has some struggles with the new language—it will be years, for example, before his tongue and teeth can approximate the *th* sound, and in the meantime he will have to tolerate laughter every time he pronounces "third" as "turd"—but at the same time he is protected. No one will ever break his heart with English words, he thinks. It is at home that he is naked. If the world outside the door is a vast and apparently arbitrary game, inside lies the familiar, which can easily bruise or cut him. No, his parents aren't monsters, nothing like that, although they may not appreciate their own power. Anyway, he has raised and nurtured enough monsters by himself to inflict pain without need of assistance. The French language is a part of his body and his soul, and it has a latent capacity for violence. No wonder he has trouble navigating between the languages at first: they are absurdly different, doors to separate and unequal universes. Books might allege they are the same kind of item, like a pig and a goat, but that is absurd on the face of it. One is tissue and the other is plastic. One is a wound and the other is a prosthesis.

Of course, the French language would not be so intimate, wrenching, and potentially dangerous to him if he had remained in a French-speaking world. There he would be bombarded by French of all temperatures, flavors, connotations. His friends, his enemies, his teachers, his neighbors, the newspaper, the radio, the billboards, people on the street, pop songs, movies, assembly instructions, lists of ingredients, shouting drunks, mumbling lunatics, indifferent officials, all would transmit in French. Pretty girls would speak French. He would pick up slang, poesy, academese, boilerplate, specialized jargon, cant, nonsense. He would not only hear French everywhere but absorb it unconsciously all the time. He would learn the kinds of things no dictionary will tell you: for example that apparent synonyms are in reality miles apart, each with its own calluses of association. By and by, *je* would become more than his private self, would find itself shoulder to shoulder with the *je* of a million others. There would be traffic and commerce between inner life and outer world. A great many things would go without saying, be taken for granted. It would seem as though language had arisen from the ground, had always been and would always be.

Instead French festers. It is kept in darkness and fed meagerly by spoonfuls. It isn't purposely neglected, of course; there is nothing intentionally punitive about the way it is sequestered and undernourished. On the contrary: it is cherished, cosseted, rewarded for just being, like an animal in a zoo. But like that animal it can only enact a semblance of its natural existence. Its memory of the native habitat grows sparser all the time, and its attempts at normality become playacting, become parody, become rote. Its growth has been stunted, and it correspondingly retains many infantine characteristics. Even as the boy grows gradually tougher and more worldly in English, he carries around a French internal life whose clock has stopped. He is unnaturally fragile, exaggeratedly sensitive in his French core. Not surprisingly, he resents it, wants to expunge it, destroy it, pour salt on its traces to prevent regeneration.

What does this say about the boy's view of his family circumstances? That is a complicated matter. French is his soul, and it is also a prison, and the same terms could be applied to his family. At home he is alone with his parents; no one else exists. It is stifling and comforting in equal measure. Out in the world he is entirely alone. He is terrified but he is free. Or potentially free, anyway; he's too young to know. But one of the things that sustains him in the world is the knowledge of his French innards. He can feel superior about it (his peers don't possess anything equivalent, and they'll never have any idea what it feels like) but it is simultaneously a source of shame. At home he may be alone with his parents, but while they have an awesome power over his infant core, his growing English self is something they don't know and can't touch. You can take all these propositions as mathematical equations. Work them out, forwards or backwards, and you will always arrive at the same reduction, the same answer: he is alone.

My attempt to put any sort of words in the boy's mouth is foredoomed. He doesn't yet have a language. He has two tongues: one is all quivering, unmediated, primal sensation, and the other is detached, deliberate, artificial. To give a full accounting he would have to split himself in two. But I don't know whether I might not have to do the same myself, here and now. To speak of my family, for example, I can hardly employ English without omitting an emotional essence that remains locked in French, although I can't use French, either, unless I am willing to sacrifice my critical intelligence. But there is an advantage hidden in this predicament: French is an archeological site of emotions, a pipeline to my infant self. It preserves the very rawest, deepest, least guarded feelings.

If I stub my toe, I may profanely exclaim, in English, "Jesus!" But in agony, such as when I am passing a kidney stone, I might cry, *"Petit Jésus!"* with all the reverence of nursery religion. Others have told me that when I babble in feverish delirium or talk aloud in my sleep, I do so in French. Preserved, too, in French, is a world of lost pleasures and familial comforts. If someone says, in English, "Let's go visit Mr. and Mrs. X," the concept is neutral, my reaction determined by what I think of Mr. and Mrs. X. On the other hand, if the suggestion is broached in French, *"Allons dire bonjour, "* the phrasing affects me more powerfully than the specifics. *"Dire bonjour"* calls up a train of associations: for some reason I see my great-uncle Jules Stelmes, dead more than thirty years, with his fedora and his enormous white mustache and his soft dark eyes. I smell coffee and the raisin bread called *cramique,* hear the muffled bong of a parlor clock and the repetitive commonplaces of chitchat in the drawling accent of the Ardennes, people rolling their *r*'s and leaning hard on their initial *h*'s. I feel a rush-caned chair under me, see white curtains and a starched tablecloth, can almost tap my feet on the cold ceramic tiles, maybe the trompe l'oeil pattern that covered the entire floor surface of my great-uncle Albert Remacle's farmhouse in Viville. I am sated, sleepy, bored out of my mind.

The triggers that operate this mechanism are the simplest,

humblest expressions. They are things that might be said to a child or said often within a child's hearing. There are common comestibles: *une tasse de café, une tartine, du chocolat.* There are interjections and verbal place-markers: *sais-tu, figure-toi, je t'assure, mon Dieu.* And, naturally, there are terms of endearment. In my family, the use of someone's first name was nearly always an indication of anger or a prelude to bad news. My parents addressed me as *fifi, chou* (cabbage), *lapin* (rabbit), *vî tchèt* (Walloon: old cat), *petit coeur.* If I'd done something mischievous, my father would laugh and call me *cûrêye* (Walloon for "carcass" or "spavined horse"—like saying, "you're rotten"); if I'd made myself especially comfortable, such as by taking up most of the couch, he'd shake his head and grin and call me *macrale* (Walloon for "witch"). I regularly got called *tièsse èl aîr* (Walloon: head in the clouds). If my mother was teasing me in mock anger, she'd call me a *petit chenapan* (little scamp); if it was my father, he'd be likely to say *"t'es ô tièssetou"* ("you're a stubborn one," in Walloon). My father's real anger was rare and grave; my mother's boiled over quickly even if it faded just as fast. She might call me a *vaurien* (good-for-nothing) or a *sâle gosse* (dirty kid), an *èstèné* (Walloon for "idiot," literally "bewildered") or a *singlé* (simpleton) or a *nolu* (Walloon: nullity). If I'd really stung her, though, she'd yell *chameau!* (camel), and I liked that, because she was acknowledging I had some kind of power. There are worse words, which still have the capacity to make me cringe: *cochon* (pig), *crapuleux* (vile, vicious), *crotté* (filthy), *mâssî* (ditto: Walloon). Those words are woven through the fabric of my early adolescence.

A few years ago, early in the morning, I was waiting to cross a street in Liège. I wasn't quite awake yet, and was lost in thought, so that when I heard someone shout *"Fais attention!*

Regarde!" I immediately stiffened. All of a sudden I was back at the age of eight or nine, being reproved by my parents. As it happened, there was a small boy standing next to me, holding a tray of empty coffee cups which he was returning to the café opposite; his father, manning a flea-market booth behind us, had observed the kid putting a toe into the street unmindful of oncoming traffic. It can easily happen to me, when faced with some officious francophone creep, shopkeeper or librarian or customs agent, that I lose thirty years and two feet off my height. If I haven't briefed myself beforehand, I crumple. This can happen even though I've kept my French alive internally through reading, and more recently have acquired friends with whom I engage in adult conversation in that language. But even in such circumstances I can find myself tripped up, suddenly sprawled. I can be reading something truly scabrous, some- thing by Georges Bataille, say, turning the pages as an imper- turbable adult, and then a phrase will shock me, not some description of outlandish vice but rather a perfectly innocent locution lying in the midst of the smut. It will throw everything else into a new relief. Suddenly it is as if one of my aunts had looked up from her coffee and started spewing obscenities.

Since I live almost entirely in English now, I can regard French with some of the same detachment and sense of the ridiculous with which I once regarded my adopted tongue. If I walk into an American discount store and the loudspeaker starts braying, "Attention shoppers!" I will consign the noise to the realm of static, switch off its ability to reach me except as an ir- ritant. On the other hand, if I am in a Belgian supermarket and the loudspeaker begins its recital, nearly always in a polished female murmur rather than the American male bark: *"Mon- sieur, madame, nous vous conseillons . . ."* I am bemused, imagining the rapport between the voice and its sleek, well-dressed target, someone so exquisitely put together that he or she can purchase low-fat frozen entrees with a withering superiority, as if picking out a *grand cru classé*. I am never the "you" of American advertising because I consciously slam the door, but in French I am never given the opportunity to spurn the come-on. I am excluded at the gate. Naturally, there is a class factor involved—in French I revert to proletarian status as easily as to childhood—but the exclusion is also due to my status as a counterfeit Belgian, an American pretender.

In Belgium I am an oddity. Having been raised abroad in a bubble of the old culture, I've retained curious verbal archaisms; I may unconsciously say *auto* instead of *voiture* to mean "car," for instance, or *illustré* instead of *revue* to mean "magazine," expressions redolent of the 1930s or '40s, if not earlier. Mingled with a distinct American flavor in my speech is a strong dose of the old Verviers Walloon accent, and the combination confuses anyone who perceives it. One day in Liège I shared the elevator with a neighbor I hadn't previously met. He asked me for the time, and when I told him he suddenly said, "How can it be that you're an American Verviétois?" (He was an actor, with a particularly fine ear.) Sometimes I just pass for a foreigner, and sometimes for a local who's a bit simple, uncertain of what bus to take or what to do with the ticket once on board. Whenever I arrive in the country my speech is halting, awkwardly translated from the American, ill-equipped for anything the slightest bit complex or abstract or for that matter adult. Conversely, terms that were not present in my parents' speech, often because they did not enter ordinary spoken language until after our emigration, can seem absurd, pretentious, empty. They seem that way, that is, until I have spent a few days in the company of French-speaking friends, and so have recovered the language, having effected an internal conversion to its rhythm, from which the idiom follows organically. By the third day I might surprise myself employing one of those brittle new phrases, as if it were the most natural thing in the world.

I can cross the border between English and French, although I can't straddle it. Years ago, when I worked behind the cash register in a store, I resented the demands of the customers and sometimes went out of my way to be rude to them, to put them in their place. After work, though, I might go to some other shop, and there, trying to find out whether the shirt came in a larger size or a darker color, would find myself resenting the arrogance and apathy of the clerks. I had jumped from one side of the fence to the other. I could no more simultaneously occupy the mentality of clerk and client than I could bat a ball to myself in the outfield. Each claim effaced the other. It was useless to try and apportion blame; customers and clerks were both rude and both justified, were in fact interchangeable. This insight is perhaps the closest I've ever gotten to understanding the psychology that lies behind nationalism. The situation is a bit like one of the famous optical illusions: you can see the vase, and then you can see the two profiles, but you can't see both images at once.

Belgium is an ill-fitting suit of a country. It is stitched together from odds and ends, represents a purely strategic decision on the part of the larger powers, has no identity as a nation, and so on. And it unnaturally couples two language groups who are both right and both wrong (actually three language groups if you add the relatively untroubled German-speaking minority—no more than seventy thousand souls in any case). And both principal language groups have ambiguous ongoing relationships with the majority stockholders of their languages, that is, the Dutch and the French. The Flemish and the Dutch in recent years have been forming cultural and trade partnerships, and apparently enjoying themselves at it. Their mutual history is somewhat more vexed, with the Dutch regarding the Flemings with a certain benign hauteur, and the Flemish viewing the Dutch as worldly, as apostates, as lacking in seriousness, not to mention virtue. But they read each other's literatures, and just as the Flemings have adopted the grammar and usage of their cousins, so the Dutch appreciate the particular flavor of Flemish expressions, and have helped themselves to dashes of the idiom. Between the Walloons and the French the situation is less comfortable. Essentially, the French feel superior and the Walloons oblige them by feeling embarrassed. There has long been a francophile segment of the Walloon population, and as the national tension has risen, so has the noise emitted by a certain minority that favors the detachment of Wallonia from Belgium and its adherence to France. The French have shown no corresponding interest in acquiring five impoverished and déclassé eastern provinces.

The linguistic situation is symptomatic. Popular manuals for the identification and eradication of *belgicismes* were published at least as far back as the eighteenth century and continue to be today. *Le Soir,* out of Brussels, has a weekly feature that reiterates the very same cautions as, for example, the writer who called himself *"un ancien professeur"* uttered in 1806: don't say *tartine,* say instead *beurrée,* and so forth. That example should serve to indicate that the wish to eliminate native expressions has nothing to do with grammatical rigor or the rectification of ambiguities, but is merely the expression of a class-bound shame. Visitors always note that Belgians say *septante* for seventy and *nonante* for ninety, whereas the French say *soixante-dix* and *quatre-vingt-dix,* respectively. I have no idea why Belgians do not also say *octante* for eighty, the three simpler expressions having been used by French-speaking proletarians of both lands for centuries; the arithmetical rebuses are owed entirely to class pretension. Similarly, the city of Liège was known to one and all as Liége until around the time of World War I, when the accent mark was switched in accordance with the lowercase *liège,* which means cork-tree and has no etymological rapport with the city's name. There was even a law passed; the old spelling only survived for a while in the name of the now-defunct *Gaʒette de Liége,* which was grandfathered. (Among my inheritances from the traditional working class is the old pronunciation of the word, which has caused auditors to look at me funny and even to correct me.) A more recent example of this tendency is what happened across the country to the name of the establishments that make and sell fried potatoes. For untold decades and throughout my childhood they were known as *fritures,* until at some point in the 1970s a humorless functionary decreed the name incorrect, since *friture* is the word for the fat in which the potatoes are fried. Now only establishments older than twenty-five or so years can continue to name themselves that way; the more recent shops must be called *friteries.*

The French, particularly through the agency of their Academy, have long policed their language in such petty ways. Neologisms and loanwords are forbidden, shifts in grammar and usage swiftly curtailed. French was once a major force in the world, among other things the international language of diplomacy. Those who wonder why it has ceded so much of its power to English need look no further than this wish to preserve a seventeenth-century cadaver. Belgians who submit their language to French rules concede twice over. But the submission is by now traditional; after all, the Walloons have done a fairly effective job of killing off their own tongue.

Walloon, the native patois of southern Belgium, is usually identified as a dialect of French, whereas it derived on its own from the Latin of the Roman legions, and is just as old as the patois of Île-de-France, which became the official language. The eleventh edition of the *Encyclopedia Britannica* in fact identifies it as the northernmost Romance language. I once posed the question to a linguist-translator: What is the line separating a language from a dialect? He replied that the situation could be summed up in a phrase: History is written by the victors. The dialect of Île-de-France was the patois of the French kings; it subjugated Walloon as well as Provençal, Norman, Lorrain, Gascon, Picard, Occitan, and so on, and reduced them from languages to dialects. The effect of linguistic imperialism is well described by the great Verviétois philologist Jules Feller (1859–1940), in his *Notes de philologie wallonne* (1912):

> Political necessity, material interest, constraint, and the moral superiority of the conqueror and his language can create within a single century the troubling phenomenon of a tongue being entirely forgotten by its nation. The first generation does its best to gabble the idiom of the foreign invaders. The second generation, if it be to its advantage, already knows the new language better than the old. The third generation for all practical purposes knows and employs only the new.

Feller uses this model to describe the impact of Latin on the Celto-Germanic population of Gallia Belgica, but it applies just as well to the effect of French upon Walloon over the last century (and, incidentally, it is likewise true of the linguistic process that accompanies immigration). Feller goes on to characterize French as "a brilliant soldier of fortune in the army of Romance dialects who has become a general," while Walloon is "a little corps of soldiers, consigned to the fringe of the battalion, who have never gotten the chance to distinguish themselves."

There are texts going back to around the year 1000 that employ Walloon words and phrases within a stew of various strains of French. These do not reflect the true state of the language, because Walloon was the tongue of the general illiterate population, from which authors of texts, mostly members of the clergy, were perforce removed. Walloon literature was inaugurated toward the end of the twelfth or the beginning of the thirteenth century by an anonymous *Moral* of some two thousand verses, and jerked its way forward for another three centuries until French began smothering its neighbors. But Walloon sprang back to life in the seventeenth century, Matthias Navaeus's 1620 *Ode* to the city of Liège being the first distinguished item in its literature. A further flowering occurred in the late eighteenth century, when the opening of a popular theater in Liège inspired the writing of a number of comic plays, some of which are still occasionally performed. Edmund Gosse, in his entry on Walloon literature in the eleventh *Britannica,* notes that in these works "the Walloon humor is displayed with great crudity; anything like sentiment or elevated feeling is unknown."

This state of affairs was to persist. As Feller implies in his metaphor, Walloon had developed far from courts or centers of power; even the prince-bishops of Liège were primarily Germans, and the dukes of Burgundy were educated in French territory. Walloon remained a language of the poor, and consequently its compass was limited to matters of the hearth, the market, the tavern, the soil. You can see this in the Walloon words that made their way into the French language during the late Middle Ages, such as *"estaminet,"* for example, which means a saloon or grog-shop; for that matter many French words that pertain to mining and to the textile trade derive from the Walloon-Picard complex. Walloon never darkened the doors of the centers of learning, even during the great transition to the vulgate that occurred around the time of the Reformation. As a result, it is a language almost entirely free of abstract concepts. An essayist writing in a Parisian review at the beginning of this century asserted that in Walloon "there are a hundred ways to say 'ginever,' but no words for 'idealism' or 'dialectic.' "

It might yet have had a chance to develop in the nineteenth century, had the Belgian educational establishment seized the opportunity afforded by independence to teach Walloon in schools. Instead the opposite occurred: steps were taken to suppress the language, and teachers took it as their mission to "cure" pupils of their native tongue. Belgians today might argue that the institutionalization of Walloon could not have been undertaken, given the friction between Flemish and French speakers, but let us recall that the attempt to erase Flemish reached its peak during the same period. One tangible result of the suppression is that Walloon has remained divided into clusters, separated by differences in vocabulary, grammar, and pronunciation. There are four principal strains: the eastern, centered in Liège; the middle, in Namur; the western, in Charleroi; and the southern, roughly centralized among the towns of Bastogne, Neufchâteau, and Marche-en-Famenne. Not only are the differences among these strains sufficiently great that speakers of the eastern and western varieties can barely understand one another, but variations, sometimes significant ones, can separate the Walloon of one town from that of its neighbor. The closest thing to a unified dictionary that exists is the mammoth *Atlas linguistique de la Wallonie,* a project that began after World War II and was still in progress forty years later. In it each word is accorded two pages, one for the variations and the other for the map on which to locate them. Anyway, the language today is scorned by the middle class, just as it was spoken almost clandestinely by their peasant ancestors a century ago. Feller reports that when he went on word-collecting expeditions in rural villages, most of the people he addressed in Walloon answered him in French, since they were certain he was out to mock them.

But Walloon did have its golden age. It was brief, lasting from the mid-1880s until just before World War I. That period saw an efflorescence of Walloon literature, plays and poems primarily, and the founding of many theaters and periodicals. The New York Public Library possesses a surprisingly large collection of literary works in Walloon, quite possibly the largest outside Belgium, and its holdings are statistically representative of the output. Out of nearly a thousand plays in the collection, only twenty-six were published before 1880. Thereafter the numbers rise gradually year by year, reaching a peak of sixty-nine in 1903, and then they fall again, down to eleven in 1913. Only twenty-one of them were published after World War I. The reasons for this decline remain a mystery; it was not occasioned by the war itself. The statistics presented by the library's holdings are backed up by others: the major era of Wal-

loon comic weeklies, for example, seems to have taken place between 1895 and 1905, after which more periodicals folded than
were begun. Literary production occurred at different paces in
different cities, but Liège, Verviers, Namur, and Charleroi led
the pack, approximately in that order.

In *Fré Cougnou,* one of several Walloon weeklies published
in Verviers around the turn of the century, not only were the
poems, stories, and jokes in Walloon but nearly all the advertisements as well. One ad features a studio photograph of a
man wearing a peasant's smock over his suit, a slouch hat on his
head, and a large curved pipe in his mouth; slung over an arm is
a wicker basket. The caption reads: "Jules Le Ruth, good Walloon writer, dealer in good cheeses." There were all sizes of tal-
ents and all sorts of people (all of them men, though) in the
movement. That the movement was (otherwise) genuinely democratic can be seen in Oscar Colson's bibliography of published works covering the prime years 1905 and 1906. The
professions of the authors are cited, and besides one university
professor, two priests, and a sizeable number of teachers and
printers, they also include a butcher, a tinsmith, two traveling
salesmen, a coal miner, a house painter, a cordwainer, a bar-
tender, a plumber, an electrician, several accountants, a copper-
smith, a bailiff, a crystal engraver, a watchmaker, an insurance
adjuster, a glassblower, a mailman, and a number of ordinary
factory workers. At its peak, Walloon literature was like a massive exhalation of breath long held in. It approached—as in
Lautréamont's exhortation—poetry made by all.

There was, however, perhaps more enthusiasm than substance. Boulevard comedy was the template for theatrical
works; the poems were primarily burlesques or sentimental
love lyrics. The movement was culturally and socially conserv-

ative: the Verviétois poet Alphonse Ramet, who wrote an ode
to Spartacus—which alarmed his colleagues, who heard it as a
call to revolution—stands out as an exception. The movement
was literally provincial, although literature of other languages
was translated into Walloon, including fables by La Fontaine,
letters by Rousseau, tales by Hans Christian Andersen, plays by
Goldoni and Chekhov. The movement had its stars, its innova-
tors, its hacks, its students. In Verviers, Henri Hurard was as
great as Scribe; his many plays were hailed in a vigorous critical
press, continually revived and reprinted, translated into Picard
and the dialect of Charleroi. A street was named after him. To
come upon the traces of all this ferment is like finding a city
buried under volcanic ash, its people frozen while shopping or
bathing or giving speeches—an entire self-contained world is
on view, but its glories and standards and shibboleths are now
completely forgotten. Among the holdings of the New York
Public Library are presentation copies of works inscribed by
one then-famous name to another, which were perhaps acquired by Americans in the ruins of World War I and since then
have barely been consulted by anyone. In my excitement at en-
countering this literature I searched long and hard for works to
translate into English. I failed. The material is frequently weak
if not evanescent; it possesses real merits, but they are entirely
bound up with the flavor of the language itself, which does not
travel.

The texture of Walloon is hard to convey in another
tongue. It resembles French in many ways—if you are conver-
sant with French you can make out the rudiments of Walloon,
on the page by sounding it out or from hearing someone speak
it slowly—but it incorporates elements of Old Low German in
its vocabulary, and it also differs in such structural matters as

the placement of the adjective before the noun (in French it nearly always comes after). Proper French is said to be *pincé* (pinched); Walloon is the opposite, broadly drawled. Indeed, like the French slang called *argot* it derives a great deal of its force from the ways in which it reverses the conventional French values of decorum, reserve, gestural economy, and elegant style. Walloon is anything but elegant. It roars and bawls and guffaws. It is a great vehicle for the mock-lament, the histrionic complaint, the self-consuming boast, the tender homely croon of reassurance. Its essential medium is the apothegm, of which there are so many that Joseph Dejardin's compilation (1891–92) comes in two large volumes of small type. It is loud, good-humored, long-suffering, self-mocking, wry, and often psychologically acute. It shares something with Yiddish in these characteristics, as well as in the unbuttoned, elbows-out roominess of its sound. The only translation of it I have ever come across consists of a few Walloon phrases in Apollinaire's *The Poet Assassinated*; the translator, Ron Padgett, had the inspired idea of rendering them into Scottish— "Y'arr a boonie lassie" gives a fair accounting of *"Vs'esteʒ one belle crapeaute di nom di Dio."* Taken on its own terms, Walloon is rich in shadings and subtleties, but those terms are inseparably tied to the ground of a lost world.

Walloon was the household tongue of all the relatives of my grandparents' generation. Their parents in turn might have spoken nothing else; that no one bothered to establish rules for the writing of Walloon until Jules Feller did so at the very beginning of this century, just in time for its decline in currency, partly accounts for the fact that nearly everyone in the family tree before my grandparents' era was illiterate. When I hear Walloon spoken, which is not often, I hear the table talk of countless generations of workers and farmers and their wives, not that I particularly wish to subscribe to notions of collective ethnic memory, but the sound of the language conveys the mentality of its speakers so vividly that it is dense with imprints, like fossils. Hearing old men greet each other— *"Bôdjou, Djôsef,"* *"Bôdjou, Françwès"*—can move me nearly to tears. It is the keenest tangible manifestation of what I've lost, even if it is now pretty much lost to everyone. In my childhood it was already a ghost, if a lively one. My mother's parents ceded to the tenor of their times; they spoke Walloon between themselves but did not teach it to their children and discouraged their bringing bits of it home. My father, on the other hand, grew up in a Walloon-speaking household in a city with a rich Walloon tradition.

If Verviers has an official legend, it is that of the *tchèt volant,* the flying cat, commemorated in a long if not actually endless set of Walloon verses written down in 1641: some local savant wished to test the proposition that a cat could be made to fly, after it had been purged with a laxative, by attaching a helium balloon to each of its limbs. Accordingly the cat was launched from the steeple of St. Remacle, but it did nothing more than flip over several times in midair, land on its feet, and run off. This episode became the founding myth of a tradition of self-satire, which informed the local Walloon literature, notably less lugubriously sentimental than that of certain other cities. Files at the Bibliothèque des Chiroux in Liège list more than seventy-five Walloon societies—amateur or semi-pro theater companies, poetry clubs, singing groups, and friendship leagues—in Verviers at the beginning of the century. My grandfather belonged to at least one of these (I don't know which) and did some acting. My father remembers appearances

by him in *Lès Sî Cint Franchimontwès* (1895) by Nicolas De-
presseux and *Li Fis dè Gârchampète* (1889), an operetta by Victor Carpentier, two warhorses from the Liégeois repertory.*
The latter went through at least four editions between 1889 and
1919, the spellings changing with every one; the preface to the
third edition, of 1903, proclaims that "it is annually performed
by all the societies in Wallonia, and every time is met with calls
for an encore."

Following in his footsteps, my father in 1946 joined Amon
nos autes, the leading theater company in Verviers at that time.
His contract stipulated that he would be paid one hundred
francs (two dollars, but in postwar money) for each performance, enjoined him to exclusivity, and posted a fine of one
thousand francs should the terms be forfeited. The company
was founded in 1932, with all the surviving major figures of the
prewar Walloon scene included in its board of advisors, and endured until the 1970s. By 1934, though, its programs already
bore the motto *Nos péres djâsît Walon* (our fathers spoke Walloon), an indication that nostalgia was now uppermost. By 1959
things had come to such a pass that the company got in trouble
for having two sets in a single scene—theaters of the second
rank were only allowed one, and the director was fined 520
francs by the court.

A few years ago I went to see Walloon theater for myself, at
the major such establishment in Liège, the Théâtre Communal
du Trianon. The spectacle was Nicolas Trockart's operetta *Li
Bohémiène,* a standard marrying-off-the-daughter period farce.

---

* The Six Hundred Franchimontois were a volunteer army who in 1368 unsuccessfully
defended Liège's revolt against Charles the Bold. The second title means "the son of the
rural constable."

Aside from a handful of very young grandchildren, I was clearly the only person in the audience under sixty. Things began promisingly: the six-piece orchestra played café-concert music passably well, and the stage was set in classic bare-bones style. Unfortunately, the effect was marred as soon as the actors came on, at least the ones younger than their audience; they spoke Walloon with drama-school French accents, and looked like soap-opera stars of the 1970s. The actors seemed to have picked out their own costumes—it quickly became clear that you could judge the merits of the performers by appearance alone the minute they walked onstage. Only the older actors spoke convincing Walloon, could pull off the requisite slapstick, and had bothered to dress appropriately for their roles. What I had taken for ineptitude might well have been contempt. I left, downcast, after the first act.

Walloon today is the province of the elderly, at least those of the working class or in rural communities, along with a few younger diehards and hobbyists in the cities. Most people regard it with a certain embarrassment, like the memory of a bastard grandsire who ate with his hands. The young, who are media fixated and thus Parisianized or Americanized, couldn't care less. To me, growing up, it was both familiar and strange. Sometimes my parents reached for an English phrase and came up with a Walloon one instead—the confusion was understandable given the Germanic strain running among Walloon's Latin roots. (An often-told story in my family related how Lucy Dosquet, when her G.I. suitor arrived looking like a slob, angrily ordered him in Walloon, *"Louke-tu el mireu!"* He understood perfectly, and studied his reflection.) Sometimes my parents said things to each other in Walloon they didn't want me to understand—pertaining to Christmas presents, maybe. I was never taught Walloon, but I had a fair-sized vocabulary anyway (there were concepts I could only express in Walloon; growing pains, for example, were always *crèhioûles*), and I simply absorbed its structure from hearing bits of it from my parents and from hearing my grandparents and great-aunts and great-uncles speak it. I can read it with ease; other applications don't present themselves. Like the lives of my ancestors, Walloon appears humble and yet mighty, elemental and at the same time complex, remote but a part of my fiber. I use what I have of it only internally. It is that sad paradox, a silent tongue.

One of the great stalwarts of Verviétois Walloon in this century was Jean Wisimus (1866–1953), who managed to combine the tasks of textile dealer, newspaper columnist, lexicographer (he compiled the only dictionary of the Verviers tongue that exists), historian, author (of *Dès Rôses èt dès spènes*—Roses and Thorns—a volume of rather affecting reminiscences of the old Verviers), and founder and longtime president of *Lu Vî Tchène* (The Old Oak), the last major Walloon organization in the city. His first book, however, published in 1921, was *L'Anglais langue auxiliaire internationale* (English, the international second language). Its publication may have been delayed by the war; in any case he begins by addressing concerns that have a distinctly pre-1914 air about them. Universal languages were all the rage then. Dr. Zamenhof's *Esperanto*, Monsignor Schleyer's *Volapük*, Sudre's *Solresol*, Dyer's *Lingualumina*, Bauer's *Spelin*, Dornoy's *Balta*, Marchand's *Dilpok*, the Marquis de Beaufort's *Ido*—all were supposed to bring about international harmony by tearing down the tower of Babel and making the crooked ways straight, and all of them smell like the sort of decorous, idealistic Edwardian science fiction that was about to be buried in the trenches of Verdun. Wisimus has no patience at all with such nonsense: "An artificial language is like canned food; it's a product without flavor or aroma." By contrast, there is English, which has the simplest and most analytical grammar, and furthermore has already invaded every domain ("you visit the *world's fair,* buy a *ticket,* go to the *bar,* watch out for *pickpockets* . . . see the *cakewalk,* the *looping-the-loop, cow-boys* from the *far-west* . . ."). Although some people will always grumble about its errant spelling *("Der Engländer schreibt 'Jerusalem' und liesʒt 'Konstaninopel' "),* its destiny is clear, and anyway, *"Un beau désordre est un effet de l'art"* (a beautiful mess is an artistic effect: Boileau). English, he predicts, will become a worldwide medium of convenience, like the telephone and the telegraph. Unless, that is, Japan conquers the planet . . .

Somehow, like some sort of Jules Vernian astronaut, I wound up making the journey from Wisimus's Place Verte into the very heart of the linguistic future. For my first communion I was presented with a dictionary whose jacket copy promised it to be "as up-to-date as Telstar!" Two years later I decided I wanted to be a writer, and having made that decision never thought of writing in any language but English. It was at hand, it was all new, it was not the language of my parents, it *was* the language of Robert Louis Stevenson and Rod Serling and the Beatles, it contained a ready-made incentive to competition, and besides, Mrs. Gibbs in the fourth grade at St. Teresa's School in Summit told me I had talent, and that clinched it. Gradually, I successfully passed myself off as another being. I was thirteen or fourteen the last time anyone complimented me on my charming accent. English became my rod and my staff, my tool and my weapon, at length my means of making a living. My mask merged with my skin. My internal monologue ever so gradually shifted from French into English; I even began to talk to cats and dogs (who understand all languages) in English. My most intimate conversations came to be conducted in English. Today, when someone addresses me as "Luke" I respond without a second thought; when I hear *"lük"* I jump as if I'd gotten an electric shock. Even though I know better, I feel as if someone had just looked down into my naked soul.

I tend to avoid speaking French unless I'm in Europe. In America I can't get my French hat on fast enough, and as a result I tend to keep French speakers at a respectful distance, and have often (undoubtedly) appeared rude. I still speak French with my parents, of course, although "French" is perhaps a misleading word there, since over the years we've developed a family dialect, a Franglais that is a lot like Spanglish: *"Nous sommes allés chez les séniores citizeunnes,"* my mother will tell me, describing a visit to the local old-folks club, *"et nous avons mangé du cornebif et du cabbage."* I am almost physically unable to talk to my parents in English, even when they are using the language out of politeness because there is an English speaker present. It would feel as if we were surrounded by the Gestapo, exchanging nonsensical pleasantries studded with code words. Or maybe it would be as if I had invited them to a wild party I was throwing for my friends.

I suppose I am never completely present in any given moment, since different aspects of myself are contained in different rooms of language, and a complicated apparatus of air locks prevents the doors from being flung open all at once. Still, there are subterranean correspondences between the linguistic domains that keep them from stagnating. The classical order of French, the Latin-Germanic high-low dialectic of English, and

the onomatopoeic peasant lucidity of Walloon work on one another critically, help enhance precision and reduce cant. They
are all operative, potentially. Given desire and purpose, I could
make my home in any of them. I don't have a house, only this
succession of rented rooms. That sometimes makes me feel as
though I have no language at all, but it also gives me the advantage of mobility. I can leave, anytime, and not be found.

xv Non-Site

One night I'm in Rhinebeck, New York, with my wife. After checking into our motel, we go out and buy a pint of Wild Turkey, so we can have a nightcap. Some weeks later, I'm in Brussels. I can't sleep because of jet lag; I pace around the tiny borrowed apartment. I root around in my luggage and find the bottle of Wild Turkey. Why did I pack it? It's nearly empty. One swallow and it's gone. I go into the kitchen and toss the bottle down the garbage chute. Later it will be retrieved and recycled by the porter. Eventually it will end up in—who knows?—reinforced concrete, maybe. The bottle has emigrated, and found itself a new purpose in another country. It will add something, however minute, to the economic profile of that country. The porter, upon retrieving it from the weekend's accumulation of junk in the cellar, might take a second to look at the label, might notice its foreign pedigree, then he will toss it into the bottle bin, where it will break. After that it will be mere particles within ever larger mounds of broken glass. Its story will be lost: the bottle factory wherever, the distillery in Kentucky, the truck, the warehouse, the weeks or months on the shelf in Rhinebeck, the interval on a shelf in Brooklyn, the gradual diminution of its liquid contents, the trip across the ocean in the hold of a 747, the slide down a four-story chute in another country. Nobody cares.

The next morning, early, I cross Brussels, heading for the southern end of Les Marolles, the old *quartier populaire*, to attend the flea market at Place du Jeu de Balle. When I enter the square the very first thing I see is a booth selling stationery supplies. I don't understand; this is not the sort of flea market where people sell tube socks and keychains and off-brand aftershave. I examine the goods: nibs, penholders, hard erasers, ink bottles, blotter pads, wooden pencil boxes with sliding lids, thin ruled notebooks with pictures of cowboys on their covers. Nothing remarkable, not even especially fine merchandise, just ordinary Belgian school supplies, the kind I used myself. And yet people are picking up these items and gazing at them rapturously. I'm baffled. Then a beefy guy with a mustache holds up one of the notebooks and, addressing a child or the stallholder or nobody in particular, exclaims, "When I was a kid I had notebooks just like this!" There's a catch in his throat. "We all did, pal," the proprietor growls. It's only then that I get it.

I've lost many things over the years, some of them important. I've left stuff behind in moves; there's stuff I had to give away because there wasn't room for it. I've thrown things out that I later regretted. I've given items drenched in sentiment and history to girlfriends in the early rush of entanglements that wound up lasting all of a month. At some point I inherited my maternal grandfather's watch chain, an extraordinary thing from the Congo made to look like a helix of entwined lianas, and first the tiny ivory elephant fell off somewhere in Rockefeller Center when I was working as a messenger, and then a few months later the chain itself was stolen during a break-in at my slum apartment. Other things were stolen, in burglaries or else by "friends" during that strange period in the early 1980s when absolutely nobody could be trusted. I sold stuff when I was trying to live by my wits and finding out their exact limitations. I lent things to people and they got lost, or I forgot to ask for them back, or forgot to pick them up, or forgot whom I'd lent them to, or lost track of the party in question. I gave away items from my childhood because I was disgusted by the thought of my childhood, or because I was on one of my crusades to lighten my material burden, or because I wanted to make a grand gesture. There are objects my parents gave or threw away without consulting me because they were angry at me or simply because it never occurred to them. There's stuff that just disappeared, things I always thought I had tucked away safely until the day I went to look for them.

I don't remember what year it is. I remember to return the phone call months after the fact. By the time I get around to checking the listings for the movie, it isn't showing anywhere anymore. I want to go have lunch at that place on Route 46, I tell my wife as we're driving, but there's no trace of it, and I realize I last saw it thirty years ago. I see a photograph by Berenice Abbott of a country store in the Bronx, of all places, and I nearly have my coat on and subway fare in hand before it occurs to me that the picture was taken in the 1940s and the place isn't likely to have survived. I see another picture, a very sharply detailed shot of the marketplace in Potsdam on a sunny day in the 1880s, and for a split second I'm convinced that I was there. I suddenly remember a package I left at the foot of the stairs in 1979 and want to retrieve it, and it takes me a minute or two before I understand that 1979 is not accessible by foot, subway, bus, car, plane, or boat. I hear a light guitar chord, and then another, and then a third, heavier one that reverberates, and then a tenor carefully enunciates, "My love must be a kind, of blind love; I can't see, anyone, but you," while guitar and bass and a piano player plinking one key somehow contrive to give the impression of an organ, a Hammond lounge organ

with Lesley cabinet, a machine emitting the auditory equivalent
of silk, and then here come the patterns shot through the cloth:
the other Flamingos crowding together to chirp, "Doo-bop
choo-bop"—and then the floor falls away and I am in midtown
Manhattan in 1960 at the close of a hot autumn day, the red sun
just sitting on the New Jersey horizon at the end of every cross
street, the sound coming from a swarm of transistor radios all
around, held by teenage girls in kerchiefs and toreador pants
and white shirts knotted at the waist, each with a cigarette in the
other hand held up and flipped back.

I comb through flea markets obsessively, not looking for
anything really, just looking. In Brussels I see red trays covered
with shellacked cigar bands, mass-produced African masks,
polished hammered-brass pitchers and jugs, albums of neatly
mounted Chocolat Jacques cards of the royal family at work
and play, objects I used to see all the time in people's homes but
had forgotten. I see wedding portraits that are the spit and
image of my parents': same lighting, pose, expressions, clothes,
hairstyles. I see boxes filled with baptismal announcements and
communion announcements and *souvenirs pieux* identical to the
ones stuffed between the pages of my grandparents' leatherbound missals. In Charleroi, along the *quai,* I see gilt oval
frames hanging from the trees, containing glaucous portraits of
taxidermized prewar citizens, exactly like the ones I enjoyed
being scared by when I'd root through my grandparents' things
in the attic of our Pepinster house when we went back in 1962
and '63. I see beer and soft-drink advertisements featuring
winking monks or beehived girls that I might have sat under in
the Café Terminus in Theux as my mother and I waited for the
bus after visiting my grandfather in the morbid seventeenth-
century hospice during the bleak spring of 1963. I see our old

radio, our dishes, our framed prints, our books, our tablecloths, our deck chairs, our slotted spoons, our calendars, even our parlor stove with its trademark of a running bipedal creature made of flames. In Liège, along Boulevard de la Constitution, I see piles of picture-sleeved 45s by Les Cousins, Les Chats Sauvages, Dick Rivers, Dalida, France Gall, Adamo, and of course Johnny Halliday (né De Smet) that Paul and André and I sang along with and practiced the Twist to. I see water-damaged panoramic photographs of the grotto at Lourdes, racks of chipped meerschaum pipes, cracked souvenir ashtrays from the '58 World's Fair, bundled stacks of moldy pamphlets of Walloon plays, rusted tin pails and shovels with patches of bright color still visible, boxes of dog-eared potboilers with crudely sensational cover drawings and pseudo-American pseudonyms, rush-caned chairs whose caning has been reduced to splinters, solo leather-topped crutches, broken vases, broken appliances, broken toys, and hundreds and hundreds of photographs of grandparents and fiancées and scout troops and 1918 war veterans and children staring out from under the giant beard of St. Nicolas. These things make me feel patriotic.

I'm saddened when I consider obsolete computer equipment, defunct videotaping systems, superannuated synthesizer keyboards, useless and outmoded duplication hardware, forgotten once-revolutionary medical gizmos, movie cameras and Polaroid cameras designed for film that is no longer manufactured. When I had a job in the university library during college I would now and then borrow a key from the front desk and go down to the second level of the stacks, where I would visit the closed annex whose shelves were populated by thousands of outdated or discredited scientific texts and serried ranks of nineteenth-century German doctoral dissertations printed in

Fraktur; I felt tenderly toward them. I want to rescue from the trash strangers' snapshots, discarded mail, orphaned diaries, widowed keepsake volumes, inconsequential random scrapbooks of undated clippings, contextless bureau-drawer contents dumped into cardboard boxes, unloved detritus of every description. I feel a stab when I come upon an old book that is falling to pieces, and the inner layer of the spine is revealed as consisting of some even older recycled text: lines sweated out by somebody somewhere. I get a chill when I think of Miss Butterbean Harvest of 1938, or the up-and-coming young Rotarian feed vendor of De Kalb County in the year before the Crash, or the Bard of Upper Canada, whose verses were memorized by schoolchildren in the 1890s, or the leading exponent of the Single Tax west of the Mississippi, or the fastest changemaker in the Rio de Janeiro rapid-transit system under the old currency, or the finest painter of devotional scenes in Moravia during the empire, none of whose accomplishments are now preserved or remembered by anybody.

The past is a quiet place where change occurs in increments of glacial slowness; it is a perpetually verdant landscape. You can go there and find that nothing much has happened since your last visit. Your relatives and acquaintances are fixed in stereotypical postures and occupations—your grandmother is still mending that same old coat! It's fairly boring to visit but sometimes you need an interval of that boredom amid the frenetic pace of your normal activities. There you can resume the life you knew from before, that you have always known. You can drop your defenses and affectations, and ease into the old ways as if they were a pair of carpet slippers that long ago took on the exact shape of your feet. You can hear the old stories all over again, exchange the same observations on the weather with the same people as on all your previous visits, eat the same meals, experience the same reassuring emotions as always. And when you return to your home in the present, you find that the calendar page and the hands of the clock stand where they were when you left! The minute you notice this, you simultaneously forget all the details of your trip, so that they can remain evergreen until your next visit. It's good to know that the past is there, always ready to welcome you, just an ocean away.

But I'm never sure what anybody means when they speak of the future. When I was growing up I assumed without thinking much about it that my early adulthood would be spent in the appropriately forward-looking, breezily confident 1950s, and that in my middle years I would graduate to a firm footing in that mature but dynamic era that you can see in movies made between 1936 and America's entry into the war, and that old age would find me at leisure in a long white beard and a cottage decked in rose trellises and wisteria vines, in the peaceful security of the 1890s. I might have doubted whether I or anybody else would ever get to the future, an ideal of such seductive promise but such stern requirements, a peak lost in the clouds. It only looks more distant from my adult window, if I can even see it at all. The future is an abandoned city, a locomotive ensnared in jungle growth, a ruined phalanstery on a high desert plateau, a manifesto written in pictograms no one living can decipher, an uprising suppressed so quickly that no pictures were taken, a live oak with an unknown word carved into it, a colony of idealists who turned to the manufacture of kitchen appliances, a design for rational living that forgot to account for toilets, an archive of unpublished masterpieces curated by the secret police, a café whose once-famous corner table was removed and replaced with a video poker machine, a few years' worth of entries in the early journals of someone who died broke, died insane, died a highly respected figure in the carpet trade.

I live in moderate comfort in the present, on a permanent resident visa, while I hold a passport issued by the authority of the past. This situation presents some minor difficulties, nothing grave mind you, just a few privileges denied me. Now and then I wonder why I maintain this state of affairs—what advantage can it possibly represent? And I have to admit that there is no particular advantage. Maybe an exit door, although by now it might open onto a wall or a pit or an enclosed vacant lot with scattered rat droppings, if it isn't in fact rusted shut. Maybe it's a matter of nostalgia, like awaiting the return of the savior, the return of the gold standard, the return of the Broadway musical, the return of Zorro. Maybe I can't bring myself to pledge allegiance to the present because I continue, obscurely, to believe in the chimera of the future—when it shows up I'll go directly to its governing agency and have my papers transferred. Or maybe my reluctance is simply due to the fact that such a pledge seems redundant. The present is everywhere, holds dominion over all, controls all discourse and all economy, has just about squelched the last pockets of resistance to its tide. Do we need to assemble every morning and confirm our agreement to the day's weather? Would the weather change if we demurred?

The past is a notional construct, a hypothesis, a poem. I hold on to its passport because it was issued at my birth, without any possibility of my assenting or not. It's not so much a document as it is a brand or a scar. I don't really endorse the past, mind you, and I don't intend to go back and settle there. My actual relation to the past is ironic, if anything, even if the irony is poisoned with sentiment; I can laugh at the past but the laughter sticks in my throat. I certainly feel more affection for it from a distance. And only from within the past can I appreciate the present, which is all things considered a dispiriting place to live. Each is a shabby, passive-aggressive dictatorship of compromise and self-delusion. Under the rhetoric, we all know this. I'm not alone because every one of us is an alien. That makes us all compatriots.

Sources

N.B. All translations within the text are by the author.

CHAPTER VII

Anon. [Charles Froment, Pierre A. F. Gérard, Henri-Florent Delmotte], *L'Hermite en Belgique, par une société de gens de lettres,* Brussels, 1827.

Appert, B., *Voyage en Belgique,* Brussels, 1848.

Bauwens, Catherine, *Le Patrimoine industriel de la région verviétoise,* Dison, 1994.

Bertholet, Paul, *Verviers et sa région en gravures,* Liège, 1981.

Bertrand, Louis, *Souvenirs d'un meneur socialiste,* Brussels, 1927.

Commission médicale de la Province de Liège (C. Wasseige), *Mémoire sur la condition des ouvriers et le travail des enfants dans les mines, manufactures, et usines de la Province de Liège,* Brussels, 1847.

Dechesne, Laurent, *L'Avènement du régime syndical à Verviers,* Paris, 1908.

——— *La Grève contre le tissage à deux métiers,* Verviers, 1897.

——— *L'Industrie drapière de la Vesdre avant* 1800, Paris, 1926.

De Raadt, J.-Th., *Sobriquets des communes belges,* Brussels, 1903.

Fassin, Arthur, *Recherches historiques sur les communes de Stembert et Heusy,* Verviers, 1890.

Fohal, Jean, "La Disette à Verviers en 1845," *Bulletin de la Société Verviétoise d'archéologie et d'histoire,* vol. 21, 1927–28.

——— *Les Évènements de 1830 à Verviers et aux environs,* Verviers, 1930.

——— *Verviers et son industrie il y a 85 ans: 1843,* Verviers, 1928.

Grosjean, Nicolas, *Quand nous courions dans les rues: La Vie populaire de chez nous,* Verviers, 1940.

Guérin, Daniel, *Ni dieu ni maître: Anthologie historique du mouvement anarchiste*, Paris, 1972.

Guillaume, James, *L'Internationale*, Paris, 1910.

Harmel, Claude, *Histoire de l'anarchie*, Paris, 1949.

Henaux, Ferdinand, *Histoire de la bonne ville de Verviers*, Liège, 1859.

Herbillon and Germain, *Dictionnaire des noms de famille en Belgique francophone*, Brussels, 1996.

Hugo, Victor, *Le Rhin*, Paris, 1838.

Joris, Dany, *Verviers en cartes postales anciennes*, Zaltbommel, 1972.

Joris, Freddy, *La Presse verviétoise, 1850–1914*, Louvain-la-Neuve, 1982.

Le Jour (Verviers), "Cent ans à la lumière du Jour," 24 March 1994.

Kropotkin, Peter, *Memoirs of a Revolutionist*, Boston, 1899.

Leblu, Arthur, *Les Règlements de Police annotés de la ville de Verviers*, Verviers, 1898.

Lejear, Jean, *Histoire de la ville de Verviers: Période hollandaise et Révolution belge de 1830, 1814–1830*, Verviers, 1906.

Léon, Paul, *Dictionnaire des rues de Verviers*, Dison, 1977.

Manifeste du Groupe de Propagande Révolutionnaire Verviétois, Verviers, 1873.

Mathieu, Joseph, *Histoire sociale de l'industrie textile de Verviers*, Dison, 1946.

———— *L'Industrie drapière du pays de Verviers*, Verviers, 1954.

Meunier, Joseph, *Tot avau l'vî Vervî*, Verviers, 1940.

———— *Verviers la bonne ville*, Paris, 1932.

———— *Verviers: Vu du loin et dans le temps*, Verviers, 1953.

Le Mirabeau: Organe de l'Association des francs-ouvriers, section verviétoise de l'Association Internationale des Travailleurs, various numbers, 1869–71.

Oukhow, Catherine, *Documents relatifs à l'histoire de la Première Internationale en Wallonie*, Louvain, 1967.

Poëtgens, Henri, "Souvenirs de Verviers ancien," *Bulletin de la Société Verviétoise d'archéologie et d'histoire*, vols. 7 and 9 (1906 and 1910).

"Psychanalyse d'une ville: Verviers," *La Maison*, March 1967.

Renier, J.-S., *Histoire de l'industrie drapière au pays de Liége et particulièrement Verviers*, Liège, 1881.

Shoumatoff, Alex, *The Mountain of Names: A History of the Human Family*, New York, 1985.

Le Soir (Brussels), "L'Industrie belge\ au temps jadis," 24 November 1995.

Stembert, Pierre, *L'Alphabet verviétois*, vols. 1–4, Dison, 1989–93.

Temps Jadis (Verviers), various numbers, 1979–96.

Verviers, Administration Communale, *Verviers "bonne ville" à trois cents ans*, Verviers, 1951.

———— *Verviers: Ville où il fait bon vivre*, Verviers, n.d.

Verviers, Syndicat d'Initiative et de Tourisme, *Chronologie de la vie verviétoise ou Verviers vu par les dates*, Verviers, n.d.

———— *Le travail de la laine. Vulgarisation*, Verviers, n.d.

———— *Musée de la laine*, Verviers, n.d.

———— *Petit guide historique de Verviers*, Verviers, n.d.

Xhoffer, J.-F., *Verviers ancien*, Verviers, 1866.

Ymart, Félix, *Carnet d'un flâneur: Le Vieux Verviers*, Verviers, 1894.

CHAPTER VIII

À l'école du bienheureux Curé d'Ars, Grammont, 1911.

L'Avenir du Luxembourg (Arlon), *Quand le Luxembourg entrait dans le XXe siècle*, Arlon, 1994.

Banneux, Louis, *L'Ardenne mystérieuse*, Brussels, 1930.

Bologne, Maurice, *Petit guide étymologique des noms des régions, villes . . . de Belgique*, Gembloux, 1966.

Granny, *Le Jardin des merveilles*, Jambes, 1927.

Hock, Auguste, *Croyances et remèdes au pays de Liége*, Liège, 1888.

Holland, Clive, *The Ardennes and Walloon Country*, New York, 1928.

Lambot, Jean-Pierre, *L'Ardenne*, Liège, 1987.

Legros, Élisée, "Les maladies portant le nom du saint guérisseur," *Enquêtes du Musée de la vie wallonne*, vol. 5, 1948–50.

Leroy, Marcel, *Les Chatons gelés*, Villance-en-Ardenne, 1995.

Livre blanc des pauvretés dans la Province du Luxembourg, Bouillon, 1988.

Monseur, Eugène, *Le Folklore wallon*, Brussels, 1892.

Serck-Dewaide, Myriam, and Simone Verfaille, *Le Vieux Bon Dieu de Tancrémont*, Tancrémont, 1987.

Stecher, J., "Superstitions wallonnes," *Revue de Belgique*, vol.19, 1875.

Thill, Abbé Jean, *Le Vieux Bon Dieu de Tancrémont*, Liège, 1982.

Yernaux, E., and F. Fieret, *Le Folklore wallon*, Charleroi, 1956.

CHAPTER IX

Anderson, Isabel, *The Spell of Belgium,* Boston, 1915.

Fischer, Michel, and Robert Delieu, *Les Wallons,* Brussels, 1978.

Fonteyn, Guido, *Les Wallons: Faire surface,* Brussels, 1979.

Fox, Renée C., *In the Belgian Château,* Chicago, 1994.

Fraipont, Charles, *Les wallons et les flamands,* Brussels, 1922.

Herremans, Maurice-Pierre, *La Wallonie: Ses griefs, ses aspirations,* Brussels, 1951.

Huggett, Frank, *Modern Belgium,* New York, 1969.

INBEL, *Geography of Belgium,* Brussels, 1990.

Lejuste, Ernest, *Leçons d'histoire nationale,* Tamines, 1925.

Pirenne, Henri, *Histoire de Belgique,* vols. 1–4, fourth revised edition, Brussels, 1928.

Rousseau, Félix, *Wallonie, terre romaine,* Brussels, 1963.

Tennent, J. Emerson, *Belgium,* London, 1841.

Waële, G. de, *Flamands et Wallons,* Paris, 1917.

CHAPTER X

Assouline, Pierre, *Simenon,* Paris, 1992.

Baudelaire, Charles, *Oeuvres complètes,* ed. Y.-G. Le Dantec, Paris, 1954.

Blavier, André, "L'envers du décor" (place and date unknown).

———— *Le Mal du Pays, ou les travaux forc(en)és,* Crisnée, 1993.

———— *Maurice Pirenne le peintre,* Brussels, 1959.

Chavée, Achille, *À cor et à cri,* Brussels, 1985.

Cohn, Norman, *The Pursuit of the Millennium,* New York, 1957.

Communauté Française de Belgique, *Les écrivains belges de langue française,* Brussels, 1992.

Gablik, Suzi, *Magritte,* New York, 1970.

Klinkenberg, Jean-Marie, ed., *Espace Nord: L'Anthologie,* Brussels, 1994.

Mariën, Marcel, ed., *L'Activité Surréaliste en Belgique,* Brussels, 1979.

Marnham, Patrick, *The Man Who Wasn't Maigret: A Portrait of Georges Simenon,* New York, 1992.

Nougé, Paul, *Quelques bribes,* Brussels, 1993.

Pansaers, Clément, *Bar Nicanor et autres textes Dada,* Paris, 1985.

Phantomas (Uccle), nos. 100/111: *La Belgique sauvage* (1972).

Quaghebeur, M., J.-P. Verheggen, and V. Jago-Antoine, eds., *Un pays d'irréguliers*, Brussels, 1990.

Scutenaire, Louis, *Mes inscriptions*, Brussels, 1976.

Sylvester, David, *Magritte: The Silence of the World*, New York, 1993.

Toussaint, Françoise, *Le Surréalisme belge*, Brussels, 1986.

Tout Simenon: Maigret à Liège, 2 June–31. October 1993 (catalogue) and individual literary works as cited in text.

CHAPTER XII

Bayer, Henry G., *The Belgians: First Settlers in New York and in the Middle States*, New York, 1925.

Carton de Wiart, Henri, ed., *Vie et aventures d'un ouvrier foulon du pays de Verviers au XVIIIe siècle, d'après un manuscrit inédit*, Brussels, 1920.

Defret, Mary Ann, et al., *From Grez-Doiceau to Wisconsin: Contributions à l'étude de l'émigration wallonne vers les États-Unis au XIXe siècle*, Louvain-la-Neuve, 1986.

Ghélin, Edgard de, *Aux wallons qui fondèrent New York*, Brussels, 1924.

Goffin, Robert, *De Pierre Minuit aux Roosevelt: L'Épopée belge aux États-Unis*, New York, 1943.

Griffis, W. E., *The Story of the Walloons*, Boston, 1923.

Heagy, "Avoir 68 ans . . . ," *Le Jour* (Verviers), 12 November 1969.

Holand, H. R., *Wisconsin's Belgian Community*, Sturgeon Bay, 1933.

Kadjik, Joseph, "La Contribution belge à la vie américaine de 1624 à nos jours," *Nouvelles de Belgique*, 1 January 1964.

Lempereur, Françoise, *Les Wallons d'Amérique du Nord: Étude principalement consacrée au wallons établis au Wisconsin*, Gembloux, 1976.

Parkman, Francis, *La Salle and the Discovery of the Great West*, Boston, 1879.

Perlot, Jean-Nicolas, *Chercheur d'or: Vie et Aventures d'un enfant d'Ardenne*, Arlon, 1897.

Smet, Antoine de, *Voyageurs belges aux États-Unis du XVIIe siècle à nos jours: Notices bio-bibliographiques*, Brussels, 1959.

Tlachac, Math S., *The History of the Belgian Settlements in Door, Kewaunee and Brown Counties*, Algoma, 1974.

CHAPTER XIV

Anon. [A. F. Poyart], *Flandricismes, wallonismes et expressions impropres du langage français, par un ancien professeur,* Brussels, 1806.

Apollinaire, Guillaume, *Le Poète assassiné,* Paris, 1916.

———— trans. Ron Padgett, *The Poet Assassinated,* Berkeley, 1984.

Atlas linguistique de la Wallonie, tableau géographique des parlers de la Belgique romane d'après l'enquête de Jean Haust, Liège, 1953–87.

Body, Albin, *Recueil de vers, chansons et pièces satiriques sur la révolution liégeoise de 1789,* Liège, 1881.

Brasseur, Léon, *À l'ombre du Vieux Chêne,* Verviers, 1910.

Colson, Oscar, *Bibliographie de la littérature wallonne contemporaine, 1905–06,* Liège, 1912.

Defrecheux, Nicolas, *Oeuvres complètes,* Liège, 1925.

Dejardin, Joseph, *Dictionnaire des spots ou proverbes wallons,* Liège, 1891–92.

Delaite, Julien, *Le Wallon est-il une langue?* Brussels, 1893.

Dory, Isidore, *Wallonismes,* Brussels, 1878.

Fairon, Émile, "In memoriam Jules Feller," *Bulletin de la Société Verviétoise d'archéologie et d'histoire,* vol. 33, 1940–41.

Feller, Jules (with Jean Wisimus), *Anthologie des poètes wallons verviétois,* Verviers, 1928.

———— "Le chat volant de Verviers," *Bulletin de la Société Verviétoise d'archéologie et d'histoire,* vol. 11, 1910.

———— *Les Noms de lieux en -ster,* Verviers, 1904.

———— *Notes de philologie wallonne,* Liège and Paris, 1912.

———— *Traité de versification wallonne basé sur la versification française,* Liège, 1928.

Fré Cougnou (Verviers), various numbers, 1899–1904.

Gosse, Edmund, "Walloon Literature," *Encyclopedia Britannica,* eleventh edition, Cambridge and New York, 1911.

Grangagnage, Charles, *De l'origine des Wallons,* Liège, 1852.

———— *Dictionnaire étymologique de la langue wallonne,* Liège, 1845–51.

Grosjean, Colas, *Fribotes d'istwère dè mouv'mint litéraire walon à Vervî,* Verviers, 1937.

Guiraud, Pierre, *Patois et dialectes français,* Paris, 1968.

Hurard, Henri, *Lès pièces du Vervî,* Verviers, 1923.

Ista, Georges, "Le Dialecte wallon," *Les Marches de l'Est* (Paris), vol. 3, no. 6, 1912.

Mawhin, Jean, *Lès Tchants d'one vêye,* Verviers, 1969.

Remacle, Louis, *Le Problème de l'ancien Wallon,* Liège, 1948.

Slangen, Marcel, *Guide des expressions en Wallon liégeois,* Bressoux, 1995.

Lu Trô d'Sottais (Verviers), various numbers, 1898–1900.

Wilmotte, Maurice, *Le Wallon,* Brussels, 1894.

Wisimus, Jean, *L'Anglais langue auxiliaire internationale,* Paris, 1921.

———— *Dès Rôses èt dès Spènes,* Verviers, 1926.

———— *Dictionnaire populaire Wallon-Français en dialecte verviétois,* Verviers, 1947.

———— *Le Mouvement littéraire wallon à Verviers,* Verviers, 1933.

Thanks

To Angelika Becker and Joseph Mullender for their crucial friendship, which changed my life, and for their guidance and tutelage, and their extraordinary kindness.

To Raymonde and Pierre Michel for equipping and sustaining my hazardous expedition into the heart of the Belgian jungle, and for nearly three decades of being virtually indistinguishable from family.

To Frank Albers, Paul Auster and Siri Hustvedt, Thérèse Beauraind-Stelmes, Judy Bernstein, André Blavier, Philippe Bordaz and Michèle Grange, Mr. and Mrs. Luk Darras, Peter Dervis, André and Brigitte Detiffe, Paul Detiffe and Danielle Grailet, Paulette and René Detiffe, Elizabeth and Richard Devereaux, Maurice Devroye, Ginny Dougary and Bruce Millar, Barbara Epstein, James Fenton, Jonathan Galassi, Malu Halasa and Andy Cox, Miguel Hernandez, Frank Kogan, José Lambiet, Robert Long, Michael McGowan, Susan Morrison and David Handelman, the late Paul Pavel, Carmen and Charles Pierson, Darryl Pinckney, Brooke and Peter Schjeldahl, Chris Stansell, Jenny Turner, the Wathelet family (especially Nelly Wathelet-Remacle, Louise Baijot-Wathelet, and Frédéric Wathelet), John Wójtowicz, and Ellen Wolk for advice, assistance, encouragement, ideas, suggestions, books, articles, letters, pictures, hospitality, friendship.

To James Atlas at *The New York Times Magazine,* Klara Glowczewska at the *Condé Nast Traveler,* and Wendy Lesser at *The Threepenny Review* for giving me assignments that helped me work out ideas leading to this book.

To all those persons named Sante who were kind enough to respond to my inquiries, some of whom went to great lengths to help.

To the staffs of many libraries, archives, and collections, especially those of the Salle Ulysse Capitaine and the Salle de Dialectologie at the

Bibliothèque des Chiroux, Liège, as well as of the Musée de la Vie Wallonne in the same city, of the International Institute of Social History in Amsterdam, and of the Utah Genealogical Society facilities in the Manhattan stake of the Church of Jesus Christ of Latter-Day Saints.

To Jan Caluwaerts, who guided my steps in the early stages of my genealogical investigations.

To the ghost of Dziga Vertov (Denis Arkadievitch Kaufman) for graciously allowing me to swipe his phrase for my title.

To the John Simon Guggenheim Memorial Foundation, which supported this project at its inception, to the Mrs. Giles Whiting Foundation, which first gave me my wings, and to the American Academy of Arts and Letters.

To Robert Polito, who (incredibly enough) volunteered to read this work in manuscript as it progressed, and who diagnosed like a wizard, showing me the places where I copped out.

To my exceedingly wise, extraordinarily patient and generous agent, Joy Harris.

To the wily and discerning Erroll McDonald, as well as to Dan Frank and Altie Karper at Pantheon.

To Mrs. Gibbs (wherever you are), without whom none of this would have been possible.

To my parents, Denise and Lucien Sante, without whom the possibility would not even have come up. They are in effect my co-authors. I can only hope that they will find the picture a reasonably truthful likeness, even if they do not agree with all of its particulars.

And above all to Melissa Holbrook Pierson, my light and my guide, who time and again removed thorns from my paw.

About the Author

LUC SANTE was born in Verviers, Belgium, in 1954. He came to the United States as a child, and has lived in New York City since the age of eighteen. He is the author of *Low Life: Lures and Snares of Old New York* (1991) and *Evidence* (1992). He is currently book critic for *New York*, a senior contributor to *Slate*, and a frequent contributor to *The New York Review of Books*, and he has written on books, movies, art, photography, and miscellaneous cultural phenomena for many other periodicals. Sante has received a 1989 Whiting Writer's Award, a Guggenheim Fellowship in 1992–93, and, in 1997, a Literature Award from the American Academy of Arts and Letters. He lives in Brooklyn with his wife, the writer Melissa Holbrook Pierson.

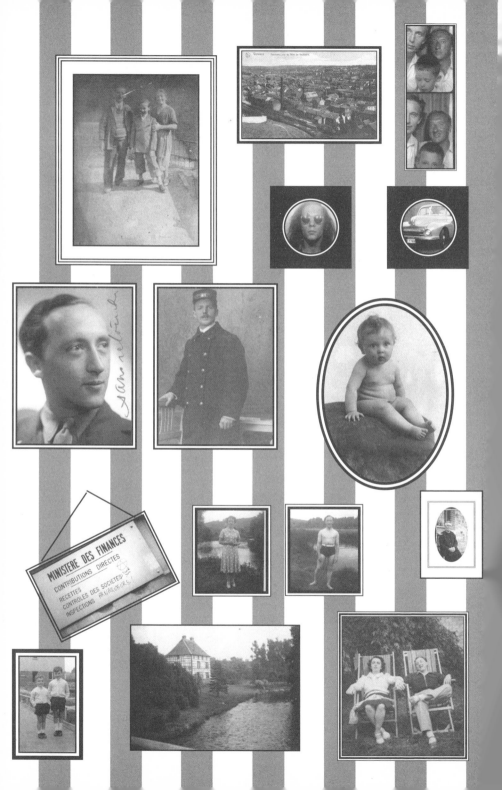